Silent Skies

The Air Traffic Controllers' Strike

WILLIS J. NORDLUND

PRAEGER

Westport, Connecticut
London

Library of Congress Cataloging-in-Publication Data

Nordlund, Willis J.
   Silent skies : the air traffic controllers' strike / Willis J.
Nordlund.
      p.   cm.
   Includes bibliographical references and index.
   ISBN 0–275–96188–5 (alk. paper)
   1. Strikes and lockouts—Air traffic control—Illinois—Chicago.
2. Air Traffic Controllers' Strike, U.S., 1981.   3. Chicago Air
Route Traffic Control Center—Officials and employees—Dismissal of.
4. Air traffic controllers—Dismissal of—Illinois—Chicago.
I. Title.
HD5325.A4252   1981.C486   1998
331.892′81387740426′0973—dc21   97–38545

British Library Cataloguing in Publication Data is available.

Library of Congress Catalog Card Number: 97–38545
ISBN: 0–275–96188–5

First published in 1998

Praeger Publishers, 88 Post Road West, Westport, CT 06881
An imprint of Greenwood Publishing Group, Inc.

Printed in the United States of America

The paper used in this book complies with the
Permanent Paper Standard issued by the National
Information Standards Organization (Z39.48–1984).

10 9 8 7 6 5 4 3 2 1

Dedicated to Kathy, John and Jeff

Contents

Tables

Acknowledgments

While the author must assume all responsibility for the character and quality of this work, other individuals provided expert guidance and assistance that materially improved the product. Central to the production of the book was the attention and expert guidance by Ms. Lynn Taylor and Ms. Linda Ellis, both from the Greenwood Publishing Group. Ms. Taylor recognized the significance of the subject matter and encouraged me to complete the manuscript. Ms. Ellis expertly coordinated the final editing and preparation of the manuscript through its many stages of development. The trials and tribulations of preparing manuscripts for publication is often a thankless task. The individual who ensured that every detail was addressed and that the final product was in camera-ready copy was Ms. Brenda Allmon. Her unfailing commitment to quality and professionalism in every aspect of the process provides inspiration to all who know and admire her work.

Introduction

Every administration has a "defining moment"; many have several. The Reagan administration will be remembered for many things, but the one event that remains in the psyche of every American is the discharge of federal air traffic controllers for failure to follow a presidential directive to return to work. When middle-aged Americans are asked what they feel is the importance of President Ronald Reagan's first term, most will scratch their heads and ponder the question. A few will point to the economic policies of Reaganomics. Most, however, will point to the firing of the air traffic controllers. The drama leading up to the event and the national trauma that followed it provide a poignant picture of raw power and the misjudgment of power.

There were numerous historical examples of workers in critical industries that struck and made it stick. Teachers, police, postal workers, sanitation workers, and others, including air traffic controllers, had used the strike weapon effectively as a vehicle for squeezing more concessions out of management— generally public sector management. These events were not always popular, but they accomplished their sought-after goals for the unions and their members. No president had ever dared exercise his prerogative of releasing large numbers of federal workers in critical occupations because of work stoppage activity. Ronald Reagan did, and he did it with great success. He broke the strike, and he broke the union. This is the story of that event and its aftermath. It is not a pretty picture, but it is critically important because the American labor movement is still "shell-shocked" by the event. A sure way to provoke emotional discussion by unionists is to suggest that what President Reagan did was reasonable and appropriate.

Whether the discharge of thousands of air traffic controllers was necessary and prudent is a question that will linger for decades. The decision to discharge the controllers was as much political as it was economic or legal. President Reagan wanted to send a signal to the unions and the American people that he would not tolerate work stoppage activity, especially in critical occupations, regardless of the risks and ancillary costs involved. The president was a lucky man during this episode of American history in that there were no large air disasters that could have been attributed to a less than perfectly functioning air traffic control system. A single major incident could have easily reversed the decision for complete and final termination of thousands of controllers. While a tragic Air Florida crash in the Potomac River five and a half months after the strike could have been the catalyst for a reversal of the sentiment of the American people, the sheer magnitude of the loss of life overshadowed any finger-pointing by either side.[1] Who was to blame for the crash has never been determined precisely. The airplane was cleared for takeoff by an air traffic controller, but as is always the case, the pilot in command (PIC) is the final authority who decides whether or not the airplane leaves the ground.

There are differences of opinion as to how the Federal Aviation Administration Professional Air Traffic Controllers Organization (FAA-PATCO) situation evolved into one of overt and direct confrontation. How did the situation gravitate into one from which there was no return? Some argue that the president was simply looking for a vehicle to use in making his inflexible opposition to unions visible, and the air traffic controllers happened to be first in line. Whether this is an accurate assessment remains to be seen; however, there can be no doubt that what happened in 1981 will have far-reaching ramifications concerning unions and particularly federal unions that consider the option of initiating a work stoppage. There can be no question that the PATCO and the FAA were at loggerheads over just about every issue. Other federal unions, including several in the postal service, have expressed serious concerns about wages and working conditions, but since 1981, none have taken the final crucial step, that is, strike.

The PATCO debacle is a perfect example of how personalities enter the labor-management arena and often play a major role in the outcome of negotiations. Long before formal negotiations began, the FAA administrator was traveling around the country, making speeches about the overpaid and underworked controllers. This public display of insensitivity about controller activities was not helpful. Controllers have enormous responsibility for the successful outcome of the air traffic control process. Controllers' responsibilities are not only to prevent accidents but also to substantially determine the degree to which airplane flights are efficient. If controllers "work to the rule," very few airplanes will be able to operate on schedule. The problem with working to the rules is that these procedures are permitted, and in fact required, by federal regulation. Most controllers know, however, that the separation of aircraft prescribed by the rules can be "modified" on occasion while ensuring complete safety. This is critically important in locations in and around the two dozen major airports in the United States. One need only watch the active runways at Chicago's O'Hare Airport to see the intensity and volume of traffic on an average weekday morning. One airplane is touching down while another is lined up on final approach directly behind the one landing. Simultaneously, other airplanes are taking off on other runways. All of this occurs with seeming order and precision. It is utterly fantastic to realize that the instructions for each of these aircraft are coming from inside control rooms located on and near the airport. All of these aircraft have been lined up for arrival without anybody seeing them visually until they are spotted by the O'Hare tower on final approach.

It may be that the air traffic controllers union was large enough to be visible, but not large enough to be irreplaceable in a relatively short period of time. The controllers may have been in an occupation in which the skills and training necessary to be effective are easily transferable to other motivated and capable employees. By discharging them, the president took the risk of having an air traffic control system thrown into chaos with the attendant risk of major air disasters. Chaos was minimal, and there were no major disasters—other than the Air Florida crash—directly attributable to the strike. This outcome was more a matter of luck than it was careful planning and strategic intervention.

The issues in the PATCO strike were simultaneously simple and complex. The Reagan administration attempted, successfully, to encapsulate the totality of union demands into a single demand, that is, money. Through public relations programs in which the agenda was determined by the administration, controllers were characterized as single-focused, money-hungry, underworked crybabies who were attempting to hold the American people hostage to the union's demands. PATCO did virtually nothing to counteract these characterizations. Rather, the union relied on the importance of its function in the American economy, the fact that earlier efforts to gain concessions had worked, and the belief that earlier statements by the president would be the "ace in the hole" when the going got tough.

The union attempted to argue that its working conditions, retirement program, and other aspects of the work environment, for example, the old and unreliable Automated Data Processing (ADP) equipment, were the major issues important to PATCO members. While there was substantial confirmation by individuals outside of PATCO that all or most of these problems had merit, the union was unable or unwilling to counterbalance the administration's public relations program effectively. The American people were unable to determine what parts of the controllers' agenda, if any, were real. The one-dimensional caricature provided by the government, that is, money, was easy to understand.

Through a series of studies by outside experts, spanning the better part of two decades, the acrimonious relationship between the FAA management and its employees was clearly documented. No one should believe that the union was without some responsibility in the creation and continuation of this difficult relationship. However, every study pointed to the same set of conditions within the FAA that served to aggravate the areas of disagreement and prevented the union and the FAA from coming to terms on important issues.

There was a certain arrogance by leaders of both the FAA and the PATCO. The FAA leaders apparently did not feel they had to be responsive to union concerns. There were clear indications that managers in the FAA viewed the union as, at best, an irrelevant outsider and the controllers as employees who were expected to comply with management orders without question. The union also did little to calm the troubled waters. Union leaders, from the infamous F. Lee Bailey to Robert Poli, consistently took actions that irritated FAA managers, voiced their concerns in the media and before the Congress, and on every occasion attempted to find fault with management decisions.

There was much to be criticized in the U.S. air traffic control system. The hardware that supported one of the most complex systems in the world was antiquated and unreliable. The volume of air traffic was increasing every year. These increases placed pressure on an already burdened system. The hardware had difficulty absorbing the pressure, and the air traffic controllers were often placed in difficult situations when failures occurred—and they occurred frequently. The industry deregulation program served to make airline scheduling less predictable. There was a tendency for the flow of traffic into and out of major airports to be "lumpy." Every airline wanted its airplanes to depart at 8 A.M. each workday and fly the most direct route to other major airports.

Management attitudes and practices were also problem areas. Virtually every study of the FAA indicated that most managers were ill-equipped for the "personnel side" of the process. Most supervisors had worked their way up through the system and therefore had acquired the technical skills needed in the air traffic control environment. What they did not acquire in that process was the set of skills needed to deal with employees. Deficient skills were evident in all aspects of the labor-management process. Managers were ineffective in providing directives to employees that did not irritate and demean those on the receiving end. Managers were particularly inept in facilitating the communications process both downward and upward. In fact, most employees did not believe there was an upward communications process.

Many of these studies noted the militaristic style of management, the insensitivity of supervisors and managers to the personal side of an employee's life—that is, vacations, long work hours, six-day workweeks, and other aspects of one's life that affects satisfaction both on and off the job. In the 1970 FAA-commissioned Corson Committee Report, many of the problems that were to surface in 1981 were reported. The report noted, for example, "There is great dissatisfaction among the controller work force about their inability to communicate upwards. They contend that individuals who express dissatisfaction to management are labeled as disloyal; the filing of a grievance is the act of a trouble maker and to 'make a wave' of any kind is a guarantee against promotion."[2]

In addition, there was controller concern about the physical and psychological demands of the job. The Corson Committee reported, "A major cause of dissatisfaction among the controller work force is the deep-seated and widely held belief that most individuals will be physically unable to continue to control air traffic (even while physically able to perform other kinds of work) well before they will have qualified under prevailing provisions for retirement."[3]

Over many years of insensitive labor-management relations, employees became convinced that the FAA did not care about them as employees and did not care about the concerns and problems they faced each day. Air traffic controllers did not believe that management wanted their views about how to improve the system. Air traffic controllers who raised issues and concerns about system operation became known as troublemakers and not team players. There was a strong sentiment that "'[m]anagement' in the eyes of a substantial proportion of all controllers, is out of touch with the working force."[4] Therefore, most controllers simply kept their mouths shut and tried to make the best of the conditions they worked in.

This is not to say that there were no problems within the union. In the year prior to the strike, there were major changes in the union that served to unbalance the system. A president of over ten years' tenure was suddenly ousted by an individual known inside the union but relatively unknown to outsiders. The manner in which the transition in power took place left a bad taste in the mouths of most union leaders outside of the PATCO. In what was characterized as a "bloodless, palace coup," Robert Poli sought and attained the fall of John Leyden as the PATCO president. Leyden had worked hard to build bridges between other national unions and the PATCO and between the PATCO and the leadership in the American Federation of Labor and Congress of Industrial Organizations (AFL–CIO). In addition, the FAA management team seemed to understand and appreciate what Leyden was trying to accomplish. There were those in both the PATCO and the FAA who believed that the relationship between the organizations was improving. However, there was sentiment within the PATCO that changes were too slow. Poli capitalized on those sentiments and ousted Leyden as president.

After the coup, Poli embarked on a campaign to change the work environment in the system dramatically and to obtain major salary gains for PATCO members. In this process, he failed to elicit or obtain support from other parts of the labor movement. Precisely why he went it alone is not known, but it seems to have stemmed from his feeling that the union was in a strategic position that was strong enough to obtain whatever goals it sought. Examination of the role of air traffic controllers in the aviation industry suggested that Poli's assessment of their strength was based on reality. One would be hard-pressed to find another group of public employees that were as highly skilled and indispensable as were the air traffic controllers.

However, what Poli and the PATCO failed to recognize and understand was the changed political climate in the nation. Americans elected Ronald Reagan on a platform for change. This change process involved downsizing government, returning governmental power to the states, deregulating industry, and initiating a dramatic change in economic policies to reshape the economic and social systems. Americans apparently found in the new president the kinds of ideas and policies that coincided with this mandate. However, what Poli and the PATCO did not see was that the goals of the union were, in large part, inconsistent with the new Reagan agenda.

More specifically, Poli and the PATCO failed to see that the method of obtaining worker goals, through union intervention, was inconsistent with the Reagan agenda. In fact, many Americans sympathized with the controllers in terms of the conditions of employment, but they appeared to have little sympathy for the PATCO as an organization.

While the factors leading to the strike and the government's response to that strike are complex, the single aspect of the controller strike that seemed to cause the president the most distress was that controllers violated their written, signed oath not to strike against the government of the United States. The oath that every government employee signs says the following:

I am not participating in any strike against the Government of the United States or any agency thereof, and I will not so participate while an employee of the Government of the United States or any agency thereof.

This deceptively simple statement became the publicly stated driving force behind the president's decision to fire the controllers and not permit them to return to federal employment.

In an interview on National Public Radio, Transportation Secretary Drew Lewis argued that the president considered the strike a "moral issue." The secretary suggested that the president felt that "these people [the controllers] took an oath of office. They haven't lived up to their responsibilities to the American public." Further, the president asked the rhetorical question, "If ever we feel that our oath of office need not be kept, how long would we have this society?"[5] While clearly the president felt strongly about the fact that controllers had signed an oath, there is irony is this belief when one considers the exploits of President Richard M. Nixon in the Watergate debacle, which occurred before the controller strike, and the pardoning of Oliver North and others by President George Bush in the Iran-Contra Affair. These individuals had also signed and spoken oaths that covered far more than a pledge not to strike against the government; however, when found to be in violation of their oaths, they were released from responsibility by executive privilege. Lane Kirkland, president of the AFL–CIO, characterized the signed oaths as "yellow-dog contracts" that were outlawed in the private sector over fifty years earlier.[6]

The second dimension of the controllers' strike was the illegality of their actions. Nobody denied that the strike was in violation of federal law. The Civil Service Reform Act of 1977 and Section 305 of the Taft-Hartley Act explicitly outlaw strikes by federal employees. In fact, federal law makes strikes by federal employees a felony because it is punishable by a fine of as much as $1,000 and imprisonment of a year or more. Administration officials other than the president seemed to have much more concern about the illegality of the strike than its moral character that so troubled the president. Individuals such as Edwin Meese, Secretary Lewis, David Gergen, Lynn Helms, and others focused on the illegal nature of the act. Gergen commented, "This union is in flagrant violation of the law. We're out to end an illegal strike." Presidential counselor Edwin Meese argued that controllers would not be rehired "because the PATCO strike is so clearly a violation of Federal law."[7]

However, while not denying that the controller strike was illegal, Congressman Guy Molinari suggested that there was room for blame that resided outside the ranks of the controllers and the PATCO. He observed;

[I]f you look at the history of job actions and strikes, we had many of them, and people weren't fired. So that when this business [the controller strike] occurred in 1981, I and others told these people, they're not going to fire you. By prior action, the Government led them to believe that they wouldn't be fired.

We were partially responsible by our past actions. If there had been an inviolate rule that up and down the line every time somebody strikes, you lose your job, well, okay. Everybody knows it. But we led them down the garden path ourselves. We led them down the garden path, and there was the feeling that, oh, they're not going to fire us. It's happened before. We had a job action in the seventies. They didn't fire us.[8]

In addition, prominent scholars Antone Aboud and Grace Sterrett Aboud argued, "Although strikes may result in public inconvenience and disruption, proponents argue, any extension of freedom entails costs, and a free society should be willing to tolerate inconvenience and disruption."[9]

It has been said several times in this book—and it warrants being repeated numerous times here and elsewhere—that there is no excuse for the PATCO's knowing violation of a federal statute. In addition, there is no excuse for individual employees (controllers) violating their written oath not to strike. Nobody can or should sanction these kinds of activities. However, nobody can or should consider these actions in a vacuum, either. Individuals and organizations do all kinds of things based on conditions or events that affect their welfare. Society abhors murder, as it should. However, we now know that society has become substantially more tolerant of murder, even if premeditated and horrific, if conditions in which the murderer found himself or herself were so untenable that there was thought to be no other course of action. Individuals raised in a violent inner-city environment who kill another in a life-threatening situation, real or imagined, may receive leniency or outright acquittal on murder charges because of how they felt about the actual or perceived threats toward themselves. Whether they were in fact threatened makes little difference—only that they acted because they *felt* threatened. Juries have factored these conditions into the judicial decision-making process.

Battered or threatened spouses constitute another area in which society has garnered leniency when one spouse kills another. Even though some in society may question why one spouse does not simply leave the other rather than kill them, juries have taken considerable liberty to invoke leniency when these types of conditions have arisen.

The point is that the PATCO and its members, individually and collectively, initiated a course of action that many in society may consider unreasoned and improper under any circumstances. They broke the law and violated their oaths. But the question is whether or not these actions warranted the intensity and tenacity of the federal response to those actions? Did the president, the secretary of transportation, and the administrator of the FAA weigh the true character of the strike in terms of its impacts on the economy, its relationship to air safety, or the consequences of their actions on individual controllers and their families? In brief, Did the penalty fit the crime?

There were inferences in some of the prestrike discussion that the strike would have an adverse impact on the president's economic revitalization program. After the strike, there is little mention of this potential problem. Throughout the strike, there is constant reassurance by the FAA, the president, the Air Line Pilots Association (ALPA), the secretary of transportation, working controllers, and others that the skies were safer during the strike than they had been before the strike. The impacts on the controllers' families were seldom mentioned in the public debate. The president did make reference to them when he said he felt sorry for the families but that he "had no other choice" other than to fire the controllers. Of course, these comments ring hollow when one considers that the administration took many steps to make the lives of controllers and their families more difficult, in some cases, long after the strike was over. For example, "Many controllers say the government has deliberately worsened the ordeal, blocking applications for unemployment benefits, ordering people into court for things done after Reagan declared the strike officially over and barring the controllers from other Federal jobs."[10] Individual states followed the lead of the federal government in denying unemployment benefits. In addition, to make controller's and their families' lives even more difficult, the United States Department of Housing and Urban Development (HUD) issued a statement denying federal aid to the fired controllers who were behind in home-mortgage payments.[11]

What, then, was the motivation for firing over 11,000 controllers? If there was no adverse economic impact, if there were no air safety problems, and if the families didn't make a substantial difference, what was the motivation? The only answer can be that the president decided that the illegal strike and the violation of the controllers' oath were sufficient reasons to destroy the union.

Maybe the president was right. However, one must ask the rhetorical question about why other strikes and violations of the oaths of federal employees, and the violation of the solemn and sworn oath by a former president, were not more egregious and equally repugnant events. Earlier strikes and oath violations by federal employees had resulted in either no adverse consequences or minimal admonishments. Richard Nixon simply left office in disgrace and tarnished the image of the office of the president. Nevertheless, he continued to live a relatively normal life, much of it supported by taxpayers through pensions, Secret Service protection, and other amenities. The controllers did not lead normal lives after they were fired, and certainly they did not enjoy federally supported benefits. In fact, the federal government took special actions to completely prevent fired controllers from having access to unemployment benefits, housing subsidies, and other federal benefit programs. In addition, they were initially barred for life from further federal employment. If the violation of one's oath is such an egregious event, one wonders how the disparity in response to similar situations can be explained by rational public policy.

Supporters of the president's actions will reply that just because former presidents didn't uphold the law or find the violation of the employees' oath repugnant does not mean that President Reagan shouldn't have exercised his power in the manner in which he did. Fair enough. However, an important principle in American judicial review and the application of public policy is that there should be consistency and predictability in those processes. In more colorful terms, the punishment should fit the crime, and similar crimes should elicit similar punishments.

All of this leads primarily to one conclusion: While there is scant evidence that President Reagan set out, in the prestrike period, to destroy the PATCO, there is overwhelming evidence that once the PATCO had committed a federal crime, there was no stopping the movement to destroy the union. The evidence is compelling that if the strike had not occurred, the PATCO would undoubtedly be representing controllers to this day. The public policy question must be, then, did the president's response to an event that the administration was at least partially responsible for constitute appropriate and consistent federal action? Was the president's response overkill in a situation in which there were other options? Was it appropriate when there were no documented public health and safety issues? Was it consistent and predictable in terms of how the president himself acted in other situations and in terms of how federal public policy developed and was administered in a historical context?

The air traffic controllers utilized the power of their unique position to "bring the nation to its knees" and in that process force the federal government to concede to the union's demands. That was the strike strategy of the PATCO. There should be no misunderstanding about how the union intended to achieve its goals. What may be important, however, is that every union, in the public and private sectors, uses the identical technique in the national context or in a more localized context. What was the intent of the postal unions when they struck? When nurses strike a hospital? When railroad unions strike? When autoworkers strike? In every case, the intent is to put direct pressure on the employing organization to concede to the union's demands. This is the purpose of the strike action, pure and simple. It is not informational; it is not therapeutic; it is not for public relations. Its purpose is to impose costs on the system so that agreement can be reached.

The method American workers have used since the first strike by Cordwainers in Philadelphia in 1776 has been the same. Not every strike has been successful; in fact, there are examples where unions faced sufficient opposition to destroy them. Never before, however, had the federal government totally destroyed an organization that was the certified bargaining agent for a segment of its employees. Some may argue that it was about time for the federal government to draw the proverbial "line in the sand." Maybe a case can be made for that position.

Certainly, those whose political or philosophical views are in opposition to unions or any worker organizations felt that the federal actions in the PATCO dispute were appropriate.

The other side of this, however, is that in a free society that finds compulsory labor by free, private citizens repugnant, the form of protest called striking is an accepted part of the system. Taxpayers strike; stockholders strike; congressional aides strike; medical professionals strike; sports professionals strike; and the list goes on. Individuals, through collective action, exert their rights as American citizens to protest through the strike mechanism.

This story is laced with ironies concerning the application of double standards to events foreign and domestic. While President Reagan was incensed by the audacity of the controllers who violated their oaths of office, he seemed to have little problem with other government officials, such as former President Nixon, who did likewise. The nation cheered when Lech Walensa and Solidarity struck the Polish government to right grievances but found no such sympathy for the grievances of American air traffic controllers. Congressman William D. Ford argued:

In all of the history of the no-strike provision in the law, this is the first time that anyone has been prosecuted as a felon for striking against the Government. It seems to me particularly embarrassing to see pictures in the media of the PATCO strikers being escorted to jail in leg irons and manacles, while we were all cheering lustily the courage of Lech Walesa and Solidarity for bringing the Government of Poland, a Communistic, totalitarian government, to a stop because of the extreme frustration. I have never heard anybody discuss the merits of the Polish Solidarity Movement, yet, there is not a Member of Congress of any stripe, liberal, conservative, or anything in between, who has not been quick to run forward and praise the courage of those people in the labor movement in a Communist country, where it is, indeed, like the United States, illegal to strike against the Government.[12]

Congressman Ford argued further:

I am reminded over and over again of the embarrassment I constantly have in talking to people from other countries about the fact that one of the common Federal policies that we share with the Russians is an absolute prohibition against our employees and their employees engaging in a strike or a work stoppage against the Government. We are the only two major countries in the world that have that kind of a flat prohibition.

I suspect that if the equivalent of PATCO went on strike in Russia tomorrow, we would have parades in the streets in support of them. We would be collecting money and sending aid. There is something very wrong when the public discourse is swayed by events to the point where nobody recognized the ramifications of what, from an historical perspective, may become one of the most embarrassing incidents in this great experiment in democracy.[13]

What follows is the story of the first federal union that violated the law and paid the ultimate price. There had been many strikes by public unions before the PATCO strike, and a handful of employees had lost their federal jobs. However, the demise of the PATCO was the first time in American history that a federal union would take on the federal government and lose. This does not mean that the Federal government and the American people won. On the contrary, the costs to the government and the American taxpayer were substantial. Retraining the controllers to replace the fired controllers cost over $2 billion. In addition, there were major impacts on the aviation industry and all of the industries that rely on air transportation. The total costs of the strike and its aftermath may never be known, but one must wonder whether the demise of the PATCO as a union and the disruption of over 11,000 controllers' lives and the lives of their families were worth it—worth it to the union worth it to the controllers worth it to the nation.

This retrospective study of the strike provides significant clues about motivation, mistakes, and missed opportunities. It provides insights into the vagaries of the administrative and judicial processes that worked less than perfectly. However, whether the nation, the American labor movement, and the American people have learned from the experience is yet to be determined.

NOTES

1. The crash of Air Florida Flight 90 in the Potomac River in mid-January 1982 resulted in the death of seventy-eight people.

2. Senate, Committee on Post Office and Civil Service, *Air Traffic Controllers*, 91st Cong., 2d Sess., Calendar No. 1016, Report No. 91-1012 (Washington, D.C.: GPO, July 9, 1970), p. 124.

3. Ibid., p. 110.

4. Ibid., p. 49.

5. "Review and Outlook: No Room for Compromise," *Wall Street Journal*, August 6, 1981, p. 22.

6. "Kirkland Blasts Attempt to Bust Air Controllers," *AFL–CIO News*, Vol. 26, No. 33, August 15, 1981, p. 2.

7. "Air Controllers Union Holds Line on Strike Despite Threats of Massive Fines, Firings," *Wall Street Journal*, August 5, 1981, p. 2.

8. House of Representatives, Committee on Post Office and Civil Service, Subcommittee on Investigations, *Working Conditions and Staffing Needs in Air Traffic Control System*, 100th Cong., 1st sess., Serial No. 100-26 (Washington, D.C.: GPO, July 29–30, 1987), p. 11.

9. Antone Aboud and Grace Sterrett Aboud, *The Right to Strike in Public Employment*, Key Issues Series—No. 15 (Ithaca: New York State School of Industrial and Labor Relations, Cornell University, 1974), p. 9.

10. John Burgess, "Cautious Hope for Area Air Controllers," *Washington Post*, December 3, 1981, p. A18a.

11. "Air Strike Starts to Wear Down All Sides," *U.S. News and World Report*, August 31, 1981, p. 22.

12. House of Representatives, Committee on Post Office and Civil Service, Subcommittee on Investigations, *Federal Labor-Management Relations and Impasses Pro-*

cedures, 97th Cong., 2d sess., Serial No. 97-50 (Washington, D.C.: GPO, February 24, April 29, May 4, July 22, 1982), pp. 25–26.

13. Ibid., p. 27.

Chapter 1

The Line in the Sand

There are events that serve to crystallize thinking about unions, the role of labor in the economy, and the relationships between institutions and public policy. Certainly, the creation of the U.S. Department of Labor in 1913, the enactment of the National Labor Relations Act in 1935, the merger of the AFL and CIO in 1955, and the executive orders of Presidents John Kennedy and Richard Nixon giving collective bargaining rights to federal government employees were focal and defining events. In more contemporary times, the single event that sent the strongest signals about unions and the role of labor in the economy—to the American people, generally, and the American labor movement, specifically— was the breaking of the Professional Air Traffic Controllers Organization union by the Reagan administration in 1981.

There are those who believe that the Reagan administration was looking for a vehicle to signal organized labor that it would play a minor, backseat role in the economic policies of the new administration. Following this line of reasoning, the PATCO strike was coincidently the vehicle that served that purpose. After all, there had been hundreds of public sector strikes throughout recent decades in both the state and federal systems that were resolved with minimal disruption. The get-tough stance by the Reagan administration that led to the demise of the PATCO was thought by some unionists to be a tactical mistake at the time, but with President Reagan's reelection for a second term, organized labor hunkered down for a period of difficult relationships.

In many ways, the PATCO strike was the ideal vehicle for forging a renewed policy of toughness toward unions. The air traffic control system is highly technical and little understood by the average American but recognized as an important part of the overall transportation system. It takes little imagination to appreciate the discomfort and apprehension millions of air travelers feel when they lose confidence in those controlling American airspace. Since the air traffic controller's functions are first and foremost ensuring the safe movement of aircraft, anything that impinges on those functions is reason for immediate concern. The Reagan administration knew all that, but they also believed that conceding to the PATCO could unleash a series of public sector bargaining efforts that could jeopardize the president's economic agenda.

Thus, the Reagan administration acquired a strike that was constrained in scope, little understood by the public, and involved relatively few—18,000—employees. Few Americans have ever met, let alone know, an air traffic controller. It was in that sense an impersonal, highly technical sort of relationship. If the nearly 1 million postal service workers had been the first to go on strike, it is not clear how the new administration would have responded. Postal workers directly and immediately affect the lives of every American citizen, and many of them are visible and known in their communities. Strikes of this nature are more personal and less technical and seldom, at least in the short term, affect the health and safety of the nation.

In this sense, the PATCO strike was a fortuitous event that the Reagan administration sensed would not incense the American people. While a risk to safety existed in the aviation industry, it was not an all-encompassing impediment to domestic transportation; furthermore, the size of the union suggested that the weight of the federal government would quickly dominate the relationship. Then, too, there was the well-known "ban" on strikes by federal employees, which tended to legitimize the tough action taken by the administration.

It was not clear in the heat of battle—even though it probably should have been—that once the strike occurred, there was no scenario in which the FAA could peacefully come to terms with the PATCO. The PATCO had crossed that proverbial "line in the sand," and no retreating or compromising was possible. It is unlikely that the administration would have backed off even if the PATCO had abandoned its demands for improved working conditions and higher salaries. The administration believed it had the law and public opinion on its side, and it wanted to send a strong, unambiguous message to organized labor. That message has many facets or interpretations, but in substance, it was that organized labor—unionism—was essentially incompatible with the emerging free-market philosophy of the administration. Any activities such as strikes, boycotts, slowdowns, or other concerted actions by organized labor, certainly in the federal sector, would be viewed as contrary to the policies of the administration. While the event occurred in the public sector, one must be certain that the signals sent by the administration encompassed union activities throughout the economy.

One can easily see how this attitude toward unionism permeated the administration's selections for the National Labor Relations Board, senior positions in the Department of Labor, the National Mediation Board, the Federal Labor Relations Authority, the Federal Mediation and Conciliation Service, and other federal agencies responsible for labor-management relations. The unblushing advocacy of the open-shop form of contracting, as opposed to reliance on unionized firms was another dimension of the application of the free-market philosophy. The persistent, though largely ineffective, attacks on the prevailing wage programs (the Davis-Bacon Act and the Service Contract Act, in particular) the nation's minimum wage and maximum hour programs, the Occupational Safety and Health Act, and other labor-oriented programs are further evidence of the administration's efforts to shift the balance of power in the nation's labor management community.

How and why did the PATCO strike occur, and why wasn't it successful? From the above, it can be surmised that it was destined to fail because of the attitude of the new administration toward these types of events. The power of the entire federal government is an awesome prospect to contemplate, especially when it is not counterbalanced by public sentiment or the sentiment of other large institutions in society. The resources that the federal government can amass in these situations—legal, financial, communications—can easily submerge any but the strongest institutions. One must be careful to note, however, that the federal government derives its power and authority from the American electorate. An institution, even a very small one, can "win" in its contest with the federal government if it has public sentiment on its side. Absent public support, the contest is likely to be one sided and predictable.

There are many lessons to be learned from the PATCO strike by both organized labor and the federal government about public sector labor-management relations. There are three adages in government that relate directly to these relationships. First, "Perception is reality." It doesn't make any difference what is real. What is important is how people perceive what is going on, because it is this perception that motivates their actions. The administration was able to paint a picture of the PATCO that was singularly focused, that is, money, regardless of the PATCO's real demands. Second, "Timing is everything." Poor timing or being in the "wrong place at the wrong time" will destroy an otherwise sound initiative every time.

Americans do not like strikes any more than they like to be told what to do by government. Who can blame them? Strikes inconvenience people at best and sometimes disrupt well-established relationships and programs. Strikes have the potential for violence that upsets and concerns people. Strikers have been known to destroy personal property, injure and kill those who disagree with their cause, and disrupt the income flows of those not directly involved in the dispute. Actions by management can and have had the same sorts of consequences. Nevertheless, the American people have a good sense of what is right and wrong, even in the most complex situations. Americans can be counted on to throw their weight behind activities that are right, fair, and equitable. They may not like the inconvenience or disruption of an action, but if they understand it and it leads to greater fairness or equity, they will stand behind it and endure the outcome.

The third adage is "Watch what they do, not what they say." We live in a political world in which the nuances of words are what separate the political winners from the losers. Politicians who are successful are politicians who can craft rhetoric that captures the imagination or confounds the issue so that nobody understands it or so that nobody is accountable. Politicians will use verbiage or rhetoric that suits their political purposes regardless of the accuracy, honesty, or integrity of their statements. Politicians will say what they have to say to win. Anybody who does not believe that to be true, or who does not understand that point, is destined to be fooled or mislead by the rhetoric. Robert Poli, president of the PATCO, believed what presidential candidate Ronald Reagan told him about how he, Reagan, would change the air traffic control system if elected president.

The PATCO did not have public sentiment and support for its cause. Regardless of the merits of its grievances, and the merits were overwhelming, the PATCO did not mount an effective public relations campaign to educate the public about conditions in the air traffic control system. What the public heard about the situation was what the federal government—the FAA—decided they should hear. The FAA argued that controllers were paid too much, that they worked short hours, that automation had made their jobs easier, that there were ready replacements for those who left their jobs, ad infinitum. The mental image the public had was that air controllers were another bunch of underworked, overpaid federal employees who did not know how good they had it. A less-than-fair assessment, for certain, but one that the federal government methodically set out to establish and was very effective in doing so.

THE EARLY YEARS OF PATCO

The Professional Air Traffic Controllers Organization union existed for almost fourteen years. It served as the exclusive bargaining agent for air traffic controllers for the last nine years of its life. Officially, the PATCO was incorporated under the laws of the state of Iowa in 1969. Its first president was F. Lee Bailey. He served for about two years in that capacity. From the very beginning, the union exhibited a confrontational attitude toward the FAA and the Department of Transportation. The union issued public statements about problems relating to safety, employee relations, antiquated equipment, near misses by aircraft, and many other issues that often caught the FAA off guard. Union officials testified before the Congress on many occasions over its fourteen-year life. For example: "Six months after the Professional Air Traffic Controllers Organization (PATCO) was formed, the union publicly decried the antiquated air traffic control system. It alleged that some FAA supervisors were sacrificing air safety by requiring controllers to reduce separation minima between aircraft to make up for other systemic deficiencies."[1] Virtually all of these encounters concerned problems the PATCO was having with the FAA. The Congress seemed to like the union and appeared to appreciate the alternative perspective it provided.

To demonstrate its muscle, the PATCO engaged in several concerted actions prior to becoming the exclusive bargaining agent for all air traffic controllers. The first concerted action by the PATCO was a slowdown initiated in the summer of 1968. This action, orchestrated under the rubric of a program called "Operation Air Safety," precipitated an immediate crisis in the aviation industry. The PATCO "instructed its members to adhere strictly to the letter of all regulations of the Federal Aviation Administration (FAA) governing the separation and control of aircraft rather than exercise their judgment, based on long experience, as to appropriate standards for prevailing conditions."[2]

One might reasonably ask, Shouldn't air traffic controllers *always* adhere strictly to the letter of all regulations? It might seem at first blush that this is prudent and in accordance with the law. After all, the regulations are designed to ensure air safety. The problem is that the separation requirements are designed for the least proficient controller, not the most experienced. A new, less experienced controller may maintain five miles or more of horizontal separation between aircraft to ensure maximum safety. An experienced controller could, with complete safety, maintain, say, three miles or less separation. More aircraft can be moved through the "three-mile separation system" than through the "five-mile separation system." The industry wanted, expected, and supported the separation and sequencing that were most efficient, even though they were at variance with the letter of the regulations. Air traffic controllers routinely accommodated the dual need for safety and efficiency. They argued then, as they argue today, that safety is the single overriding objective in the air traffic control system.

Therefore, once the system functions on closer separation standards and flights are scheduled that are consistent with those standards, obvious problems arise when controllers go back to the "letter of the regulations." Suddenly airplanes are thrown off schedule, they are delayed on the ground awaiting takeoff, they are placed in holding patterns awaiting arrival instructions, and they may be controlled to altitudes that are not optimally efficient. What this translates into is more expense for the airlines, unhappy customers, and less efficient use of the air traffic control system. However, importantly, it is perfectly legal.

In the late 1960s, four unions were representing segments of the air traffic control work-force. To facilitate the payment of union dues to the unions, the FAA had initiated a checkoff in which dues are automatically withheld from a member's paycheck and provided to the union on a prearranged schedule. However, in response to the PATCO's actions, "[o]n July 27, 1969, FAA terminated its dues withholding agreement with the union. Pointing out that the dues checkoff arrangement is based on mutual interest, FAA Administrator John H. Shaffer said he ended PATCO's checkoff because 'it is clearly no longer in the public interest to assist an organization which is involved in a work stoppage.'"[3] Eliminating the dues checkoff was more symbolism than substance because the PATCO collected the same amount of dues. It simply did so less conveniently.

The first substantive legal action against the PATCO occurred in response to a sick-out orchestrated by the PATCO in early 1970. As court testimony showed, "[o]fficers of PATCO publicly announced their intention to stop work on March 25, 1970 unless their demands upon FAA were met, and they encouraged the Air Controllers to claim that they were ill and to stay away from work."[4]

Sympathetic controllers responded to the PATCO overture. They responded with several hundred calls in cities across the country

on March 25th and 26th, 1970, that they were too sick to work. Air Transport Association of America (ATA) and thirteen member airlines brought the first action, 70-C-400, against [the] Professional Air Traffic Controllers Organization (PATCO), its officers and directors and various of its leaders in the metropolitan area, and approximately 200 individual members, to enjoin the work stoppage, to direct them to perform their statutory duties and for damages.[5]

While the calls were identified as coming from "cities across the country," the vast majority appeared to come from the New York City region. The ATA complaint alleged "that an illegal work stoppage has occurred by concerted action of the defendants, based on false assertions of illness, that this is a strike, and that it has caused serious financial damage to the airline plaintiffs and interferes with their normal operations."[6] The ATA sought to enjoin the PATCO from continuing the sick-out, but "[a]n injunction acceptable to both sides, conditioned on impartial mediation, proved impossible because it was pointed out that PATCO has not been certified as a representative of the air controllers."[7] The PATCO had attempted to receive certification as a controller representative, but the FAA had opposed this action, and formal certification was pending.

The success of the sick-out hinged on the number of controllers who honored the union directive and remained off the job. It was a short job action—two days long—but as court proceedings noticed: "Since March 25, 1970, the number of absences from work by air controllers on account of alleged illness has increased from the normal average of 4 percent to a total of more than 60 percent at the facilities in the New York area."[8] This action, the sick-out, is perhaps the first substantial indication that air traffic controllers favored PATCO-style militancy rather than the less direct methods utilized by other employee representatives. Working to the "letter of the regulations" is not a violation of the law; failing to work because of alleged illness when illness is in fact not present is a concerted action that is illegal. This action in March 1970 was the first indication that air traffic controllers were prepared to take actions that directly challenged the application of law and regulations.

Early recognition by the judiciary that there may be more than one side to the controllers' problems occurred in the review of this action. "The court considers also that a substantial number of relatively highly paid men with specialized skills would not violate the law unless there was some provocation that they thought justified it, even though their belief in the justification might be erroneous."[9] The court provided an excerpt from the 1970 Corson Report [10] as further evidence of the joint problems in the PATCO-FAA relationship. The

Corson Report noted:

No single cause accounts for this crisis in the relation between FAA's management and the organizations representing its employees. Yet our observations suggest that among the most important is the failure of FAA's management at all levels to truly understand the role of the employee organizations and to accept them as not only legitimate, but hopefully as collaborators in building understanding, satisfaction, and an *esprit de corps*.

The court recommended, among other things, that the FAA "[e]xpedite, in good faith, the resolution . . . of all existing labor-management problems."[11]

During its formative years, the PATCO competed with four other unions that also sought to represent the air traffic controller work-force. In a representation election in September 1972, the "PATCO collected 83 percent of the votes cast and became the exclusive national bargaining agent of the 15,000 air traffic control specialists then employed by the FAA."[12] Based on the election, the PATCO was recognized as the exclusive national bargaining representative for all federal civilian air traffic controllers on October 20, 1972.

Five months after certification, "[o]n March 20, 1973, FAA and PATCO signed a labor agreement which for the first time recognized PATCO as the controllers' sole bargaining agent."[13]

The agreement provided for a full complement of union recognition, dispute resolution, and work rule provisions customarily found in these types of agreements. In addition, the FAA-PATCO Collective Bargaining Agreement provided for familiarization (FAM) flights by controllers. Called the SF-160 Program, the agreement provided that "[t]he parties recognize that any air carrier may suspend or abridge their participation in the SF-160 (familiarization flying) at any time and that the Employer [the FAA] has no authority to direct the conduct of the program by individual air carriers."[14]

The design and intent of FAM flights were to provide air traffic controllers free flights on scheduled airline flights to "familiarize" the controllers with the procedures and demands found in the cockpit. Since the vast majority of air traffic controllers were not pilots, this procedure made sense. The contract provision stated that the airlines could accommodate FAM flights or not, at the airlines' choosing. Air traffic controllers understood this aspect of the contract but believed strongly that all airlines should opt for participation in the FAM program.

These FAM flights played an important role in the PATCO-FAA relationship. In fact, some believe that the elimination of these flights was one of the most important events that ultimately led to the 1981 strike. In any event, not all carriers provided the FAM flights provided under the March 1973 agreement. When these flights were denied by individual carriers, PATCO members became annoyed.

In *Air Transport Association of America* v. *Professional Air Traffic Controllers Organization*, the ATA [Air Transport Association] alleged by affidavit that "Upon information and belief, [Mr. John F.] Leyden stated that the controllers are 'angry' and 'fed up' with these airlines, predicted a 'spontaneous' slowdown could hit 'today, tomorrow or anytime,' and observed that the airlines 'can allow us a free seat or spend some money burning fuel.'"[15]

While there were a number of "events" during the early years of PATCO's existence, the longest period of relative labor peace between the FAA and PATCO "occurred between the end of April 1970, and the end of July 1976. Although PATCO made isolated threats of slowdowns or 'strict compliance with procedures' there were no significant increases in controller absenteeism nor delays to the airspace user."[16]

The leaders in the PATCO recognized the importance of international air transportation. They knew that anything they wanted to do domestically would ultimately involve foreign carriers and, by inference, foreign air traffic control organizations. Air traffic control between the U.S. and Europe, one of the heaviest traveled air routes, requires cooperation by Canadian controllers, British controllers, and often, Spanish, Portuguese, and French controllers. The air carriers had their domestic and international associations representing their interests. The International Federation of Air Traffic Controllers Associations (IFATCA) was established precisely for these types of coordination purposes for air traffic control employee organizations. The PATCO affiliated with the IFATCA. However, the relationship was short-lived. PATCO leaders did not believe their affiliation provided enough in terms of mutual support activities, and they were unhappy about contributing more financial support than other IFATCA affiliates. Thus, in 1976, the PATCO disaffiliated. This action may have weakened PATCO's strike activity in 1981, because soon after the strike began, it entered the international sector.

In 1977, the PATCO established a strike fund known as the National Controller Subsistence Fund. The national organization allocated 15 percent of the membership dues that were submitted to the union for support of the fund. "By August 1981, over $3 million was in this fund, and three controllers who had been discharged for strike activity were receiving payments from the fund equal to their full salaries."[17]

Problems between the FAA and the PATCO were unresolved during the "period of relative labor peace," and pressure for more direct action began to mount. On May 25 and 26, 1978, and June 6 and 7, 1978, the PATCO conducted a slowdown. The results were predictable—disruption in air traffic flows and threats of lawsuits. The slowdowns were of short duration but demonstrated the vulnerability of the industry to concerted actions, short of an actual work stoppage. These actions demonstrated once again that the PATCO could apply pressure on the industry anytime the union chose. "The final disruption before 1981 occurred at Chicago's O'Hare International on August 15, 1980. Following the FAA's refusal of a PATCO demand for an annual tax-free bonus of $7,500 to compensate for the alleged greater stress on the job at that busy airport, PATCO members there initiated a slowdown that caused 616 delays of 30 minutes or more and cost the airlines more than one million dollars in wasted fuel."[18]

As demonstrated by the selected events just described, the PATCO was not a status quo organization. It continued to challenge the FAA through concerted actions during its entire fourteen years. It was successful in some but unsuccessful in a major one. The remainder of this book describes the unsuccessful event. It all ended when the Professional Air Traffic Controllers Organization was decertified on October 22, 1981, because of its strike against the Government of the United States on August 3, 1981. Robert Poli resigned the presidency of the PATCO on December 31, 1981.

ACADEMIC REVIEW OF THE PATCO STRIKE

One of the frustrating aspects of the PATCO strike and its aftermath is that the precise factors that caused the strike may never be known. In 1984, distinguished labor relations scholar Herbert Northrup wrote an article in the *Industrial and Labor Relations Review* entitled "The Rise and Demise of PATCO." His article attempted to describe the motives of both sides, the prestrike and post-strike activities, the role of external parties to the dispute, and so forth. It's an interesting analysis that paints a picture of a union-gone-bezerk in its thirst for power over factors and conditions that it did not control. The Northrup analysis provides an important perspective about the strike, but its omissions of fact and perspective were criticized by Richard Hurd and Jill Kriesky in a long article in the same journal in October 1986. Northrup attempts to refute the criticisms raised by Hurd and Kriesky but, unfortunately leaves the character and tone of his analysis tainted by a clear bias supporting the actions of FAA management officials. A careful reading of the article and the two rejoinders does not provide compelling evidence for the one-sided role of either PATCO or the Reagan administration that the authors portray.[19] There was certainly enough blame to go around for the onset of the strike and the failure of the parties to resolve it.

Workers have gone on strike in both the public and private sectors for the better part of a century for a whole range of important and not-so-important reasons. Many of those actions were motivated by greed, some by the need to correct injustices, some on the basis of misinformation or stupidity. As one reads the Northrup–Hurd–Kriesky interchange, what becomes clear is that all of these factors—and probably others—played a role in the onset of the strike. Was PATCO exuberant and overly optimistic about its ability to bring the industry to its knees and therefore compel compliance with PATCO's agenda? Probably. Was the FAA insensitive, overly militaristic, inflexible, and belligerent toward the PATCO? Probably. Did the PATCO make some tactical and strategic errors that made success almost impossible? Without a doubt. Did the FAA and the Department of Transportation (DOT) adopt a response to the PATCO that attempted to diminish the union's role and as a consequence frustrated both union members and leaders? Assuredly.

These general observations do not excuse those who violate the law; these general observations do not excuse those who incite actions that may be counterproductive because of poor personnel practices; they do not excuse those who poison the system with misinformation or who tell part truths to bolster their positions. What these observations do tell us is that this story, too, has at least two sides to it. It is not a story of a bunch of horrible air traffic controllers and their union attempting to extract their pound of flesh from an innocent federal agency who is just doing the best it can to protect the public interest. Neither is it a story of some horrible federal autocrats bent on destroying the PATCO or any other union that does not comply with their wishes. It is a more complex story based on many years of acrimonious relationships between two organizations that spun out of control on August 3, 1981. This is not to suggest that it spun out of control accidently; that both parties were surprised by the action; that there were no ways of preventing the event; or that everyone in the process acted above board and in good faith.

There is evidence that the strike on August 3, 1981, was misfocused and probably poorly timed. The PATCO must, to a large extent, be held responsible for that action. There is also evidence that the FAA and the DOT established positions that prevented any possibility of resolving the strike amicably. They must be held responsible for the ultimate destruction of the PATCO and the firing of over 11,000 federal employees. One might say that the PATCO was responsible for the firing of the 11,000 employees because if the strike had not occurred, none of the workers would have been fired. A fair point, but not particularly relevant. One could also argue that if the management style and substance of the FAA over many years of documented history was not so inflexible and confrontational, the strike would never have occurred.

While these types of tussles relating to "who shot Joe" will probably continue as long as there are people around interested in the issue, nobody will be able to convince everybody with a "grand theory" that unites all the pieces. Much of the problem of placing blame goes to motivation. We can observe public statements, public actions, responses to actions of others, and a variety of knowable events without ever witnessing firsthand the real motivation for their actions or events. A second important element in the dialogue relates to who knew what, when. Some may argue that it's not important to know who knew what, when because all that really matters is that a strike occurred, over 11,000 controllers lost their jobs, and the PATCO was destroyed. However, nobody will disagree that communication is probably the single most important part of the collective bargaining process other than raw power. While both sides argue that they tried to be open with each other and communicate effectively, it's unclear how either side approached this process. Its very clear that there had been communications problems between the FAA and its employees for many years prior to the strike. It's generally accepted that the FAA did not embrace the role of the several unions that represented its employees and in fact attempted to minimize or diminish their representation role.

On the other hand, the PATCO apparently did little to ingratiate itself with the FAA leadership but, rather, communicated its concerns and problems through the media and in the political process. The precise reasons for this approach to communications is unclear, but it obviously did little to enhance the stature of the PATCO within the FAA. Management was often caught off balance and unprepared to address problems and issues that could have been resolved more amicably.

The FAA was undoubtedly tired of wrestling with the PATCO, the exclusive bargaining agent subsequent to 1972, and may have been looking for a vehicle to put an end to this irritation. What better vehicle for garnering public support and for the appearance of taking the "high road" than an illegal strike? This is a particularly interesting proposition because of the mood of the country in the early years of the Reagan administration. Americans were tired of "big government" and seemingly wanted major reforms in the role and consequences of government, particularly the federal government, in economic and social affairs. In fact, several of the planks of the Reagan economic program were designed to further these objectives. Decreased government regulation, while started in the Carter administration, became the rallying cry of the Reagan administration.

There is a twinge of irony in the PATCO situation in that the American people were apparently willing to see—and support—one of the most highly regulated agencies in the federal government exert its power to crush the union. Admittedly, the public did not see federal regulation as the issue in this environment, but there can be little doubt that much of the monopoly power the FAA exerted then and exerts today is due to the high degree of regulation and regimentation in that agency. The role of the FAA as the exclusive repository of control over air traffic, pilot certification, hardware testing and certification, regulatory enforcement, and other aspects of this high-technology industry provides it a mechanism for initiating and maintaining high-handed personnel and labor relations policies.

All of these tantalizing activities, events, and attitudes should have been the fodder for not one significant article and two rejoinders but dozens of books, articles, and doctoral dissertations. Far less important events have been the focus of extensive research and numerous publications.

WHY HAS SO LITTLE BEEN WRITTEN ABOUT SUCH AN IMPORTANT EVENT?

Why has there been relatively little written about the PATCO strike and its aftermath? The answer has several parts. First, organized labor was not happy with the strike, how it was conducted, what may have caused it, and certainly not with the administration's response to it. The American labor movement would just as soon put the PATCO behind it and move forward. Second, the federal government accumulated some political capital in the early months of the crisis, but in the longer term, it came to realize that the public was not overly enamored with how the government responded. Yes, the controllers did break the law. Yes, there were periods of mild disruption and inconvenience. Yes, something decisive had to happen. However, there were other options. The federal government came down on the PATCO in a way that smacked of overkill and overreaction that tainted the public's view of the situation. Had the government explored all other options before choosing industrial death for the PATCO? Clearly not. Was there merit to some or most of the issues and problems advanced by the PATCO that played a role in the strike? Clearly, there was merit.

The third reason that little has been written is that many academics have written off or started to write off labor unions in America. Some academics apparently feel that the unions got what they deserved—and so what else is new? In the context of the ascent of market economics, academics have hitched their wagons to the dogma of noninterventionist economics, of which labor unions are the antithesis. By writing about them, one brings them to public attention. Since the PATCO story raises serious questions about the government's motives and processes, and in the final analysis may not cast as dark a shadow over the PATCO as some would like, there are dangers in unraveling this story. The PATCO and the labor movement may not come out as vilified as some would like, and certainly the federal government will come out with blood on its hands.

One must not infer from this general observation that the PATCO had pristine motives and was acting in an up-front, good-faith manner with the FAA or the American people. The PATCO broke the law, pure and simple, and there was a price to be paid. There were undoubtedly some clandestine motives lurking in the minds of the PATCO leadership that somehow the federal Congress and the executive could be brought to their knees and the PATCO shopping list obtained. Other unions had succeeded in the federal sector, and there was little to suggest that the PATCO would not succeed as well. However, the PATCO could have exerted pressure on the system through means other than a strike, too. One gets the distinct flavor of greed in the character of the PATCO demands and in the tenacious nature with which it hung on to those demands. Robert Poli was not a man with a small ego. In this respect, however, he is little different from other leaders in every aspect of American life. Certainly, Ronald Reagan, Drew Lewis, and Lynn Helms would not be characterized as "small ego" men.

Probably because there has been a reluctance to tell the entire PATCO story is this writing effort so important. Over fifteen years have passed since the strike occurred, the union was decertified, and Robert Poli resigned as PATCO president. A new union has arisen in the FAA to represent air traffic controllers.[20] While not necessarily unprecedented, the rather quick formation of a new union with members who were *not* part of the PATCO strike says something about labor-management relations in the FAA. Unions form where there is a need for unions. Unions form where workers want a voice in their destiny and in resolving issues that are important to them. If all was well between the FAA and its controllers, would a new union have sprung up so quickly? Did the FAA learn from the PATCO experience, or is FAA management proceeding in a business-as-usual fashion?

This book is not going to delve into the new controller union or the current FAA management practices. Its purpose is not to regale the current relationship between the FAA and its controllers or the new controller union—the National Air Traffic Controllers Association (NATCA). Rather, it is intended to tell the story in as complete a manner as possible so that someone else can draw the inferences and apply the lessons that were learned by this experience. The PATCO experience has been termed a "tragedy," a "disaster," a "debacle," and a "calamity." I suppose it is all of these things, particularly for the more than 11,000 controllers who lost their jobs permanently. We cannot go back in time and change what happened, but we can learn the lessons that the experience taught us to improve conditions in the future.

Will we learn and apply those lessons to improve conditions in the future? Probably not. As a people, we now know what not to do in situations of confrontation in the federal sector, but there will be confrontations in the future. The leaders of federal unions and federal officials are human beings, and they make mistakes in judgment, read into conditions and situations much that is not there, and permit ego and self-serving motivation to flavor the decision-making process. So, what else is new? This is all part of the human condition, and it is unlikely to change much in the future. Nevertheless, the PATCO strike and its aftermath are an important part of American labor history and should be studied carefully by those with a stake in the success of the governmental process and the role of workers and their representatives in the economic system. In brief, that means every one of us.

A BRIEF HISTORY OF FEDERAL LABOR-MANAGEMENT RELATIONS

Labor-management relations between the FAA and its unions are determined by federal law, regulations, and customs. Private sector labor relations are controlled by a variety of federal statutes including the National Labor Relations Act (the Wagner Act), the Labor-Management Relations Act (the Taft-Hartley Act), the Labor-Management Reporting and Disclosure Act (the Landrum-Griffin Act), and a variety of state statutes dating back over fifty years. The basic framework within which federal activities occur was initiated by Executive Order 10988, issued by President John Kennedy on January 17, 1962. This order was modified by Executive Order 11491, issued by President Richard Nixon on October 29, 1969, and subsequently by the Civil Service Reform Act (CSRA) of 1978. The CSRA, effective on January 11, 1979, superseded the two executive orders but, for the most part, codified their provisions. As a result, there were few major changes in how the federal government performed its labor-management relations activity.

The CSRA created a three-member Federal Labor Relations Authority (FLRA) to perform essentially the same functions as those performed by the National Labor Relations Board (NLRB) under the National Labor Relations Act. Union representation questions and the prosecution of unfair labor practices are the two main functions of the FLRA. The FLRA has a general counsel who oversees the daily functions of the organization. FLRA decisions can be reviewed in the courts.

The CSRA prohibits strikes by federal employees. In addition, the law prohibits compulsory unionism. The Congress maintains authority over many of the conditions of federal employment such as wages and salaries, length of the workday and workweek, benefit packages, and so forth. Federal employees cannot generally "bargain" about these issues. There are examples, however, in which agencies and their unions discussed and negotiated changes in the nonbargainable areas. When this occurred, the agency and union usually approached the Congress jointly in an effort to effectuate their "agreement." The FAA and the PATCO had a relationship along these lines prior to the August 3, 1981, strike. In fact, Herbert Northrup believes that the PATCO and the FAA had succeeded in negotiating a wage package that was the first step in breaching the nonbargainable collective bargaining issues. Included within the permissible bargaining sphere are work hours, overtime pay, holidays, work schedules, promotions, and the like. Grievances that remain unsettled during the term of the contract are settled by arbitration. However, the arbitration award is not necessarily the final word. Either party can ask the FLRA to review an arbitration decision.

During negotiations, unresolved issues are first referred to the Federal Mediation and Conciliation Service (FMCS). If the FMCS cannot resolve the impasse, the issues are referred to the Federal Services Impasses Panel (FSIP). Created by Executive Order 11491, the FSIP has the authority to resolve the impasse through whatever means are necessary. The prevalent form of resolution is to submit the issues to binding arbitration.

Under the CSRA, strikes by federal employees constitute unfair labor practices. Strikes and other concerted actions by unions and their members are illegal under other federal statutes as well. If a union promotes, encourages, or participates in a strike against the federal government, a possible penalty is decertification of the union. In addition, the penalty for participants in the strike may involve imprisonment and fines. The law is clear about strike activity and its penalties. Nevertheless, the issue of striking federal employees is one that deserves more careful attention. It may seem to some to be a black-and-white issue, but to most it is anything but clearly defined.

AIR TRAFFIC CONTROLLERS AND THE RIGHT TO STRIKE

There are two polar positions relating to the question of whether or not the PATCO had the right to strike. Obviously, President Reagan did not think it had the right to strike. The controllers and much of organized labor, foreign and domestic, believed they did have that right as human beings. The right to strike by public employees is a philosophical as well as an economic and legal issue. A number of states in the United States have given public employees legal right to strike under certain conditions. Most states and the federal government ban public employee strikes by statute.

Virtually all collective bargaining agreements in the private sector contain language that prohibits strikes during the term of the contract. Nevertheless, there are conditions in private industry that permit strikes even though contractually they are prohibited. For example, if workers believe that their health or safety is at risk, they have the right to walk off the job, that is, strike. Assuming that the courts can verify that there was in fact a probable cause to believe a life-threatening condition existed, workers are unlikely to be fired or disciplined in any other manner for their actions.

The right to strike by the air traffic controllers is a specific instance of the general question concerning public employee strikes. Throughout history, public sector unions at both the federal, state, and local levels have gone on strike. In some cases, striking workers were discharged. In the vast majority of cases, however, striking workers were permitted to return to their jobs without sanction or punishment. In a small number of cases, public jurisdictions rehired fired employees on a selective basis.

The terrain is not smooth, and the application of the law has been less than uniform. Why is there so much confusion about how to deal with striking public employees? The types of questions that must be addressed include: Is there a difference between the rights of public sector employees and the rights of private sector employees? If there is a difference, what gives rise to the difference? In a free society, does it make sense to enact laws that make criminals out of those who withhold their labor services? Should all public employees be prohibited from striking, or are there types of employees that should be permitted to strike? If public employees are prohibited from striking, what are the alternative dispute resolution mechanisms?

If Americans on the street are asked about this issue, the answers are likely to range from support of an absolute strike prohibition to support for complete freedom of individual and collective action. One can be almost certain that public sector managers will opt for complete prohibition of strike activity by public employees. They will cite the law as the primary support for their position. Union officials will always start their response to "the" question by saying that they respect the law. However, they will then articulate circumstances and situations in which strike activity should be permitted in spite of the law. Union officials argue that there are two sides to any labor dispute, and one must weigh the contributing factors by both parties. Typical of the union response was that provided by Moe Biller, president of the American Postal Workers Union, in response to a question as to whether the U.S. government should give amnesty to the striking air traffic controllers. Biller replied:

I acknowledge the law, but it's far too stringent. Ours is the only democracy in the world that sentences its government workers to "economic capital punishment"—that takes their jobs away because they choose to strike. That's something which should be reexamined. In dealing with the air-traffic controllers, the government must acknowledge its own role in causing this strike. It failed to redress their grievances and their problems—and there is a long history of problems in this area."[21]

When Drew Lewis, secretary of transportation, was asked what was wrong with granting amnesty to the air traffic controllers, he responded with the notion, "Now we're in a position that the very core of this democracy—the very system of law that we've developed over the last 200 years—is in jeopardy."[22]

One can see that there is very little overlap between these two positions. The grandiose assertion by Lewis that the "core of this democracy is in jeopardy" is typical of the generalization of the law when attributed to these situations. One wonders why when the postal workers, shipyard employees, and many others struck that these actions were not a threat to our democracy. Nevertheless, the question of public sector strikes is one that deserves serious attention. Many scholars have given these issues careful thought and have developed a useful framework within which to think about these actions. It is unlikely that the balanced and careful analysis provided by these individuals will alter the position espoused by either Moe Biller or Drew Lewis, but it is useful to sketch the arguments nonetheless.

THE THEORY OF PUBLIC SECTOR STRIKES

On the one hand, the United States does not permit forced labor; on the other hand, the federal government is the sovereign and exercises sovereign power. Withholding of labor, individually or collectively, is a strike. Strikes are a sanctioned part of the collective bargaining process in the private sector. Are there differences between employees in the public and private sectors that compel treating them differently? Federal government employees sign an oath that says they will not strike or assist a strike while employed by the federal government. Is this enough to preclude strike activity by these employees? After all, one can always resign from federal service if dissatisfaction with the work or work environment becomes unbearable.

Sovereign power is ultimate power in society. It is the sovereign power of the state, after all, that permits the state to impose capital punishment for certain types of crimes. In the United States, the government is empowered by the people and can be changed by the people. In this sense, the people collectively constitute the sovereign power in American society. Striking against the sovereign is tantamount to striking against oneself. More important, striking against the sovereign undercuts the ultimate authority or power structure in society.

All of this is well known and generally accepted. However, it does not address the real questions related to freedom of action and freedom of choice faced by federal employees as they fulfill their work responsibilities. One thing is certain: Legally prohibiting strikes will not stop strikes. Does it make sense to legally prohibit striking and require employees to sign an oath when it is clear that conditions can and do arise that compel workers to withhold their labor services? Strike opponents would argue that it does make sense and that these prohibitions should be strengthened. Strike supporters argue that it makes little sense to make committed federal workers criminals for exercising one of their fundamental human rights.

To permit further consideration of this issue, it may be useful to delineate the major arguments on each side. Those arguments in opposition to public sector strikes will be described first.

The Sovereign

The sovereignty doctrine argues that the government is the "embodiment" of the people and those who are entrusted to perform governmental functions (federal employees) may not impede those activities. Presidents, liberal and conservative, and the judiciary have upheld this doctrine throughout much of American history. In 1951, in *Norwalk Teachers Association* v. *Board of Education*, the Connecticut State Supreme Court provided as clear a description of the sovereignty doctrine as it applies to employee rights as can be found anywhere. The court argued:

In the American system, sovereignty is inherent in the people. They can delegate it to a government which they create and operate by law. They can give to that government the power and authority to perform certain duties and furnish certain services. The government so created and empowered must employ people to carry on its task. Those people are agents of the government. They exercise some part of the sovereignty entrusted to it. They occupy a status entirely different from those who carry on a private enterprise. They serve the public welfare and not a private purpose. To say that they can strike is the equivalent of saying that they can deny the authority of government and contravene the public welfare. [23]

The courts have occasionally gone further. They have viewed strikes by public employees as a form of uprising that can lead to chaos and anarchy. In that process, individual rights become meaningless. A task of the sovereign is to maintain balance within the society and to be the sole source of power to determine public policy.

While the concept of sovereignty is absolute, there are varying degrees of sovereignty within a political system. The federal government, in the American political system, is the ultimate sovereign because it contains the final judicial appeal mechanism, has the authority to print money, can declare war on a belligerent adversary, can consummate international trading agreements, and so forth. Out of this system of absolute power arises the recognition that all of the power is in fact derived from the people. The U.S. constitutional democracy provides for the separation of powers and for the location of ultimate power in the hands of the states. Only the power or authority the states give to the federal government resides in the federal government. Unless the several states give the federal government specific power or authority, this power and authority remain with the states.

Human Rights

The sovereignty arguments seem persuasive and compelling. After all, we are a nation of laws, and nobody is above the law. We are a nation that feels strongly about the role of law and the fairness of application of the law. Due process, the right to a fair and speedy trial, self-incrimination, and a variety of other legal principles are what set our society apart from totalitarianism. It is not a perfect system, and justice does not always prevail, but it is a system that is responsive to the needs of a free people.

In this context, society develops and maintains a set of rights or obligations to which participant citizens must adhere. However, many will argue that there is, as a part of the human condition, a body of rights that are even more basic. Those rights are human or individual rights. In essence, as human beings, we have the right to perpetuate our lives, to seek and enjoy liberty and freedom, and to advance and perpetuate actions that maximize the quality of our lives, as we perceive that quality as individuals. Some may encapsulate these ideas in a more contemporary framework of "individualism." In fact, in the United States we pride ourselves on individualism and self-reliance. We view the government as secondary in achieving self-fulfilling goals. Most Americans would not argue with the concept of pursuit of individual, human rights.

However, as one thinks about this set of relationships, one is struck by the obvious inconsistencies. Either the sovereign is sovereign and can exercise supreme authority—or it cannot. Either we have a right to basic human rights—or we do not. If the government—the sovereign—can take away those human rights, then we, in fact, do not have them. But that isn't the end of the story either. While obviously the government can take away some of our human rights, we are the government. In that sense, we are *permitting* the government to exercise this authority for the maintenance and continuance of society. If we don't want the government to perform that role, we remove that authority, and it reverts to individual citizens. Some would argue that it reverts to anarchy.

One can see the circular nature of this relationship. It is unique, in large part, to Americans. In a civilized society, there must be order; there must be generally accepted rules of conduct. On the other hand, the vagaries of the human condition are such that individuals find themselves in conditions in which the rule of law cannot be applied. If it is applied, then, on an individual basis, persons may sacrifice their freedom and ultimately their lives to maintain a legal principle. This is the essence of the dilemma: Where do human rights begin and the rights of society end?

This is precisely the nexus of the arguments relating to the Professional Air Traffic Controllers Organization. Controllers believed that their health and longevity on the job were threatened by conditions of employment. After years of unsuccessful bargaining with the FAA to resolve these problems, the vast majority of controllers believed that their only remaining remedy was to withhold their labor services. The fact that upwards of 90 percent of controllers leaving employment with the FAA on medical disability, years earlier than most people retire, suggests that there may be a case for their actions.

However, it is difficult to determine the immediacy of their problem. It seems qualitatively different from the presence of bare electrical wires or leaking gas in a production environment. The latter types of situations have precipitated immediate strikes that have been upheld by the courts. Nevertheless, concerns involving nontraumatic injuries are the fastest-growing category of injuries in the Federal Employees' Compensation Act program.[24] Even though these types of injuries are not traumatic injuries, they are nonetheless important maladies in the lives of employees that deserve and receive attention. Must individuals endure a work environment so stressful that their emotional and physical being are damaged before they have the right to strike? Most reasonable people would argue that if there is no "road map" for resolving these types of employment conditions, a strike may be the only avenue of action left. One need not, it is argued, be required to endure danger or damage in the public work environment any more than one need be required to endure danger or damage in private sector production processes.

This discussion about the right to strike by the Professional Air Traffic Controllers Organization is not a definitive review of the legal concepts relevant to a complete review of the strike issue. Rather, it is designed to sensitize the reader to the kinds of issues and how one might think about those issues so that the context in which the PATCO strike occurred can be better understood. The thrust of the discussion so far is that the "right to strike" by public employees is a sensitive and largely unresolved problem. It is likely to remain that way. Work stoppages are never pleasant, but neither is infringement of the basic human rights of dignity, equity, safety, and fair play.

SUMMARY

The Professional Air Traffic Controllers Organization emerged as the exclusive bargaining agent for 18,000 air traffic controllers. It assumed this position in large part because controllers believed that it (the PATCO) would aggressively take on the FAA to resolve serious problems of long standing. The five years of "relative labor peace" convinced many controllers that the FAA was not going to change things unless more direct action occurred. The PATCO demonstrated its ability, on several occasions, to immediately and directly affect operations in the airline industry. This realization commingled with the inability or unwillingness of the FAA to resolve problems affecting controller working conditions, provided the environment for increasingly aggressive controller actions. "Working to the rule" didn't seem to solve their problems. Slowdowns didn't seem to solve their problems, either. Therefore, the PATCO initiated "its greatest challenge," a "definitive strike" against the government of the United States.

The strike failed, and over 11,000 air traffic controllers lost their jobs. Reason suggests that this event deserves more than cursory review and attention. However, regardless of its importance, very little has been done to explain and understand fully what happened and why it happened. While the Northrup–Hurd–Kriesky attempted to bring focus to this event, justice has not been done to a seminal occurrence in American labor history.

The PATCO strike forced the nation to once again focus on the issue of strikes in the public sector. While there is substantial scholarly consideration of this issue, what remains is the recognition that while strikes by federal employees are illegal, they cannot be prevented. Until the nation adopts a mechanism(s) for addressing federal employee grievances that is accepted by federal employees as fair and effective, federal employee strikes will remain as the vehicle of choice for serious problem resolution.

NOTES

1. Gregory L. Karam, "The Legal Consequences of a Deliberate Air Traffic Controllers Slowdown," *Northern Kentucky Law Review*, Vol. 8, No.1, January 1981, p. 159.

2. Senate, Committee on Post Office and Civil Service, *Air Traffic Controllers*, 91st Cong., 2d sess. Report to Accompany S. 3959, Report No. 91-1012 (Washington, D.C.: GPO, July 9, 1970), p. 25.

3. Karam, "The Legal Consequences of a Deliberate Air Traffic Controllers Slowdown," p. 160.

4. *Federal Supplement*, Vol. 313, F. Supp. 181 (St. Paul, Minn.: West Publishing Co., 1970), pp. 181–190.

5. Ibid., p. 183.

6. Ibid.

7. Ibid., p. 185.

8. Ibid.

9. Ibid.

10. The Corson Report, as described later, was the first significant study, commissioned by the FAA, that examined air traffic controller problems. The report was published in the late 1970s.

11. Ibid., p. 188.

12. Karam, "The Legal Consequences of a Deliberate Air Traffic Controllers Slow-down," p. 168.

13. Ibid.

14. Ibid., p. 169.

15. Ibid.

16. Ibid., p. 167.

17. Ibid., p. 171.

18. Ibid., pp. 170–171.

19. The three articles comprising this review are Herbert Northrup, "The Rise and Demise of PATCO," pp. 167–184; Richard W. Hurd, "Communications: The Rise and Demise of PATCO Reconstructed," pp. 115–121; and, Herbert Northrup, "Reply," pp. 122–127.

20. The new union is called the NATCA (National Air Traffic Controllers Association). It became operational in 1987, six years after the strike.

21. "Should the U.S. Grant Amnesty to Air Controllers?" *U.S. News and World Report*, August 24, 1981, p. 18.

22. Ibid., p. 19.

23. Kurt L. Hanslowe and John L. Acierno, "The Law and Theory of Strikes by Government Employees," *Cornell Law Review*, Vol. 67, No. 6, August 1982, pp. 1061–1062.

24. Willis J. Nordlund, *A History of the Federal Employees Compensation Program* (Washington, D.C.: GPO, August 1992), p. 174.

Chapter 2

The Air Traffic Control System

Those who fly in the U.S. air traffic control system should feel confident about the integrity, safety, and efficiency of the system. Many people never think about it, but when they board an airplane, they are placing their lives immediately and irrevocably in the hands of somebody else. Often, they do not even know who that person is, and in most cases, they have never laid eyes on the person. When that jumbo jet rotates at the end of the takeoff roll, each passenger's life is in the hands of a stranger. Admittedly, there are several key players in this scenario, but the pilot, flight engineer, and air traffic controller handling each segment of the flight are the ones who make the decisions about the success of the flight. When the cabin door slams shut and is locked, each passenger is placing his or her trust with somebody in a more direct way than when he or she enters the operating room for major brain or cardiac surgery.

Regrettably, there are occasional problems relating to antiquated computer systems, the loss of radar coverage, power failures, and other events that grab the headlines. These events, while they have caused problems, generally cannot be tied to any particular accident or death in the American system. Why not? The answer is simple: The U.S. air route traffic control system is the most sophisticated air traffic control system in the world. It is not the most up-to-date system in terms of ADP hardware, but it has the most effective and efficient overall control system to be found anywhere in the world. The FAA continues to test and upgrade new technical systems to improve safety and efficiency.

THE EVOLUTION OF THE AIR TRAFFIC CONTROL SYSTEM

The American air traffic control (ATC) system started in 1936. Air traffic controllers used mechanical devices such as aviation maps, blackboards, slide rules, and other basic tools to help them calculate the positions of aircraft flying on established routes. These routes were limited in number, and they connected a dozen or so of the largest American cities. With no automated equipment, controllers used mental calculations to determine separation between aircraft. It was a primitive system by modern standards, but it provided the basis upon which to begin the automation processes in the 1950s, 1960s, and 1970s.

The governmental functions supporting the ATC system have changed in substantial ways. Several of these changes placed increased burdens on the air traffic controller. The 1938 Civil Aeronautics Act created the Civil Aeronautics Authority as an independent federal agency. The Civil Aeronautics Authority functions included the power to issue certificates to air carriers that determined the routes they were authorized to fly. In addition, the authority was charged with regulating airline fares.

President Franklin Roosevelt split the Civil Aeronautics Authority into two parts—the Civil Aeronautics Board (CAB) and the Civil Aeronautics Administration (CAA). The CAB was responsible for safety rule-making, accident investigation, and economic regulations related to civil air carriers. The CAA assumed responsibilities including safety enforcement, aircraft and airmen certification, and the ATC system. The CAA began controlling takeoff and landing operations just prior to the nation's entry into World War II.

Serious concerns about the capabilities of the air traffic control system to accommodate the growing volume of U.S. air traffic started in earnest shortly after the Korean War. In May 1955, President Dwight Eisenhower asked William Barclay Harding to provide a report on aviation facilities requirements and to provide recommendations concerning a long-range study of the air traffic control system. The Harding Report recommended that the president appoint a distinguished American with a national reputation to conduct a study of the system. Based on the Harding Report recommendations, the president appointed Edwin P. Curtis to conduct the study. The character of his assignment was to echo through a variety of subsequent study commissions. President Eisenhower instructed Curtis "to develop a 'long range study of the nation's requirement,' to develop 'a comprehensive plan for meeting in the most effective and economical manner the needs disclosed by the study,' and 'to formulate legislation, organizational, administrative, and budgetary recommendations to implement the comprehensive plan.'"[1]

Eighteen months later, in May 1957, the "Curtis Report" was submitted to the president. This report was the first in a long series of reports that purported to provide definitive guidance to federal policy makers to fix the air traffic control system. The Curtis Report recommended the creation of an independent agency to manage all of the civil and military aviation activities in the United States. As an interim step, the report recommended the creation of a "modernization board" to begin the development of requirements for "future systems of communications, navigation, and traffic control needed to accommodate the nation's air traffic."[2]

Based on the Curtis Report, the Airways Modernization Act of 1957 cre-

ated the Airways Modernization Board. As Congress enacted the stopgap legislation, they invited the president to recommend legislation to create a permanent agency to address the nation's aviation needs. In 1958, the Federal Aviation Act created the Civil Aeronautics Board and the Federal Aviation Agency.
The agency superseded the Civil Aeronautics Authority and assumed responsibility for all safety rule-making with the exception of accident investigation. In
addition, the new Agency was given responsibility for developing a system of
air traffic control and air navigation for both the civilian and military sectors.
The CAB, created originally in 1941, retained authority for establishing air
routes, for reviewing tariffs, and for determining the probable cause of accidents.

A second concept in the Curtis Report provided for extensive involvement
of pilots in conjunction with a nationwide computer system to determine the
precise location of aircraft. This highly automated system, using basic radar
systems, replaced much of the slower voice communications procedures. The
prototype system was called the Data Process Central System. Portions of the
new system were installed in the Atlantic City research facility for testing. After
months of testing, it became apparent that the system could not be implemented.
It was canceled in 1961.

Three months after his inauguration as president of the United States, President John Kennedy directed the FAA to conduct a scientific study of the nation's
air traffic control system. The president wanted the FAA "to prepare a long-
range plan to assure safety and efficient control of all air traffic within the United
States."[3] Based on the president's directive, on November 7, 1961, the FAA
produced a report entitled "Project Beacon" that established general guidelines
for a state-of-the-art air traffic control system. Ten years after the submission of
the "Project Beacon" report, "no significant element of the new air traffic control system recommended in that report [was] in operation."[4] The lack of progress
in enhancing the system was compounded by the growth in the aviation sector.
In 1960, there were about "50 million domestic revenue passengers enplanements
and 30 billion domestic revenue passenger miles."[5] While the number of commercial aircraft increased from 2,135 in 1960 to 2,689 in 1970, enplanements
increased to 157 million passengers, and almost 100 billion domestic revenue
passenger miles were flown in 1970.[6] General aviation aircraft increased in number from about 76,549 in 1960 to over 133,000 in 1970.

All of these changes occurred in spite of few improvements in the air traffic
control system needed to accommodate them. One of the disturbing consequences
of these changes was, by the end of the 1960s, the complete saturation of some
of the nation's major airports. Airports in New York, Chicago, Washington, and
Los Angeles were placed on strict operational quotas to prevent complete break-
down of the system. These airports and many others near saturation simply
could not accommodate the volume of air traffic and the new demands placed on
the system by high-speed jet aircraft.

Since the FAA demonstrated its inability to develop and implement a responsive air traffic control system, the Congress decided to undertake a "fundamental review" of the agency's development efforts to ascertain what problems prevented the development of "Project Beacon" recommendations.

What became clear was that the air traffic control system required the simultaneous development and implementation of new technology in conjunction with the overall expansion of the system. The growth of the aviation sector never gave the air traffic control developers time to stabilize the system. As a consequence, for every advance that occurred, there were three or four more difficult problems to resolve. The users of the system, the air traffic controllers, became increasingly dissatisfied with the operational environment. After the concerted actions by the air traffic controllers in 1968 and 1969, the secretary of transportation appointed the Corson Committee to study working conditions and other problems affecting air traffic controllers.

When the Department of Transportation was created in 1967, the Federal Aviation Agency became one of the DOT's organizations and was renamed the Federal Aviation Administration. Also in 1967, the CAB accident investigation responsibilities were transferred to the newly created National Transportation Safety Board (NTSB), where they reside today.

This structure was the one that found its way into a relationship with its employee unions. One year after the FAA was absorbed by the DOT, the PATCO began its first concerted actions to motivate change. These actions escalated to a sick-out in 1970 by over 3,000 controllers and ultimately contributed to the strike in 1981.

By the mid-1970s, the ATC was a crude but workable marriage of radar and early computer technology. These systems automated many routine tasks of the controllers and permitted them to focus more on aircraft separation requirements. However, as the ATC processes became more complex and in some ways reliable, the problems associated with traffic volume continued to plague the system. While the automated processes undoubtedly enhanced the "quality" of the control process, from this early period, the growth of air traffic continued to outpace the capability of the ATC system to handle it. Traffic volume was a problem related to the 1970 slowdown, it was a contributing factor in the PATCO strike, and it remains an issue in 1998. Automation can, and has, improved the air traffic controller's ability to maintain safe separation and efficient operation, but the sheer volume of traffic into and through the ATC system places increased pressure on all aspects of aircraft control. For every 100 airplanes in a controller's sector this year, there will be 105 airplanes next year. With an annual growth rate of controlled traffic of about 5 percent, those 105 aircraft will become 110 in the following year. Automation can assist in many ways, but every one of those airplanes must take off and land. Every one of those takeoffs and landings involves an air traffic controller.

AIR TRAFFIC CONTROL SYSTEM OBJECTIVES

The objectives of the air traffic control system are bewilderingly simple. The bedrock goal is the separation of airplanes in the air and on the ground to ensure maximum safety for all users of the system. A corollary, but presumably subordinate, goal is system efficiency. Moving passengers and merchandise from point A to point B at least cost, in the shortest period of time, is the essence of the goal.

There are numerous subordinate goals related to on-time departures and arrivals, preferential routing, noise abatement, passenger comfort, and so forth. While different air carriers may place different weights on the collateral goals, the primary two goals have provided the motivation behind the development of the air traffic control system for most of the last four decades.

Why has the achievement of these two primary goals been so difficult? The first reason is that the demand for safety is absolute. It is not good enough to argue that the system is 90 percent safe or 99 percent safe. American air travelers want to believe that the air traffic control system is safe—period. That means that it is 100 percent safe. What air travellers are asking is that the hardware be totally reliable and controllers mistake free. One hundred percent safety is, of course, impossible, but system designers and developers cannot propose anything less than 100 percent safety. As a consequence, there must be built-in redundancies and complexities that increase costs, complicate development and installation, require extensive training and retraining, and so forth. From the perspective of system safety alone, the task is daunting.

Add to the safety requirement the quest for system efficiency, and one can immediately appreciate the enormity of the task. Air carriers maximize revenues and profit by scheduling flights at peak passenger hours, departing on time, and flying the most direct route at the most efficient altitude. As traffic density and aircraft speeds increase, the probability of complications increases. The five-mile separation requirements during the enroute segments of flights provide substantial margins of safety. However, as controllers begin funneling arriving airplanes into narrower flight paths and less than five-mile sequencing, the margins of safety may decrease. On final approach, aircraft may be sequenced at one- or two-mile intervals. If controllers increased the separation to four or five miles, less than half the traffic could be handled with existing facilities. In this sense, there is a direct trade-off between safety and efficiency.

The second reason is that no one can foretell the character and speed of technological changes or the ability of human beings—pilots and controllers—to adapt to the changes. Technology can, should, and does assist pilots and controllers in the decision-making process, but it is difficult to keep all participants at a consistent level of proficiency. Training and retraining constitutes an expensive, complex, perpetual process that is not uniformly effective. Like maintenance, training may be delayed without immediate adverse consequences. Long-term effects may be more difficult to assess.

Third, in all systems involving human beings, there will be acts of God that simply cannot be explained and cannot be prevented. Steps can be taken to avoid icing, thunderstorms, metal fatigue, human error, and myriad other events that occur within a fantastically complex human-machine system. However, there is no method of avoidance that will work all of the time. Consequently, system designers who attempt to create systems with sufficient redundancy or sensitivity to detect and avoid these types of events will find their task beyond attainment. As noted earlier, no designer can concede these types of events, but in the backs of their minds, they know 100 percent effectiveness is beyond human attainment.

A fourth reason may be the slavish goal of removing human beings from the process. There is a seeming preoccupation with system automation that will replace people in system operations. The reasons for this preoccupation are several. One reason undoubtedly is fueled by the belief that the human element in the air traffic control system is an area of vulnerability. Machines, that is, computers, make fewer errors than people. Thus, the reasoning goes, replacing people with machines should reduce some areas of vulnerability. Another reason for replacing controllers with machines is to weaken the organizations, that is, unions, that represent air traffic controllers. Managers will vehemently deny that the second rationale for automation motivates their decisions, but history does not support their views. This does not suggest that automation is motivated by employee relations issues, but managers certainly see it as an important collateral rationale.

THE SYSTEM

To understand the overall structure of this system and the role of air traffic controllers in it, visualize the United States as a large land mass over which there are concentric, overlapping circles covering the entire country. The circles are all-inclusive and in fact extend some distance beyond the nation's territorial borders. While the circles may be of different size, depending on the area of the country they are in, several things are important to note. First, no matter where a pilot is in the country, he or she will be in one of the circles. Second, on a typical trip, the pilot may pass through two or more of the circles before reaching his or her destination. Third, the circles have horizontal and vertical dimensions that vary, depending on the location of airports and other "special use" airspace.

Within the centers, there are other facilities that contain air traffic controllers. Recognize that air traffic is "controlled" from the time an airplane leaves the passenger gate at the departure airport until it arrives at the passenger gate at the arrival airport. Thus, air traffic controllers work in airport towers, in departure and arrival facilities (TRACON facilities), and of course, in the enroute centers. The issues, problems, and concerns of controllers in all of these functions are substantially identical. Therefore, most attention will be focused on the "center controller" even though all three categories are equally important. In fact, controllers often move within and between these three functions as they move through their air-controlling careers.

The FAA calls these concentric circles "centers." There is a New York Center, a Washington Center, a Cleveland Center, a Jacksonville Center, a Dallas–Fort Worth Center, and so forth. No matter where a pilot flies in the United States, he or she will be in a center somewhere. This doesn't mean the pilot will be in communications with the center, but he or she will be in a center's airspace.

The official name of these centers is the Air Route Traffic Control Centers (ARTCCs). They are the basic building blocks of the FAA control program in the United States. Today, there are 21 centers covering the United States. The ARTCCs handle an incredible volume of traffic. Table 2.1 shows 1995's ten busiest ARTCCs and the volume of aircraft traffic handled at each.

Table 2.1
1995's Ten Busiest ARTCCs

ARTCC	Aircraft Handled (in millions)
Chicago	2.883
Cleveland	2.736
Atlanta	2.461
Washington, D.C.	2.315
Fort Worth	2.316
Indianapolis	2.117
New York	2.095
Minneapolis	2.006
Memphis	2.003
Miami	1.976

Source: FAA administrator's *Fact Book—Air Traffic*; obtained on the Internet at http://www.tc.faa.gov/ZDV/FAA/administrator/airtraffic.html#10.

While they vary in geographic size, a typical center may cover 100,000 to 200,000 square miles of airspace extending into several states. Each center is broken down into sectors that provide smaller geographic areas for aircraft control. Illustrative of the size configuration of an ARTCC and its related airspace is the tower, TRACON, and Chicago Center. The O'Hare tower is responsible for about 56 square miles of airspace; the TRACON handles about 2,826 square miles of airspace; and Chicago Center covers about 120,000 square miles of airspace.

The ARTCCs are staffed by air traffic controllers and other support personnel. The intensity and complexity of these operations place major stress on everyone. There are no easy jobs in the ARTCC. Not everyone in the ARTCC is a controller, of course, but all functions serve to support the air traffic control functions. There are huge ADP facilities, radar facilities, radio communications operations, and electrical support machinery for mainline operation and backup operation that work to support the efficient and safe movement of aircraft in every part of the country. In the entire air traffic system, of which the ARTCCs are one part, the types of facilities shown in Tables 2.2 and 2.3 were on-line in 1996.

Table 2.2
Air Navigation Facilities

VHF omnidirectional radio range (VOR)	1,027
Instrument landing system—LOC	1,197
Approach light system	108
Runway end identification light	732
Runway visual range equipment	533
Visual approach slope indicator	1,308

Source: FAA administrator's *Fact Book—Air Traffic*; obtained on the Internet at http://www.tc.faa.gov/ZDV/FAA/administrator/airtraffic.html#10.
LOC = Localizer

Table 2.3
Air Traffic Control Facilities

Air route traffic control centers	21
Air traffic control towers	476
Automated radar terminal system	195
Flight service stations	94
Airport surveillance radar—terminal	228
Air route surveillance radar—enroute	118
Remote center air ground facility	701
Remote communications outlet	1,726
Direction finder equipment	202

Source: FAA administrator's *Fact Book—Air Traffic*; obtained on the Internet at http://www.tc.faa.gov/ZDV/FAA/administrator/airtraffic.html#10.

Over the interval from 1994 to 1996, every category of air navigation and air traffic control facilities increased with the exception of two—flight service stations declined from 131 stations in 1994 to 94 stations in 1996, and direction finder equipment declined from 220 in 1994 to 202 in 1996.

THE AIR TRAFFIC CONTROLLING ENVIRONMENT

The first thing you notice when entering the ARTCC facility's operational environment is that it is dark. Not pitch dark, but dimly lighted so that one can walk around without bumping into things. It is relatively quiet except for the low background murmur of controllers communicating with aircraft, control towers, clearance delivery systems, and so forth. As you approach a controller's station, the most conspicuous thing is the large circular screen that is covered by a jumble of lines, symbols, letters and numbers. If the screen is watched for a few minutes, the symbols, letters and numbers change. Some simply change in magnitude while others flash. It's a spectacular sight for the uninitiated. The first thing that goes through your mind is, How do they keep track of everything displayed on the screen? This is doubly perplexing when one realizes that the screen images display a "sector" within the "center's" controlled airspace that may cover hundreds or even thousands of square miles. It is an awesome process that has a tightly controlled set of procedures and processes operating in conjunction with a constantly varying and unpredictable set of uncontrolled variables.

Most of the controller's workload is routine arrival, departure, and en route control of aircraft. The procedures and processes relating to "controlled aircraft" permit an orderly flow into and out of the controller's jurisdiction. However, there are frequently large numbers of uncontrolled aircraft that, in the jargon of the controller, "pop up" on the radar screen with no warning. How, one may ask, can this happen? The answer is simple: The American aviation system and the laws and regulations relating to this system permit people to fly their airplanes without telling anyone. Just as a driver's license is necessary to drive your car legally, you must obey traffic signals, and you must have insurance to protect other drivers, there are similar requirements in the aviation sector. However, if you decide to take a 500-mile trip this weekend to see Aunt Martha in Cincinnati, you do so without telling anyone about how you plan to get to Cincinnati, how fast you plan to drive, how often you plan to stop, or when you plan to arrive. You simply get in your car and go.

The same applies to airplanes. There are several hundred thousand airplanes owned by private citizens, scattered across the United States. Some of these airplanes are located at major airports, while others are in smaller local airports and others are on grass strips far from major population centers. An individual owning one of these airplanes can also decide, as an alternative, to fly to Cincinnati to see Aunt Martha without telling anyone. It may be foolish to do so, but it is not illegal. Then, there are also the "weekend warriors" who simply enjoy the thrill of flying. They go out to their local airport or grass strip, fire up the old bird, and launch into flight. Many of them don't really go anywhere. They circle the "home" field and shoot "touch and goes." Others venture off in unpredictable directions to take a few pictures of the home place, belittle the poor suckers tied up in traffic jams on the nearby interstate, or simply practice steep turns or stalls in the local practice area. If they venture much above a thousand feet above ground level in most localities, they will appear on the controller's radar screen.

One should not say that these "pop-ups" are unwelcome by the controller, but it is fair to say that if they are numerous and the volume of controlled traffic is heavy, they can cause significant disruptions in the normal flow of controlled flights. In some areas, weekends, particularly Saturdays, are murder. On warm, sunny days, it seems that every airplane owner decides to take a few "loops around the patch." What was an orderly process of arrival and departure for the controller suddenly becomes a swarm of bees around a hive. Airplanes are moving in every direction, some fast, some slow. Some are climbing, while others are descending. Commingled with these pop-ups are controlled aircraft that are in predictable places, operating at known speeds, heading in known and predictable directions.

The controller handles his (or her) controlled traffic well because he knows the performance characteristics of all categories of aircraft, and even if he doesn't know, he can instruct the pilots to conform to speeds, directions, and altitudes that the controller needs for an orderly process. The controller knows all about the controlled airplanes. He knows what kind of airplane it is, how fast it is flying, what altitude it is flying at, where it came from and where it is going, what radio and navigational equipment is onboard, and so forth. Then there is the pop-up. The controller knows none of the above. He simply sees this symbol on the screen and hasn't the vaguest notion what will happen next. Depending on where the pop-up is, the controller is likely to know something about it. If it is in the vicinity of an airport known to have a lot of training activity or weekend warriors, he can reasonably assume that the airplane will stay in the vicinity of the airport. But he can never be certain. The pilot may circle the airport a few times, shoot a few landings, and then decide to beeline to the coast for a hot cup of coffee. The controller has to be prepared to deal with any possibility. When you multiply the number of "bees" darting around in an area by 100 or 200, the situation can become very interesting, very fast.

To better understand the basic processes within the air traffic control system, it is important to describe the two fundamental types of flying. One type of flying is conducted by visual flight rules (VFR). Referred to in the business as VFR flight, this type of flying requires that the pilot adhere to certain procedures within the overall system, the most important one being that he or she remain in meteorological conditions permitting "see and avoid" techniques. Basically, the pilot must be able to see vertically and horizontally sufficient distances to see other aircraft and take appropriate actions to avoid encounters. The pilot must remain clear of clouds, fly at specific altitudes, and have certain navigation and radio equipment onboard and functioning. For short, local flying, most pilots utilize VFR flight. There are variations to basic VFR flight in which under special conditions the pilot can deviate from normal procedures. These conditions need not be described here to understand the controller's work environment.

The second type of flight is conducted under instrument flight rules (IFR). Referred to as IFR flight, it involves very stringent rules and procedures that permit the controller to maintain order in the system. When the pilot files an IFR flight plan, a long list of very specific conditions are required. The pilot must identify the type of aircraft flown, time and place of departure, initial cruising altitude, flight path identified by known navigation fixes, the number of people onboard, types of navigation and radio equipment onboard and functioning, and so forth. When this flight plan enters the air traffic control system, it becomes the road map the controller needs to place the particular aircraft into the system most safely and efficiently.

Importantly, filing an IFR flight plan is only the first step. Before the pilot can takeoff, he or she must obtain a "clearance" from the appropriate control facility that activates the flight plan. At this point, the pilot is told when he or she can takeoff, what altitude to climb to, what radio frequency to contact the control facilities on, when to switch from one controller to another, and so forth. Under IFR rules, the controller has complete knowledge about and control over the flight. With today's radar and radio facilities, the controller has a better picture of exactly where the airplane is than does the pilot. In fact, if the pilot deviates from the direction of flight or altitude assigned by the controller, he or she will receive a polite but stern instruction to correct the situation.

Obviously, en route, things may change to some degree. The pilot may encounter winds aloft that are stronger or lighter than those forecast for the flight; the controller may have to alter the filed flight plan to accommodate faster or slower traffic in the vicinity; the pilot may decide to deviate to a different airport for personal or other reasons. The system is set up to accommodate these types of changes. Since the pilot is in direct and continuous radio communications with the ARTCC, he or she can request changes in the flight plan to address any reasonable need. The point is that the controller knows about the current situation, can assess the impact of any requested changes, and can control the outcome to make the overall process safe and efficient.

It's instructive to note that when a pilot files an IFR flight plan and receives a clearance to fly that plan or a modified one, a "tunnel" of airspace is reserved for that flight by the ARTCC. This tunnel may be visualized as having a certain height and width that follows the flight path provided in the clearance. The controller's job is to ensure that this tunnel of airspace is unobstructed by other aircraft or that if other aircraft enter the space, the pilot knows about it. In close proximity to airports, the tunnel of air is about three miles wide and 1,000 feet in depth. In the enroute sectors, the tunnel widens to about five miles with a depth of 2,000 feet.

It may now be clearer that the uncontrolled traffic can cause the controller and controlled traffic major problems. Consider a situation in which the controller has a variety of inbound and outbound aircraft all lined up and sequenced for smooth arrival and departure. Everyone has assigned times, altitudes, air speeds, and so forth. All of a sudden, into the middle of the whole process meanders a pop-up. Since safety is the paramount consideration, until the controller knows where the pop-up is going, other clearances must be amended. Aircraft may be diverted to other locations, placed in holding patterns, or delayed from taking off until the situation is clarified. One can easily visualize the complications involved in this situation when potentially hundreds of aircraft are involved in a large terminal area.

At the center of this storm is the controller. He or she must convey all the "bad" news that may mean delay for commercial carriers, additional flight time for passengers, the consumption of additional fuel, inconvenienced airport personnel, and a host of related problems. The controller's job is to ensure that all IFR traffic is handled in a manner that is safe. This means that all aircraft are vectored or placed in holding patterns in such a way as to maintain required horizontal and vertical separation. Delays in large aircraft can be very expensive. For example, a recent *Washington Post* article indicated that a 15 minute delay for American Airlines' smallest plane, the Fokker-100, will cost the airline about $1,800. The same delay for American Airlines' largest airplane, the McDonnell-Douglas MD-11, will cost the airline over $8,000.[7] Little wonder that pilots and airline officials become anxious over delays that add expensive time to their flights.

In fairness to the problems the pop-up produced, similar situations can arise involving weather conditions or, an incident at the airport, for example, a power failure or other unpredictable event. Aircraft may be lined up or sequenced to a major airport when an afternoon thunderstorm rumbles through the area. Airport operations may be suspended temporarily until the storm is passed or conditions improve enough for safe operation. An airport may experience a power failure that eliminates the runway and approach lighting systems needed for safe nighttime operations. Aircraft converging on the terminal area may have to be diverted or placed in a holding pattern until the problem is corrected.

Any of these types of problems can instantly place the controller at the center of a difficult and stressful situation. The hours and hours of routine traffic control can be instantly converted into an undetermined period of intense stress that will test the mettle of the most experienced controller. Aircraft cannot be simply frozen in place as happens with a traffic jam on the highway. People's lives are at stake. Airplanes consume prodigious amounts of fuel, crews on long flights are tired, and aircraft tend to continue converging on a terminal area even after the problem has occurred. Sorting out this menagerie of vehicles in constant motion, all with different speeds and capabilities, is a natural stress producer.

One should not get the impression that there are constant problems in the skies that portend disaster at any moment. This is not a correct picture. In fact, while problems can and do occur, controllers utilize procedures and rules that permit problems to occur without leading to instant disaster. Aircraft are controlled to airspace and "approach fixes" that are purposely chosen to minimize potential conflicts. If a pilot is given a clearance to proceed along his or her route of flight, the clearance has a "limit" placed on it so that if certain conditions are not met, the pilot must take appropriate action. Even on the ground, pilots are given departure clearances that must be executed before a specified time, or they are void and a new clearance must be obtained. There are built-in safeguards and redundancies that permit the controller and the pilot time and options to engage in safe and efficient flight.

Increasingly today, airplanes at the departure airport are kept on the ground if traffic or weather conditions at the destination airport are not favorable for an expeditious flight. On flights from, say, New York's LaGuardia Airport to Washington's National Airport, it is prudent and more economical to hold an airplane on the ground at LaGuardia rather than have it in a holding pattern enroute to National. Airplanes do not simply takeoff anymore with the pilot hoping that conditions at the destination airport will clarify themselves or that weather will improve. In conjunction with this type of procedure, aircraft at busy terminals are given landing "slots" into which they must fly. Basically, the pilot is given a time slot within which he or she is supposed to arrive at the destination airport. Occasionally, one will see airplanes at a major airport sitting in a parking area with their engines running while other aircraft taxi by and depart. More than likely, the airplanes holding do not have a slot at their destination, and therefore the center will not give them a departure clearance. If a flight is late and misses its slot, it can take a while before the controllers are able to free up a new slot to accommodate the flight. One can be sure that the pilot is busily trying to negotiate a new slot at the earliest possible time. It is expensive for airplanes—particularly heavy jets—to sit and idle, and passengers tend to get perturbed when flights are delayed. In some instances, the weather at a destination airport may preclude the successful culmination of the flight. Controllers will hold the airplane on the ground until conditions resolve themselves.

A TYPICAL EXAMPLE OF OPERATIONS IN THE ARTCC

Pilots in commercial, private, and military operations have the capability to receive valuable detailed information and data about their flights that permit safe and efficient operation throughout the system. Controllers work under stringent rules relating to aircraft separation, emergency procedures if there are failures in the ARTCC system or in individual aircraft, arrival and departure operations, weather problems, and the like. There is an adage in the flying business that says something like "The *pilot* is the ultimate decision maker inside the cockpit and is solely responsible for the safety of the flight." In a conceptual sense, this adage is true. However, modern-day communications and navigation involving the ARTCC system serve to help the pilot make the flight safer and more efficient than would occur if the pilot acted on his or her own.

After all, the pilot can see certain things within and outside the cockpit that the controller cannot see. An obvious example is the local weather condition. The controller *may* be able to see large weather patterns on the radar scope but would typically not be able to see a particular "cell" that is readily visible to the pilot. The pilot could ask and receive a modification in his or her clearance that would permit navigating around the storm cell. On the other hand, the controller can "see" all of the other aircraft in the vicinity of the pilot's aircraft that the pilot probably cannot see. Certainly, if the pilot is flying in the clouds, he or she is unlikely to see any other aircraft. However, even when not in the clouds, it is extremely difficult to see other aircraft even when they are pointed out to the pilot by the center. This is surprising to most people. There is a perception that the pilot can see everything for hundreds of miles in all directions. The truth is that a pilot can easily make a 500-mile flight on a crystal-clear day and never see a single airplane in flight. This doesn't mean that there were no other aircraft in the locality: but it does mean that they were very difficult to see.

The controller can tell what altitude each aircraft is at, their air speed, direction of flight, destination, and so forth. This information would not be readily available to the individual pilot. In this sense, the controller has the "big picture" of all aircraft operating in his or her sector. This information can be critically important in determining sequencing for arrivals and departures, establishing holding patterns, rerouting aircraft to avoid potential conflicts, and so forth. A safe and efficient flight requires that both sources of information be merged together and used effectively.

So how does it work? We can follow a typical flight from one major airport to another. The same principles would apply for any flight in controlled airspace, but there would be slight differences such as radio frequencies or routing patterns for different kinds of aircraft. Let's assume that the pilot has obtained his or her weather briefing and filed an IFR flight plan from Washington's Dulles Airport to Denver's Stapleton Airport. Denver's Stapleton Airport is no longer the primary airport for flights to the Mile-High City, but we will use this example, nonetheless.[8]

To assist in visualizing how a flight originates and terminates, it may be useful to characterize the air traffic control system as three concentric circles in the form of a bull's eye. At the center of the "target" is the local controller. Individuals in this part of the system are primarily the tower controller, the ground controller, and clearance delivery. The next circle in the target is the approach and departure controller. These individuals provide the communications and guidance in the transition from the ARTCC to the local controller. The outer circle in the target is the ARTCC. Every flight originates in the center of a target and ends up in the center of a target. Except for very short flights, pilots will fly through all three rings of the target during departure and all three rings of the target during arrival.

While the air traffic control system is set up generally as described, there are other actors in the system that are also important. Fundamentally, the flight service stations (FSSs) act in an advisory capacity to provide weather and other information to the pilot but usually do not "control" anything.

In any event, on our hypothetical flight, the conversation between the aircraft and the ARTCC system would be something like the following:

Aircraft [Flight 851] to Dulles Clearance Delivery: Dulles Clearance, Flight 851, Gate 17, IFR to Stapleton.

Dulles Clearance: Roger 851, cleared as filed, runway heading, climb and maintain 4,000, squawk 5-1-4-4, contact Departure on 1-2-3 point 9 [for clarity, both the pilot and controller would say "niner" rather than "nine"].

Flight 851 would read this clearance back to Clearance Delivery. In the flight plan, the pilot identified a route of flight that he preferred to follow between Dulles and Stapleton. The ARTCC system provided the pilot with a "cleared as filed" clearance, which tells the pilot that the system has accepted his planned flight as submitted. This does *not* mean that the ARTCC system will not modify the plan as the flight progresses. Pilots who fly the same routes on a regular basis know what routing the controllers will accept. To save time and increase efficiency, pilots try to file flight plans that they know the controllers want and need for orderly departure sequences. In the ARTCC system, there are both departure and arrival "fixes." These are simply navigation facilities that are appropriately located to ensure safe and efficient procedures. For example, when Dulles Airport is operating on a southern departure regime, aircraft departing for western locations are virtually always routed to Casanova VOR and then handed off to a Washington Center controller.

Pilots know this procedure, the departure controllers know the procedure, and the Washington Center controllers expect the procedure. It is much easier for the center controllers to identify an aircraft when it is over or enroute to a VOR. The Casanova VOR is conveniently located southwest of Dulles Airport and therefore serves that purpose well.

These are standard procedures that are well known to everyone using the system. On a clear Sunday morning when there is no other traffic in the vicinity of the airport, the controllers may deviate from the usual procedures. Northwest from the Casanova VOR is the Linden VOR. An aircraft departing Dulles could be vectored directly to Linden if it would facilitate the flight and not create problems for other aircraft. Controllers have a lot of flexibility in how they handle aircraft. While it is true that the pilot is the final authority for the safe operation of his or her aircraft, all savvy pilots work well with the controllers and know that these highly trained professionals have an important role to play in the safe and efficient operation of the overall system. One occasionally hears a pilot get "snippy" with a controller when he (or she) does not get the routing that he wanted or is told to change course or altitude. Generally, changes in the flight path are likely to add to the length of the flight. These instances may cause the pilot to be late to his destination and use additional fuel. In these cases, which are infrequent, the controller will usually tell the pilot why the changes were necessary, and in most cases, that is the end of it.

The clearance stipulated "runway heading." This simply means that the pilot is expected to takeoff on a particular runway and continue the initial part of the climb out on the runway heading. On this heading, the pilot is authorized to climb only to 4,000 feet MSL (mean sea level) and, unless instructed otherwise, maintain that altitude. There are several reasons for a runway heading clearance, the most important of which is to permit quick and accurate identification of the departing aircraft. All of the controllers in the sector have the runways of major airports painted on their control screens. When an aircraft departs and flies on a particular runway heading, all controllers can instantly zero in on his or her needs.

The "squawk" code is a discrete frequency for the aircraft's transponder that permits the controlling facility to easily pick out the aircraft in congested airspace. The transponder receives an "interrogation" signal from the radar transmitter, amplifies that signal on the discrete frequency, and sends it back to the radar receiver. The controller can then locate the aircraft on his or her radar screen without ambiguity. Visually, when a pilot is instructed to "ident," it means that the controller is attempting to unambiguously identify the airplane in the controller's sector. When the transponder is activated, the visual symbol on the control screen flashes a much brighter color than other aircraft in normal radar contact.

Contacting "Departure" on 1-2-3 point 9 is simply an instruction that provides the pilot with information about the frequency the "departure controller" will be on for the sector into which this flight will proceed.

With the clearance in hand, the pilot will say:

Flight 851: Ground, this is 851, Gate 17, IFR to Stapleton.

Dulles Ground: Roger, taxi to Runway 1-9 Left.

This instruction tells the pilot that he or she can taxi to Runway 19L, crossing all taxiways and other runways enroute. It also tells the pilot that he will be departing on Runway 19L. Therefore, he can identify the appropriate frequencies for the instrument landing system (ILS) for that runway. We will talk about the importance of the ILS later.

Since Runway 19 Left is oriented to the south, which is 180 degrees, the pilot knows he will be taking off to the south and his initial route of flight will be on a heading of 190 degrees.

The conversations throughout the ARTCC are typically short and crisp. They provide specific information and are usually peppered with words and phrases that have particular application to the aviation industry. They sound like mumbo-jumbo to the uninitiated ear but in fact are crisp and lucid to the pilot and controllers.

The pilot taxis to Runway 19L and performs a series of system checks and, a run-up of the engines, if needed, and prepares for departure. At this point, in the main cabin, flight attendants are telling passengers to check their seat belts, be sure all articles are securely stowed, seatbacks are in their upright position, and so forth. When the pilot is ready to takeoff, he contacts the Dulles tower.

Flight 851: Dulles Tower, 851, ready for takeoff.

Dulles Tower: 851, taxi into position and hold.

Flight 851: Position and hold.

At this point, the pilot is cleared onto the active runway, in this case Runway 19L, and is instructed to hold that position. He is *not* cleared to takeoff. The controller must maintain separation between aircraft. A recently departed airplane may not have flown far enough from the departure runway to permit the next aircraft to depart. When the situation warrants takeoff, the tower will say:

Dulles Tower: 851 cleared for takeoff, runway heading, climb and maintain 6,000, contact Departure on 1-2-3 point 9.

This transmission provides the pilot with instructions to takeoff on Runway 19L, and they reiterate some of the crucial information for the first part of the flight. Note that the pilot is instructed to climb and maintain 6,000 feet MSL. This means that sometime after the time the pilot received his initial clearance, conditions warranted a higher initial altitude. The pilot is now authorized to disregard his initial clearance to 4,000 and to climb to and maintain 6,000 MSL.

The pilot applies appropriate takeoff power, and the aircraft accelerates down the runway and lifts off. For most passengers, this is the most exciting part of the flight. The increasing crescendo of the engines, the acceleration, the rotation of the nose upward, the sudden smoothness as the wheels leave the ground—all provide a sense of excitement and exhilaration.

As the pilot begins the climb out, the tower will say:

Dulles Tower: 851, contact Departure on 1-2-3 point 9, good day.

Flight 851: Roger.

The pilot then changes radio frequencies to the departure controller and says:

Flight 851: Departure, Flight 851, climbing to 6,000.

Dulles Departure: Roger 851, radar contact, climb and maintain 10,000.

Since there had been a change in his clearance by the Dulles tower, this savvy pilot told the controller that he was "climbing to 6,000." If there had been a misunderstanding earlier in the clearance process, the departure controller would have picked it up. In this case, conditions warranted an even higher initial altitude, and the pilot was cleared by the departure controller to 10,000 MSL. The pilot is still flying runway heading.

Departure Control: Flight 851, turn right to 2-4-0 degrees, direct Casanova, flight plan route, maintain 10,000.

At this stage of the flight, the pilot is given a "vector" to a heading of 240 degrees to a navigational aid called "Casanova." This navigational aid is called a VOR (very high frequency omnireceiver). It provides directional guidance to the pilot both inbound and outbound to the VOR. The departure controller then gives the pilot instructions to fly his planned flight and to maintain 10,000 MSL.

Generally, as the pilot passes over Casanova, the departure controller "hands him off" to the Washington Center controller. This is accomplished when the departure controller positively identifies the aircraft and the Washington Center controller has positive identification. At this point, the departure controller says:

Departure Controller: Flight 851, contact Washington Center on 1-2-5 point 2.

Flight 851: Roger, 1-2-5 point 2.

After changing frequencies to the Washington Center controller, Flight 851 says:

Flight 851: Washington Center, Flight 851, with you at 8,000, climbing to 10,000.

Washington Center: Roger, 851.

The pilot generally provides the center controller with his current altitude, in this case 8,000 feet MSL, and the altitude to which he is climbing. This is done so that the center controller can cross-check to be sure that the altitude he is displaying on his screen is accurate (it should show 8,000 MSL) and that the altitude clearance limit is what was assigned to this flight.

At an appropriate point, with traffic conditions permitting, the pilot is cleared to a higher altitude and proceeds on his way. Depending on his route of flight, the en route controllers may hand the pilot off to other sector controllers within the Washington Center jurisdiction and ultimately to the neighboring controller, probably Cleveland Center or Kansas City Center.

Before this hypothetical flight arrives in the Denver area, another important aspect of the air traffic control system must be described. Airplanes in the system flying under IFR procedures utilize a highly sophisticated, electronic system for guidance and aircraft control. Throughout this hypothetical flight from Washington to Denver, the pilot was in constant radar contact with the ARTCC, and he utilized a variety of electronic devices to ensure efficient and safe operation. As the aircraft approaches the Denver area, the pilot will be transitioned by the en route air traffic controller to make either a visual approach or an instrument approach, depending on weather conditions. A visual approach permits the pilot to land the airplane using visual references to the ground and visual separation from other aircraft. This example assumes that weather conditions require that the pilot utilize an instrument approach procedure. Under this procedure, the pilot will navigate solely by reference to instruments inside the cockpit.

THE INSTRUMENT LANDING SYSTEM

For the uninitiated, sitting in the interior of the airplane with only a curtain or a cabin door to look at can be a disconcerting experience. How can one be sure that the pilot knows where he is going and that he will be able to land the aircraft safely at the end of the flight? The Denver Center controller hands the flight off to a Denver approach controller, who hands it off to Denver tower, who hands it off to the Denver ground controller. All of these actions are crisp and well coordinated. At no time during the flight is the pilot out of radar and radio contact with the ARTCC system.

Since the weather is unfavorable in the Denver area for a visual approach, the pilot will be instructed to expect an instrument approach to the active runway. He will be told what approach to expect, the tower frequency, and other pertinent information. At this point (actually, most good pilots monitor control frequencies long before they arrive in the vicinity of the Denver airport and therefore know what runways are being used and what weather conditions exist), the pilot sets up his radios and navigation equipment for an instrument approach and landing. There are two types of instrument landing procedures in the instrument system—precision approaches and nonprecision approaches. The procedures in each type are somewhat different, but we will only describe the precision approach because it is the one most typically used today.

When the pilot is told to "expect" an ILS approach to runway 1-6 Left, a series of cockpit actions take place. The pilot knows that he will be making a precision approach and will be landing on runway 1-6 Left; that is, he will be heading 160 degrees at touchdown and will be on the left runway of two parallel runways.

Each instrument landing system has a discrete frequency (actually, it is two frequencies, but they are coupled together so that the pilot needs only to set his radio for one frequency). The pilot sets his radio to the frequency for the ILS and completes his prelanding checklist. Out of the end of the runway, or nearly so, are two radio beams that are at a specific width and frequency. If one could see these radio beams, they would appear to be two "flat" radio beams beginning from a point (the transmitter) and pointing up the expected flight path. The two radio beams intersect each other at ninety-degree angles so that if one were to look at them "end on," they would appear in the shape of a cross.

Inside the aircraft are the radio receivers that are tuned to the appropriate frequencies. These radio receivers pick up the signals and determine where the aircraft is relative to the center of the approach course. The cockpit radio contains a "course deviation indicator" (CDI) and a glide slope indicator, which tells the pilot which way to fly. If the CDI is to the right of the center line, the pilot makes a correction toward the right. If the glide slope indicator is low on the instrument, this means the aircraft is flying high, and the pilot should decrease his altitude. The pilot will continue to make corrections until the CDI and glide slope indicator show a pattern similar to the crosshairs in a rifle telescope. If the pilot maintains this position, he will fly directly to the threshold of the 16L Runway. There is a decision height (DH) expressed in feet above the ground, at which the pilot is required to abort the flight and "go around" if the runway is not in sight and a safe landing cannot be made. Generally, the DH on standard ILS approaches is 200 feet AGL (above ground level).

LANDING IN DENVER

After flying through several centers, the sequence within the Denver Center would be about as follows. The Denver Center Controller would handoff the aircraft to the approach controller. The approach controller would tell the pilot to expect an ILS to 16L. The pilot sets up his navigation and radio gear. The approach controller vectors the aircraft to ensure that it intersects the ILS at a specific altitude. As the pilot approaches the ILS, the ILS head in the airplane will suddenly "come alive." The CDI and glide slope indicator will begin dancing around, and the "no signal" flag will disappear. The pilot now knows he is intercepting the "localizer" and the glide slope. Once the vectoring process is nearing completion, the approach controller will clear the aircraft for the final ILS approach. At this point, the pilot assumes complete control over the approach procedures and is responsible for executing the approach procedures as published in authorized publications. At the final clearance point, generally called the "outer marker," the pilot is told to contact the tower on a specific frequency.

At the final approach fix, the pilot contacts the tower and says, "Flight 581, outer marker, inbound, on the ILS, Runway 16L." This tells the tower controller exactly where the airplane is in the approach sequence and when he can be expected to touch down for landing. The tower controller ensures that no other aircraft are on the active runway until Flight 581 lands or executes a missed approach.

The pilot of Flight 581 breaks out of the clouds at 800 feet AGL, and he looks directly down the center stripe of Runway 16L. He is likely to see an intense flashing strobe light that starts a mile or so off the end of the runway and zips toward the threshold. This light is called the "rabbit" by pilots. He will also see the runway side-marker lights, the airport rotating beacon, and other lights on the airport. It is an impressive sight, even for high-time pilots who have made thousands of similar landings. The pilot flares the airplane over the runway threshold, and the wheels screech gently on the concrete runway. The aircraft quickly slows down through appropriate braking and reverse thrust procedures. As the airplane exits the runway, it is handedoff to a ground controller. Following the ground controller's instructions, Flight 581 arrives at the gate on schedule.

This procedure is repeated thousands of times each day. Every flight is handled by the air traffic controller in essentially the same manner. Methodically following established procedures that everybody in the system understands and applies ensures safety in the system.

There are many players in the air and on the ground that coordinate and cooperate to ensure a safe flight. The procedures used are standardized and implemented routinely. There are built-in procedures for both the pilots and controllers in the event there are system failures in the airplane or in the ground facilities. For example, there are procedures in the centers that are initiated if the computers supporting the radar system malfunction. Controllers are trained to use noncomputer radar systems to ensure adequate separation between controlled aircraft. In the airplane, the pilot is trained in conducting his (or her) flight on a precise time and navigation aid procedure that permits successful completion of the flight if radio communications are lost or interrupted.

How effective are controllers in the functions they perform? There are several sources of information that suggest that controllers, while not perfect, operate with high levels of safety. The General Accounting Office (GAO) noted in a 1981 study that out of 12,344 general aviation accidents over a two-year period, only 39 involved air traffic control personnel as a cause or factor in the accident. Reviewing the handling of 4.7 million aircraft by air traffic controllers in calendar year 1980 found only 39 system errors. None of these errors involved an accident.[9] The number of aviation industry accidents is very small by any measure. Table 2.4, shows the numbers of fatalities in airplane accidents, in the United States, over a thirteen-year period.

On average, about 230 people die in aviation accidents each year. This compares to about 125 to 150 people who die each day in automobile accidents in the United States. The number of deaths per million aircraft miles is exceedingly small. In 1992, for example, the 25 deaths amounted to about 0.0006 deaths per million aircraft miles flown. From this, one can infer that air travel is very safe. The difference may be that when a scheduled airplane accident does occur, it usually results in a fairly large number of people being killed in a single location.

Table 2.4
Airplane Accidents Involving Passenger Fatalities,
U.S. Airlines (Part 121) 1983–1996

Year	Accidents	Pax Fatalities
1983	2	8
1984	0	0
1985	5	486
1986	0	0
1987	4	212
1988	2	255
1989	5	259
1990	2	8
1991	2	40
1992	1	25
1993	0	0
1994	3	228
1995	1	152
1996	3	319

Source: Internet address:http://www.ntsb.gov/Aviation/Paxfatal.html.

While the number of controller-involved incidents is small, controllers tend to work long hours of high intensity. In the GAO study noted earlier, controllers worked an average of five hours actually controlling air traffic for each eight-hour shift.[10]

There was, however, considerable variation of traffic volume during an eight-hour shift. From 8 P.M. until 5 A.M., controllers used about 40 percent of their time actually controlling airplanes. At other times during the day, controllers used as much as 60 percent of their time actually controlling traffic. One must actually see controllers at work at the radar screen to appreciate the concentration and level of quick decision making needed to function safely and efficiently.

At a particular moment, a controller may have the lives of thousands of passengers and flight crews in his (or her) hands. He provides instructions and conveys information that is critical to the successful completion of the flight. This is an exceedingly important job. However, one should not get the impression that the air traffic controller is in a state of constant stress and high demands on his skills. This is simply not true. A particular controller may encounter extremely stressful periods followed by periods of relative calm. A flight surgeon for the FAA compared the roles of a center controller with those of a flight center employee. The doctor concluded that the flight center person was considerably more stressed than was the center controller. This was true primarily because the intensity and pace of work in the FAA flight service stations are unrelenting. The FSS specialist never has time to sit back and simply relax.[11]

SUMMARY

This description of the U.S. air traffic control system provides insights into some of the conditions affecting air traffic controllers. This hypothetical description of a flight from Dulles Airport to Stapleton Airport glossed over many of the enroute procedures and did not describe a situation involving substantial changes in the route of flight or flight conditions. As a consequence, this flight was typical and routine. Importantly, the vast majority of flights are of this nature.

To truly understand the nature of working conditions for air traffic controllers, it is important to differentiate between "en route" controllers and "terminal area" controllers. In some cases, a controller may perform both functions for certain types of aircraft. The next chapter describes this occupation and the unique role controllers play in aviation safety.

NOTES

1. House of Representatives, Committee on Government Operations, Subcommittee on Government Activities, *Problems Confronting the Federal Aviation Administration in the Development of an Air Traffic Control System for the 1970s*, 91st Cong., 2d sess., Report No. 91-1306, Union Calendar No. 623 (Washington, D.C.: GPO, July 16, 1970), p. 10.

2. Ibid.

3. Ibid., p. 1.

4. Ibid., p. 2.

5. Ibid.

6. Ibid.

7. Richard M. Weintraub and John Burgess, "U.S. Seeks Shift in Air Traffic Control," *Washington Post*, May 2, 1994, p. A1.

8. Denver's new airport is the Denver International Airport.

9. General Accounting Office, *Controller Staffing and Training at Four FAA Air Traffic Control Facilities*, CED 81-127 (Washington, D.C.: GOP, July 9, 1981), p. 25.

10. Ibid., p. 30.

11. W. E. Anderson, "Medical Observations of Flight Service Specialists," in Hearings before the Subcommittee on Post Office and Civil Service, House of Representatives, *Air Traffic Control* (Washington, D.C.: GPO, September 30, 1980), pp. 46–48.

Chapter 3

Air Traffic Controllers
and Their Unions

AIR TRAFFIC CONTROLLERS IN THE AVIATION SECTOR

As these words are being read, there are certainly hundreds and possibly thousands of commercial airplanes flying in the U.S. air traffic control system. As described in the previous chapter, every one of these airplanes is flying under a set of instructions provided by an air traffic controller. The controller's job is to ensure that every airplane departs from and arrives at its destination in a safe and efficient manner.

Air traffic controllers are civilian federal employees. In 1981, there were a total of 16,375 air traffic controllers, of which 13,170 were classified as full performance level (FPL) controllers. In 1988, there were a total of 15,520 controllers of which 8,904 were FPL controllers.[1] Starting in 1982, the FAA created a category of employees called "air traffic assistants." In 1988, there were about 1,500 employees in that classification. While FPL controllers and developmental controllers are usually in the GS-11/12/13, those in the "developmental pipeline" are in the GS-5/7/9 levels. There were about 5,815 employees in the development controller and developmental pipeline in 1982. Five years later, there were about 3,750 employees in these two categories. The number of area supervisors, managers, and chiefs was 3,056 in 1981. This category of employees decreased each year to a level of 2,640 in 1986.[2]

Air traffic controllers occupy one of the most stressful and demanding occupations found anywhere in the world. At any point in time, an air traffic controller may have several hundred airplanes with thousands of passengers occupying the airspace over which he or she has control. If this volume of activity were not enough, consider that each airplane is traveling at a different air speed, in different directions, at different altitudes. Each airplane has limitations on its performance in terms of ability to climb and maintain altitude, change air speed, and overall maneuverability. To accommodate a slower airplane ahead of a jumbo jet, the controller cannot require a Boeing 747 to slow down to 80 or

90 knots. Similarly, the controller cannot require a Cessna 172 to speed up to 200 knots to maintain the proper spacing between it and a faster jet or turbo-prop.

Each year, air traffic controllers control flights that carry about 1 billion passengers in the domestic aviation sector. Over 19,000 scheduled flights take-off and land each day under a variety of weather conditions from large airports and small airports. Airplanes in the system fly at hundreds of miles per hour along prescribed airways and other known navigation routes.

In 1993, there were 18,317 airports in the United States. In 1995, that number had decreased to 18,224 airports. Of the 18,224 airports, 5,415 were classified as public use airports, and 12,809 were private use airports. In 1995, 667 airports were "certificated airports" that served air carrier operations with aircraft seating more than thirty passengers. Air traffic controllers accept flights into and out of virtually all airports, public and private. While not all airports have instrument landing facilities such as VORs, area surveillance radar, ILSs, and required communications capabilities, air traffic controllers permit pilots to approach and land at those facilities from specified navigational fixes. Pilots departing from these types of facilities can obtain a clearance in much the same manner as a pilot would at an airport with extensive navigation and communications systems.

Air traffic controllers work in a highly technical but narrowly constrained part of the aviation sector. They are responsible for the safe movement of aircraft operating under IFR rules within, into, and out of the United States. In this process, controllers have relatively few "handles" they can pull to ensure aircraft safety. At present, there are four points at which the controller can "control" the system. First, aircraft can be held on the ground to lessen the number of aircraft on the airways or arriving at an airport at a specific time. Second, once an airplane is en route, the controller can restrict forward movement by placing the aircraft in a holding pattern. This procedure is primarily used to keep airplanes at known locations while other airplanes are permitted to proceed to land. Third, rather than stop forward progress of the airplane, the controller can reroute traffic to avoid conflicts. This process is used frequently to route transient aircraft around busy terminals or to permit faster or slower aircraft to pass one another. The fourth handle the controller can pull involves the actual operation of the individual aircraft. If needed, the pilot can be asked to increase or decrease air speed or to change altitude. These procedures are also used to avoid conflicts between aircraft. In some cases, pilots will request to change altitude in search of smoother air, to improve operating efficiency, or to obtain a more optimum head wind/tail wind relationship.

One may visualize the control process as a three-dimensional chess game in which all the pieces are constantly in motion. As reported in *Smithsonian* magazine, "Controllers use the analytical talents of a chess grand master, the mental calculations of a mathematician and the terse language of a police dispatcher. They're taught to perform their jobs with the cool assurance of a bullfighter."[3]

The controller can "move" the pieces in certain prescribed directions and speeds but cannot stop the overall process once the pieces are set in motion. The only process the controller has to "stop the action" is the holding pattern, but even then the pieces on the board keep moving in circles. Here, too, the amount of time an airplane can be kept in a holding pattern is determined by the amount of fuel and reserves in the circling airplane. Thus, holding patterns are not as innocuous as they seem at first. Airplanes in holding patterns are burning fuel, some at a prodigious rate. Controllers may receive requests from pilots to terminate the hold due to low fuel or for other reasons.

Air traffic controllers are different. Regardless of what pilots say about them, what the Federal Aviation Administration says about them, what the Air Transport Association says about them, what individual members of Congress say about them, or what the public believes about them, they are different. That upwards of 90 percent of controllers retire with a medically significant condition suggests something about their work. Brain surgeons and astronauts do not experience anything approaching these types of maladies. Pilots, themselves, are often in stress-producing situations that test their mettle and call on all the expertise and experience they possess. No one begrudges the pilot his or her earnings of $100,000 to $150,000 a year or more for serving as pilot in command of a Boeing 747. Passengers just love to see that pilot with the four shoulder stripes walk smartly into the cockpit and close the door. They know he (or she) is in complete control of the flight and that he is trained to handle any emergency that may arise. The pilot knows every aspect of the mechanical machine he is flying; he knows navigation and communications; he knows how to avoid danger or cope with it if it cannot be avoided. Children look up to the pilot and dream about the time they may be able to assume that responsible role. Kids and some adults dream about Sky King in his Cessna 310, diving, turning, and climbing, all without incident. Who has not seen those flying aces in recent wars who blasted enemy fighters out of the air with grace and skill? Who has not heard about General Chuck Yeager breaking the sound barrier? Who is not aware of the flying exploits of the Gulf War? These are all very powerful visual images that serve to make pilots stand out as something special or different in the American psyche.

What would one think if someone were to say, "That is all wonderful, but what about those individuals who, on a daily basis, are responsible not for one airplane and a hundred people but for hundreds of airplanes carrying thousands of people?" Complicate this scenario by noting, as described earlier, that the hundreds of airplanes are flying in hundreds of different directions, at hundreds of different air speeds, at dozens of different altitudes. There are large airplanes, and there are small ones. Some are low on fuel, while all want to conserve fuel. Some have weather-avoidance equipment onboard, while others have little other than a simple two-way radio and required navigation equipment.

In this system of endless variety, there is order and calm. The pilot is required to fly according to rules and procedures that are designed to minimize airborne "conflicts." All airplanes, regardless of the type of flying being performed, are required to fly at altitudes that prevent airplanes flying in opposite directions from meeting head-on in flight. If the pilot is flying "east" from 001 degrees to 180 degrees on the magnetic compass, he is supposed to fly at "odd" altitudes, that is, 3,000, 5,000, 7,000, and so on, feet above mean sea level. If the pilot is flying "west," he is supposed to fly at "even" altitudes. This convention is designed to ensure that no two airplanes are converging head-on at the same altitude.

There are very specific arrival and departure procedures designed to ensure that two airplanes do not attempt to occupy the same airspace simultaneously. Obviously, these rules and procedures do not work infallibly. Errors or lapses in judgment occur in all complex and demanding situations that create hazardous conditions, and the law of large numbers tells us that occasionally these errors will result in an accident.

Thrust into the middle of this situation is the air traffic controller. These individuals are directly and personally responsible for the safe and efficient movement of all controlled air traffic through, into, and out of the United States. Everything they say, every action they take, every mistake they make is recorded for review and criticism. This monitoring alone is enough to raise the blood pressure of most individuals, but virtually everyone would agree that it is necessary to ensure integrity in the system and to provide feedback for system operational and safety improvements.

In addition to the level of responsibility suggested above, how are controllers different? The differences reside primarily in three areas. First, the type of work they perform requires exceptional concentration, good judgment, quick thinking, and good communications. Once a controller assumes responsibility for a sector, the airplanes in that sector never stop moving. Like a chess player, he or she must not only know exactly where all the "pieces" are at the present but anticipate where they will be under a variety of different scenarios. Unlike the chess player whose pieces move only when he moves them, the pieces on the controller's radar screen are constantly in motion. It is a dynamic, ever-changing configuration that requires judgments and actions to prevent conflicts.

Depending on where the controller's sector is, the volume and complexity of the situation can be very different. En route traffic over Idaho, Montana, and North Dakota may require a substantially less intense demeanor than, say, traffic converging on Chicago's O'Hare Airport or JFK Airport in New York. As the "funnel" gets narrower, the physical separation between airplanes becomes more and more critical.[4] Controllers must be able to visualize every airplane in their sector in terms of direction of flight, altitude, and performance capability. There must be instinctive responses to ever-changing conditions, with safety always the overriding consideration.

The second difference is the sustained intensity of the job. Everyone has experienced stress in their jobs, some more than others. In some instances, the stressors serve to stimulate more responsive or creative problem solving or actions. Appropriate actions or responses occur, and the stressor disappears. Can one scarcely imagine a more stressful situation than that involving a brain surgeon when unexpected, uncontrolled hemorrhaging occurs during an operation? Decisive, quick action is needed to save the patient's life. The successful surgeon is trained to take those actions and is compensated commensurately. After the crisis is over, the surgeon retires to the lounge or engages in more sedate counseling or other less stressful activity. Similarly, one can imagine the stress on a pilot when there is an in-flight emergency such as losing an engine or other potentially catastrophic event. The pilot is trained to take decisive, quick action to stabilize the situation and ensure successful culmination of the flight. After the flight is ended or the emergency has been corrected, the pilot resumes a fairly routine and sedate operational posture. The successful pilot is also paid commensurately with the skills and responsibilities he or she assumes.

The air traffic controller is different. While the pilot can "punch the autopilot" and relax for a while or assign the flying responsibilities to the copilot, the controller does not have an autopilot or a "cocontroller." Admittedly, some controllers have higher-volume sectors than others, but the irony of the job is that as one gains expertise and proficiency, he or she is assigned to the higher volume, more stressful sectors. It makes sense to assign the most demanding sectors to the most proficient controllers, but the outcome of that process is that stressors tend to escalate as the experience of the controller increases. A small mistake or miscalculation relating to traffic over Montana can be embarrassing; a similar mistake in the proximity of Los Angeles International Airport (LAX) can spell disaster.

Thus, this second difference in the controller's occupation involves the persistence of stress. There may be times in the controller's workday in which the volume of traffic is low and the potential conflicts few. However, when these conditions arise, the FAA has a procedure for "consolidating" sectors so that a controller assumes jurisdiction over two or more adjacent sectors. In more normal conditions, the controller has a full plate of controlled traffic throughout all or most of his or her assignment. Every day the workload is the same. Stress starts when sector control begins and ends when sector control is relinquished to the next controller.

Congressman Guy Molinari examined the environment of the air traffic control system firsthand. He reported:

The controllers are a special breed and, boy, at Washington Center last week I sat there and watched this one fellow. I plugged in a headset and watched him take care of an awful lot of traffic, and his knees were drumming constantly; and you could see the type of tension and pressure he's operating under. The man had been there eighteen years. That's not an unusual situation. You see that all the time. But you can see the pressure cooker there. You can see the operating environment. We expect an awful lot of them. They give an awful lot. But they need more help, and that's what we're here for.[5]

The third difference is that controllers do not receive the attention and appreciation from their employer, the airline industry, or the public they serve. In fact, the FAA has adopted and sustained a management structure that is viewed as primitive, petty, arcane, insensitive, unfortunate, intolerant, and "in conflict with the expressed intent of the Federal labor management relations statute."[6] The FAA has been unsympathetic to problems identified by controllers and unresponsive to recommendations for change. Former FAA administrator Langhorne Bond observed that there is "no more tension in air traffic control than there is in driving a bus."[7] This statement hardly demonstrates a sense of understanding or a signal that there is something different about air traffic control work. Even when study groups commissioned by the FAA have recommended improvements, the agency has been reluctant to implement them. Thus, there is a sense of friction, distrust, and discomfort that exists between the controller at the screen and supervision and management at all levels. Controllers do not believe that management has their interests at heart, and the FAA has taken every opportunity to confirm this belief. If there ever was an environment that demonstrated the need for organized employee response, it is the air controller situation.

It may be possible to find similar differences in other occupational groups as well. Certainly, there are other groups of employees not appreciated by their employers in both the public and private sectors. There are other groups of employees working under demanding and stressful conditions. However, the importance of the observations about the air traffic controller is that all three differences converge in one occupation. It just so happens that the fourth element in the equation is the American public, who is dependent on the air traffic control system to control the aviation sector efficiently and safely.

Air traffic controllers are aware of the importance of their jobs and the interrelationships within the aviation sector. There must be air traffic controllers, just as there must be policemen, orchestra conductors, and corporation managers. There must be somebody who has the whole "enterprise" in focus and who can orchestrate the individual pieces to ensure safety and harmony. Note that the three corollary examples contain one or more of the differences noted above but not all of them.

Orchestra conductor—high pay, considerable prestige, some stress during performances, no safety considerations.

Corporate managers—high pay, considerable prestige, limited ongoing stress, some, but few safety considerations.

Policemen—low pay, periodic stress, periodic and intense stress and safety concerns, some recognition of importance, important safety considerations.

When was the last time that an air traffic controller was singled out for public recognition for the excellent work he or she had done? The last public recognition was probably related to a controller being responsible for a problem such as a near miss or an airplane crash. In some ways, this is precisely the point. When air traffic controllers are doing an excellent job—which is about 99.9 percent of the time—there is little understanding of or appreciation for their skills, commitment, and expertise. When something does not work as it should, the air traffic controller is likely to be singled out and criticized for not taking an action or taking an inappropriate action. There is little balance in the process. When a controller "screws up," he or she should be held accountable, just as any professional person is held accountable for his or her actions. However, when air traffic controllers exhibit exemplary performance, as they typically do, under less than ideal conditions, recognition should be made of that process as well.

With the exception of several Department of Transportation officials, virtually everybody who has become familiar with the air traffic control function and the professionals who engage in the air traffic controller occupation have come away with a great deal of respect and admiration for air traffic controllers. They are not similar to other employees in either the public or private sectors working in more typical occupations.

The 1970 Corson Committee Report observed, "This system [the air traffic control system] is a 'labor intensive' system, that is, one in which dependence is placed primarily upon human effort rather than capital equipment, and in such a system the development of that central resource—the human work force—is of prime consequence." [8]

While the typical controller is not a college graduate, each has had extensive professional training in the set of skills and aptitudes needed for safe operation of the system. It takes between two and three years of formal classroom training and on-the-job training to become a full performance level controller. Even then, controllers are assigned to control sectors with lower traffic volume so that they can gradually acquire the judgment and skills to move to higher-volume, more congested control positions. The judgment and knowledge to control hundreds and occasionally thousands of aircraft effectively and safely can only be acquired through extensive training and experience. A single bad decision or misjudgment can result in the deaths of hundreds of people. As air traffic converges on high-volume airports—Chicago's O'Hare, New York's Kennedy, Washington's National, Atlanta, Los Angeles, Dallas–Fort Worth, and many others—airplanes are in relatively close proximity to one another and are traveling at high speeds. The knowledge, judgment, and acumen needed to ensure that no two airplanes occupy the "same airspace, simultaneously" has been likened to a three-dimensional chess game, described earlier. Once a controller assumes responsibility for a sector, he or she cannot push a button and stop all the action, rock back in a chair, and take a breather. The intense concentration needed to control in three dimensions, with the realization that a single error can be disastrous, leads to stress, high blood pressure, gastrointestinal problems, and a host of other maladies.

Combining this type of work environment with a shortage of qualified controllers, compulsory overtime work, the inability to take breaks when needed, and the inability to schedule vacations or other relaxing events when needed can lead to intolerable work conditions. An important caveat to all this is that not every controller is in a pressure cooker control environment, and not every controller is in an unrelenting control environment as described earlier. However, a significant proportion of controllers occupy the control positions described above, and equally important, as noted, as controllers gain experience, they are assigned to more and more demanding control positions. Therefore, a controller can expect to occupy a highly stressful position for a major portion of his or her controlling career.

Writers in *U.S. News and World Report* captured the essence of how controllers differ from other federal employees and other employees in general.

The people who staff the air-traffic centers and towers are, by all accounts, an unusual assortment of government workers. Mostly high-school graduates, they passed stiff examinations to get their jobs and endured years of training. But complaints abound about the demands of their work—odd hours, tension, demanding responsibilities. Perhaps because of their isolated work lives, controllers have little to do with other federal employees or other public-employee unions.[9]

As early as 1970, the unique character of this occupation and the demands it placed on those who worked as controllers was noted by the Corson Committee. As the 1970 Report observed, it was impressed with the unique character of air traffic controllers in the federal workforce. The committee noted that many occupations in the federal service require similar talents, and many may contain the "exacting responsibilities" inherent in the controller's job, but the committee reported that few occupations have the combination of these traits that make the controller's job exceedingly demanding.[10]

However, significantly, controllers themselves viewed the work they performed as different. As reported in *U.S. News and World Report*, "Years of acrimonious relations with the Federal Aviation Administration forged the controllers into what one close observer calls a 'fanatical' group."[11] Even the leadership of the union viewed the members differently. "Poli himself admits that PATCO 'is not a union, it is a religion' to its members."[12]

Controllers believed that the work they performed was as critical to the safety of and efficiency of the movement of passengers and cargo as was the work of the pilots. As a consequence, "[t]hey came to compare themselves . . . with the pilots whose planes they guided—and many wanted the same $100,000-a-year salaries."[13]

Do air traffic controllers have the most important job in the world? Probably not. But if you fly commercially or in private airplanes, you would certainly think so. Do air traffic controllers have the most difficult job in the world? Probably not. However, it doesn't take much imagination to understand the complexity and stress involved in the work they do. The average person, even when flying in an airplane, never thinks much about how the orderly, generally on-time movement of airplanes occurs. It does not occur by accident. Arrival on time at a distant location after several hours in the air is not a random event. (Some people who have had a less than acceptable flight may argue with that notion.) The federal air traffic control system is a vastly complex, highly automated system that requires continual intervention by human beings twenty-four hours a day, 365 days a year.

This brief description of how controller's function in the air traffic control system provides clues about how stressful the occupation is relative to other types of work. Controllers generally like the tasks they perform; they find them challenging and there can be no question that their work roles are an integral part of an important industry.

FAMILIARIZATION (FAM) FLIGHTS

Throughout the fourteen-year relationship between the PATCO and the FAA, many issues concerning wages and working conditions served to divide the two parties. One of the issues was not actually a working condition in an immediate sense, but it affected how controllers related to the traffic they controlled. To help controllers understand what the needs and procedures were in the cockpit, a process involving FAM flights was initiated.

Safe operation in the commercial airline industry requires the cooperation of several important participants. Aircraft manufacturers, mechanics, flight attendants, air traffic controllers, cockpit crew, ground service personnel, and others work together to ensure safety in the industry. Since most air traffic controllers are not pilots, it is difficult for them to understand and appreciate the conditions and needs of the cockpit crew in commercial aviation. Conversely, most pilots have not experienced the problems that affect how a controller handles his or her job. One method for addressing this information gap was the initiation of familiarization flights for air traffic controllers. These FAM flights were designed to put the controller in the cockpit, as an observer, on scheduled airline flights.

While the intent of FAM flights was to educate the controllers, it wasn't long before these flights took on the character of an occupational "perk." Controllers looked forward to these flights, and there was considerable interest in their continuation. Significantly, the Corson Committee, too, fully supported these activities. The committee recommended that "[g]reater use of FAM trips be allowed by the FAA to provide greater understanding of the pilot's environment by controllers. As rapidly as the staffs in facilities can be increased, the objective should be to provide each controller with at least one FAM trip on regular duty time each year."[14]

Since FAM flights were essentially costless to the airlines, many airlines participated in the program. Pilots, too, recognized the wisdom of having controllers experience cockpit needs firsthand.

There is no evidence that controllers abused this perk, but airlines participated in the program voluntarily. Since it wasn't a mandatory program, the airlines controlled the number and frequency of FAM flights. The FAA-PATCO collective bargaining agreement provided for familiarization flights by controllers. Called the SF-160 Program, the agreement provided that "[t]he parties recognize that any air carrier may suspend or abridge their participation in the SF-160 (familiarization flying) at any time and that the Employer has no authority to direct the conduct of the program by individual air carriers."[15]

In spite of the clear contract language, air traffic controllers felt that they had acquired a right to these flights. To demonstrate the importance of this perk, in 1978 U.S. international carriers unilaterally abolished these free rides. In response to this action, the PATCO called a "spontaneous" slowdown at major airports in the United States on May 15–16 and June 6–7, 1978. These actions delayed departures and arrivals, increased fuel usage, and in general disrupted the smooth flow of air traffic. Controllers signaled the airlines that these types of flights were important to them and that they were not going to simply sit back and take what the air carriers provided to them. When these flights were denied by individual carriers, PATCO members became annoyed. As noted earlier, John Leyden argued that the controllers were "angry" and "fed up" with the airlines for not participating in the FAM program. This anger and frustration set the stage for a spontaneous slowdown that could happen at any moment. It was in this context that he said that the airlines could either participate in the FAM program or spend some money with their airplanes in holding patterns, at less efficient altitudes, or on less efficient flight paths.[16]

This issue hung on as an irritant throughout the turbulent years of PATCO's existence. In fact, some believed that the FAM issue was an important catalyst in PATCO's strategy to escalate its job actions from slowdowns and sick-outs to strikes. As reported in the *Wall Street Journal*:

The circumstances that drove the tiny 15,000-member Professional Air Traffic Controllers Organization to launch an illegal strike and battle with the government began developing about three years ago. At that time, PATCO thought it had negotiated an agreement with the controllers' employer, the Federal Aviation Administration, for free overseas trips. In return, PATCO signed a three-year pact with the FAA, the longest ever.

But the airlines balked at giving the controllers the free trips abroad, and PATCO's leadership emerged with egg on its face. The union, which previously conducted only sick-outs and slowdowns, began girding for a full-fledged strike.[17]

While the PATCO leadership was upset with the FAA over the FAM program, it is unlikely that this single issue was of sufficient importance to precipitate the 1981 strike. The PATCO had a plethora of issues involving working conditions and money that certainly dominated the process. Nevertheless, in the overall scheme of things, the FAM flights were an important rallying point around which leaders could coalesce strong sentiment.

To demonstrate the emotional aspects of FAM flights to controllers, an incident occurred in the skies over Florida in 1980 that brought the issue to the forefront. The skies over Florida were not solidly overcast, but there were scattered thunderstorms over much of the southern half of the state. It was early spring, and thousands of air travelers were arriving in Miami for their vacations. None of them on Braniff Flight 343 had any reason to believe that the relationship between the Federal Aviation Administration and its employees placed their lives in danger. As it turned out, none of the passengers knew that the event that follows even happened until they read about it in the newspaper.

Controller: Braniff 343 turn right heading 170, vector for spacing, expect two-seven right at Miami.

Pilot: Oh great, that's right in the stuff [thunderstorm] 170.

Controller: Well, I want you to, uh, make sure you get this information back to your vice president Brown. You know what I mean.

Pilot: No. I sure don't.

Controller: Well, most of the pilots don't. You taking anybody in your jump seat today?

Pilot: Nah, sure not.

Controller: Now you understand what I mean.[18]

This twenty-second dialogue between a veteran air traffic controller and a Braniff flight nearing Miami's International Airport captured the attention and typified the frustration that characterized the relationship between the Federal Aviation Administration and its unionized employees. This particular instance demonstrated the lengths to which an air traffic controller would go to drive home a point. Braniff Flight 343 had 105 persons onboard. The pilot was flying in controlled airspace in the proximity of one of the nation's busiest airports. The pilot could reasonably believe that he was receiving instructions from the air traffic control system that permitted the flight to terminate in a safe landing in Miami. Intentionally vectoring an airplane into a thunderstorm to drive home a point that could not be driven home through normal processes is sheer madness.

Modern aircraft of all sizes and types are exceedingly durable machines. Occasionally, an airplane will inadvertently fly into a thunderstorm. Without exceptional luck and piloting skill, the results of that encounter are likely to make headline news. Thunderstorms are one of several devices in nature that pilots dread the most. A mature thunderstorm can rip the wings off an airplane or cause the pilot to lose control of the flight for a short or extended period.

Controllers also know the power and danger of thunderstorms through their controller training and general knowledge of meteorology. Flight 343 landed successfully at Miami, and the controller was fired. Nevertheless, the inexcusable, dangerous, foolhardy behavior displayed that fateful day in early April 1980 was not an isolated event. While it was the action of a single individual that captured the headlines, the real problems in the American aviation system were much deeper and more ubiquitous.

The American public, the FAA, and for that matter, the PATCO could not and should not tolerate behavior of the type displayed by the controller. While the skies over Miami were undoubtedly busy on April 10, as they are most days, it is inconceivable that Flight 343 could not have been vectored around or above the thunderstorm. While the pilot had radar onboard and could see much of the weather in his vicinity, he could not see, on radar or through visual observation, the other airplane traffic in his vicinity. Aircraft radar is not designed to identify other airplanes in flight. The pilot is therefore dependent on the controller to provide him with instructions that will keep appropriate separation between other airplanes competing for the airspace.

Air controllers have demonstrated time and again that they have considerable power over routes, speeds, and altitudes that controlled aircraft fly. Large jets and turbine aircraft are more efficient at high altitudes than they are at low altitudes. Pilots therefore request high altitudes particularly on long flights, and they want clearance to the higher altitudes as early in the flight as possible. High altitudes are generally an efficiency (profit) issue and not directly related to safety.[19] Controlled aircraft can request higher altitudes, but the controller is the one who determines if and when their requests are granted. No pilot will leave an assigned altitude in either a climb or descent unless cleared by the controller (emergencies are the exception, of course). As a consequence, controllers have within their power considerable latitude to directly and immediately affect the operating efficiency of an air carrier.

Pilots can and occasionally do get irate with a controller who vectors the flight away from the requested route, places the flight in a holding pattern, instructs climbs or descents that prolong the flight, or instructs the pilot to fly slower or faster than is customary. Large aircraft burn thousands of gallons of aviation fuel an hour. It is easy to see why delays or other instructions that prolong the flight cost the carrier money. Then, too, pilots do not like to carry more fuel than necessary because it uses more fuel to carry more fuel, and there may be safety considerations as well. Therefore, a pilot will estimate his or her fuel requirements determined by the weight of the aircraft, winds aloft, and applicable safety margins needed for a specific flight. If the pilot receives flight-extending vectors or holds, it may mean that the flight will have to land somewhere else to refuel before completing the flight. The costs and passenger irritation dimensions of that process are easily understood.

Importantly, while controllers have the discretion to affect the efficiency of a flight directly, their first and uppermost concern is safety. While the Flight

343 event happened, one should not conclude that this type of activity is frequent or customary. It is neither. Air traffic controllers understand their role in the system, the importance of their function, and that safety is the primary consideration. When flights are vectored or placed in holding patterns, there is virtually always a good reason for the action. In some cases, weather at a destination airport is poor and flights cannot land, conflicting traffic requires the action, or an emergency has occurred on or near the destination airport (a power failure, for example) that requires the action or other events beyond the controller's control. If pilots ask the controller what the reason is for the action taken, controllers virtually always explain the reasons for delay.

When relationships deteriorated between the PATCO employees and the FAA, these "voluntary" familiarization flights were conveniently "forgotten" by major carriers. The air traffic controllers enjoyed these flights, and they cost the airlines virtually nothing. Some of the familiarization flights were to Europe and other foreign destinations. One can easily understand why the air controllers were so enthusiastic about participating in these flights and why it caused them unhappiness when they were excluded from them.

Familiarization flights were an operational prerequisite that air controllers became accustomed to. Nevertheless, these flights were not designed to give air controllers carte blanch access to flights around the world, and they certainly were provided at the discretion of the individual air carriers. On the other hand, there were few reasons not to provide these opportunities to the air controller, and when they were removed, the air carriers should have expected dissatisfaction.

In spite of the more cordial relationship between the FAA and the controllers, the FAM flight issue remained contentious. When some of the carriers refused to provide free overseas FAM flights to controllers, the PATCO engaged in the May and June 1978 slowdown. Rather than call these slowdowns "working to the rules," the PATCO called the actions "withdrawal of enthusiasm" by the union members. The result was the same: immediate delays in flights and increased congestion around the higher-volume airports. The slowdown didn't have appreciable affect on working conditions within the system. Once the crisis was passed, everything settled back into its prestrike pattern.

PATCO members were becoming increasingly irritated by the cavalier attitude of the FAA and their unwillingness to accept recommendations for improvement or to actually improve the system. In late 1978,

[i]n response to rank-and-file discontent with a three-year contract signed earlier that year [1978], President John Leyden established a committee to begin planning for the next round of negotiations. Each of the seven regional vice-presidents selected a rank-and-file leader (the seven original "choir boys") to be a member of the '81 Committee, with Executive Vice-President Robert Poli representing the national office. Leyden asked the committee to plan a legislative agenda, conduct a public relations campaign, and as a last resort prepare for a strike.[20]

Leyden was struggling to maintain balance in the system. However, he knew that the PATCO would need to be creative and forceful in its initiatives and in its dealings with the FAA. He needed information from the regions, and he needed a mechanism to whip the "troops" into action. As a result, he created the "choir boys." They "were typically activists chosen for their ability to articulate positions and for their influence with the rank-and-file."[21]

In this milieu, Robert Poli notified John Leyden that he, Poli, would be challenging Leyden for the PATCO presidency in the next election. This announcement irritated Leyden. To his surprise, some members of the PATCO executive board expressed support for Poli. To bring the matter to closure,

[b]oth Mr. Poli . . . and Mr. Leyden resigned at a union executive board meeting in Chicago in a policy disputed that revolved, in part, around complaints that Mr. Leyden had not been militant enough in his negotiations with the Government. The board accepted Mr. Leyden's resignation but refused to accept Mr. Poli's. He [Poli] took over as interim president and was elected to a full, three-year term in April 1980.[22]

In one swift Machiavellian move, Poli had removed Leyden from office and installed himself as Leyden's replacement. This action, while viewed with admiration by those on the outside of the labor movement, caused substantial dissension inside organized labor. After all, Leyden was a respected labor leader who made it a practice to develop and maintain professional relationships within the labor movement. Most important, the president of the Air Line Pilots Association (ALPA), John J. O'Donnell, resented the sacking of his friend John Leyden deeply.

In the span of several days, the entire complexion of the PATCO-FAA relationship changed dramatically. The tone for the next year and a half was set by the early actions of Poli. The role of the 1981 committee shifted dramatically. After he ousted Leyden in January 1980, "Poli allowed the '81 committee to focus its attention more single-mindedly on the mechanics of strike preparation."[23]

There is some disagreement about the role Poli planned for the 1981 committee and whether or not its single focus was strike preparation. Congressional testimony by Poli seemed to indicate that a strike was not an option in the process. However, as noted elsewhere, individual controllers clearly believed that a strike was a viable and probably necessary action. One thing is certain: The initial role of the 1981 committee to engage in an effective public relations campaign did not become operational under Poli.

Robert Poli was now the man in charge of the PATCO. He was a different sort of leader. He appeared impatient and moved to immediate action rather than working through the established processes for communications and problem resolution. Maybe Poli had a better pulse on the PATCO and understood that the FAA was not going to change their procedures and personnel policies without being pushed to do so. There was substantial evidence that the FAA did not accept the PATCO as a union and as a legitimate representative of the controllers. An excerpt from the Corson Report in a 1970 court document noted:

No single cause accounts for this crisis in the relation between FAA's management and the organizations representing its employees. Yet our observations suggest that among the most important is the failure of FAA's management at all levels to truly understand the role of the employee organizations and to accept them as not only legitimate, but hopefully as collaborators in building understanding, satisfaction, and an *esprit de corps* and which recommends among other things that the FAA "Expedite, in good faith the resolution . . . of all existing labor-management problems."[24]

There appeared to be some improvements in the relationship between the FAA and the PATCO during the early part of the decade of the 1970s, but the resolution of all existing labor-management problems as suggested by the Corson Committee did not occur. The problems were endemic and pervasive. Managers at all levels were ill prepared to implement personnel policies effectively and conduct labor management relations processes in a manner that did not frustrate and demean the workforce. Hurd and Kriesky reported: "Based on the information in the three consulting reports and the Bowers article, we conclude that FAA management never accepted PATCO as a legitimate representative of the air traffic controllers, and the union predictably responded with an aggressive, confrontational approach. The controllers' support for PATCO and its strategies is best viewed as a reflection of management's failures."[25]

Further evidence that the FAA had been unable to conform to the Corson Committee recommendations appeared in the report by the Jones Committee after the PATCO strike. The Jones Committee Report,

endorsed by all three members of the task force, provides direct evidence that the "para-military, heavy handed style" of FAA management contributed to the PATCO strike. The report describes the "rigid and insensitive system of people management within the FAA." It concludes that "the strike by air traffic controllers [is] consistent with what might have been expected negative organizational conditions, treatment, and experiences, not peer pressure, caused most individuals to decide to strike."[26]

Throughout his ten years in office, John Leyden worked mightily to improve the environment but to little avail. Robert Poli decided to take a different approach. He knew his approach engendered risks. When asked about his bargaining posture, Poli responded, "Oh, certainly, I'll go to jail. I'll carry this through to the fullest."[27] He could not have known that his bargaining attitude would ultimately lead to the destruction of the union.

SUMMARY

Air traffic controllers and their unions were unable to develop a working relationship with the FAA that could lead to labor peace. In spite of several "study commissions" that provided specific recommendations to change the FAA's relationship with its employees and its unions, conditions continued to deteriorate. As the decade of the 1970s drew to a close, there were storm clouds on the horizon. New leadership in the PATCO, the election of a new president of the United States, and continued problems within the air traffic control system provided the conditions for major changes.

NOTES

1. "House Approves Plan to Rehire Former Air-Traffic Controllers," *Congressional Quarterly*, April 2, 1988, p. 899.

2. General Accounting Office, *FAA's Definition of Its Controller Work Force Should Be Revised*, Report to the Chairman, House Subcommittee on Investigations and Oversight, Committee on Public Works and Transportation, GAO/RECD-88-14 (Washington, D.C.: GPO, October 1987), p. 11.

3. James R. Chiles, "Preparing for Takeoff as Air Traffic Controllers," *Smithsonian*, Vol. 20, No. 10, January 1990, p. 123.

4. For controlled aircraft approaching O'Hare Airport, controllers generally maintain about five miles horizontal separation while the airplane is in the center's jurisdiction. When the airplane enters the TRACON's jurisdiction, horizontal separation lowers to three miles. When the tower controller takes over, the horizontal separation may decrease to two and one half miles.

5. House of Representatives, Committee on Post Office and Civil Service, Subcommittee on Investigations, *Working Conditions and Staffing Needs in Air Traffic Control System*, 100th Cong., 1st sess., Serial No. 100-26 (Washington, D.C.: GPO, July 29–30, 1987), p. 17.

6. House of Representatives, Committee on Post Office and Civil Service, Subcommittee on Investigations, *Air Traffic Control*, 96th Cong., 2d sess. (Washington, D.C.: GPO, September 30, 1980), p. 17.

7. *Washington Post*, August 16, 1981, p. B4.

8. Senate, Committee on Post Office and Civil Service, *Air Traffic Controllers*, 91st Cong., 2d sess. Calendar No. 1016, Report No. 91-1012 (Washington, D.C.: GPO, July 9, 1970), pp. 50, 74.

9. "Challenge to the Government," *U.S. News and World Report*, August 17, 1981, p. 17.

10. Senate, Committee on Post Office and Civil Service, *Air Traffic Controllers*, p. 9.

11. "Challenge to the Government," p. 18.

12. Ibid., p. 17.

13. Ibid., pp. 17–18.

14. Senate, Committee on Post Office and Civil Service, *Air Traffic Controllers*, p. 60.

15. Gregory L. Karam, "The Legal Consequences of a Deliberate Air Traffic Controllers Slowdown," *Northern Kentucky Law Review*, Vol. 8, No. 1, January 1981, p. 169.

16. Ibid.

17. "Air Controllers' Strike Will Be Broken with Goals Thwarted, Analysts Think," *Wall Street Journal*, August 4, 1981, p. 3.

18. "Controller Faces Firing in Endangering Jetliner," *Washington Post*, May 2, 1980, p. A14.

19. The one aspect of safety related to altitude involves the accumulation of airplanes at altitudes below 18,000 MSL. The vast majority of general aviation flights and significant numbers of commercial flights operate below 18,000 MSL. Therefore, many pilots seek to climb above this altitude as quickly as possible to minimize potential conflicts.

20. Richard W. Hurd and Jill K. Kriesky, "Communications: The Rise and Demise of PATCO Reconstructed," *Industrial and Labor Relations Review*, Vol. 40, No. 1, October 1986, p. 118.

21. Ibid.

22. Jonathan Fuerbringer, "Militant Controller Chief: Robert Edmond Poli," *New York Times*, August 4, 1981, p. B23.

23. Hurd and Kriesky, "Communications," p. 118.

24. *Federal Supplement*, Vol. 313, F. Supp. 181 (St. Paul, Minn: 1970), West Publishing Co., pp. 181–190.

25. Hurd and Kriesky, "Communications," p. 118.

26. Ibid., p. 117.

27. Fuerbringer, "Militant Controller Chief," p. B23.

Chapter 4

Escalation of Animosity

In the months immediately preceding August 3, 1981, there was intense concern about the contract with the FAA that had expired on March 15, 1981, but the union had been down that road before. Everybody knew there would be some public posturing, chest-beating, threats of serious problems if agreement was not reached, and all the other charades customarily found in labor-management relations and the collective bargaining processes. The one major difference that some recognized—but not too many dwelled upon—was the new PATCO president. The new contract was being negotiated by the new president and most PATCO members did not know how he would handle the negotiations. The new president, Robert Poli, had been involved in negotiations before, but this would be the first time that he was ultimately responsible for the final product—the collective bargaining agreement.

Poli had spent many years within the PATCO and knew the system well. As described in the previous chapter, he knew the system and its participants well enough to orchestrate the ouster of John Leyden. However, as one looks at the period immediately preceding the strike, the one thing that seems to stand out is that involving the demeanor, attitude, and collective bargaining goals of Robert Poli.

WHO IS ROBERT POLI?

This is an important question because one of the significant reasons for the PATCO strike is believed to be a function of Poli's perceptions, attitudes, and temperament as a union leader. He had spent a number of years as a controller in the U.S. Air Force and then in the Chicago and Cleveland Centers. Therefore, he knew, firsthand, the types of problems controllers faced. Robert Edmond Poli was born in Pittsburgh, Pennsylvania, on February 27, 1937. He was a graduate of Pittsburgh's Wilkensberg High School. After working as an air controller in the Cleveland Center, he became executive vice president of the union in 1973. In that role, he orchestrated the day-to-day activities of the union from the inside. He worked extensively with the union's executive council in crafting union policies and in the implementation of those policies.

However, Poli was not well known in the labor movement, which should not seem surprising. The role he played ensured that he would retain certain anonymity, and there is evidence that Poli liked it that way. He was not an overly outward person. His work was accomplished through one-on-one and small group meetings within the PATCO rather than through large public meetings. Therefore, he became well known within the PATCO, but not well known to those outside the union. He was an enigma to many in his own union, but obviously they understood him well enough to follow him out on strike.

In retrospect, one would have to conclude that Poli was not an effective politician or that he did not fully understand presidential politics. Most of his strength came from his organizational skills and his ability to convince those around him to support his ideas and ideals. After the 1980 coup in which he unseated John Leyden as PATCO president, Poli failed to capitalize on his strategic position by bolstering support from other unions and the public. Rather, he embarked on a course of action that smacked of arrogance and contempt. He knew because everyone else knew that he had ruffled the feathers of many in the labor movement including the leadership of the AFL–CIO and, most important, the president of the ALPA. In the short span of time between his ascendancy to the PATCO presidency and the strike, it may have been unreasonable to expect Poli to make peace with ALPA president John J. O'Donnell, but there is no evidence that he even tried.

Poli found time to meet with presidential candidate Ronald Reagan and found areas of presumed mutual agreement, but he was unable to meet and confer with those around him in the labor movement. Perhaps he believed that with the support of the soon-to-be president, he didn't need his labor allies. In hindsight, this could very well be the single most important strategic error he committed. Once the president decided to abandon support of the PATCO, Robert Poli was left alone in his struggle.

Poli was not a sophisticated communicator either. Perhaps here, too, he believed that he did not have to make his case to the public, the Congress, the labor movement, or the media. After the strike was lost, he said that "the only thing he would have done differently would have been to tell his union's story better. He said he goofed by allowing the media to portray his discontent solely as a struggle for $10,000 more a year for controllers who are paid an average annual salary of $33,000. 'If that was a mistake, it was mine.'"[1]

Perhaps he believed that the strength of the PATCO in the aviation industry was sufficient to prevail in whatever course of action he initiated, and therefore public relations were less important. He knew what prior slowdowns and sickouts had done to the industry, and there was little to suggest that other concerted actions would not be similarly effective.

Nobody suggested that Robert Poli was not smart enough for the position of PATCO president. In fact, he was viewed by many as a clever, crafty, rather articulate union official. A congressional aide described Poli as "very, very smart and exceptionally militant in protecting his workers."[2] An official from the Carter administration who dealt with Poli described him as "calculating and more militant than his predecessor."[3]

There were some who marveled at his ability to work internally to unseat John Leyden after Leyden's decade-long tenure as PATCO president. Others, of course, took a much less charitable view of these actions. They saw Poli as devious, manipulative, scheming, disloyal, and opportunistic.

It may be reasonable to conclude that Robert Poli was impatient with PATCO's progress under Leyden's leadership and sought to take the organization to new heights much quicker and more directly. After the coup, Poli observed, "I had stronger convictions about what had to be done and I felt I could do a better job."[4] Furthermore, "It was a difference in philosophy. I guess I'm more a militant than he [Leyden] is."[5] If the PATCO strike had succeeded, Poli would probably be in an even more key position in the labor movement today. The stakes were high but, from all that was apparent, achievable. Poli had a vision of correcting what he felt were injustices of long duration experienced by air controllers. These injustices, real or imagined, sold well with air controllers. The inability of the FAA to mount an effective employee relations program made all that Poli said, to air traffic controllers, credible and imperative.

Robert Poli was a clever organization person. He was able to build on the structure of air controllers put in place by Leyden. This structure provided a network of union members who were motivated and insistent on action and change. There is some evidence that the membership may have become too motivated and too involved in the direct operation of the union. Once there was movement in the government's bargaining position, Poli may have been unable to constrain PATCO membership to accept less than its full package of demands. This situation, if real and not orchestrated, is one of leadership. A leader keeps control of the reigns of power to ensure that the vision they espouse has the maximum probability of succeeding. Leaders see the whole picture and have contingency plans when one avenue of change is shut off. Poli seemed to have whipped up the membership so that when it seemed reasonable to shift gears or change directions, he was unable to keep the rank and file in his corner. Leaders are not perfect, of course, and it may be unfair to characterize the entire debacle as a failure of leadership. Leaders make mistakes in strategy and tactics that from hindsight seem amateurish and foolish. Hindsight is always perfect, and it is easy to throw rocks at prior decisions. The emotions of the moment and the information that the leader has are what permit and mandate a particular decision. Emotions were running high, and there was great expectation by PATCO members that they were invincible. Few, including Poli, had fully grasped all of the changes under way in the political system that were just beginning to emerge.

ROBERT POLI AND CANDIDATE RONALD REAGAN

Robert Poli has been described as bright, articulate, aggressive, inflexible, and scheming, among other things. No one suggested that he was politically astute. This does not mean that he wasn't astute, but it is a character trait that was not attributed to him. Is this where Poli stumbled? Did he misread or misinterpret the political signals, or was he mislead into believing something that was simply not true? Did he lose control of the PATCO membership? Did he act on the belief that what he had been told by principals in the dispute was true?

Rule number one in politics is that you watch what they do and not what they say! The old euphemism "Talk is cheap" is certainly applicable to politics. Politicians will tell you anything to get your vote. These tired old clichés have a ring of truth in them, and not heeding them has tripped up many in the history of this Republic.

Robert Poli was newly elected PATCO president in 1980, and he wanted to find some way to "deliver the goods." The controllers had not been particularly successful under President Jimmy Carter, and Poli felt, rightly or wrongly, that supporting a new president would permit development of a more successful bargaining atmosphere. Poli knew about candidate Reagan's association with the Screen Actors Guild and that Reagan had led the first strike by Guild members. At various points in the campaign, the Republican presidential candidate had talked about support for union causes in a general sense. This support was not good enough for Poli, and he decided to meet with the Republican candidate and see if there was specific support for the controllers' demands.

On October 23, 1980, a private meeting was scheduled between Reagan and Poli in Florida to discuss PATCO issues and presumably possible support for the Republican candidate. Since the meeting was private, no one other than Reagan and Poli know exactly what was discussed. However, one thing is clear; Robert Poli came away from that meeting with a strong belief that candidate Reagan was sympathetic to the controllers' concerns. Based on that meeting and discussion, Robert Poli, president of the PATCO, endorsed Ronald Reagan for President. The nine-member PATCO board voted unanimously in support of the endorsement. Poli had strenuously criticized President Carter for not paying enough attention to the air traffic control system and for "consistently denigrating federal employees." Poli was assured that Reagan would provide the best leadership for Federal employees and that he would move quickly to improve the condition of the air traffic control system.[6]

One could argue that Poli misunderstood what Reagan said or read into their discussion things that were simply not true. Maybe. It would not be the first time that a word smith craftily constructed a position on an issue that was contrary to how he felt or planned to proceed. Certainly, Poli may have misconstrued the soon-to-be president's verbal assurances that things would be better for controllers if Reagan were elected president. What is important, however, is that the assurances were not simply verbal. On October 20, 1980, three days before their meeting, candidate Reagan wrote a letter to Poli providing his views on conditions in the air traffic control system and what he would do if elected President. Addressed to Poli, the letter said in part:

I have been thoroughly briefed by members of my staff as to the deplorable state of our nation's air traffic control system. They have told me that too few people working unreasonable hours with obsolete equipment has placed the nation's air travellers in unwarranted danger. In an area so closely related to public safety the Carter administration has failed to act responsibly.

You can rest assured that if I am elected President, I will take whatever steps are necessary to provide our air traffic controllers with the most modern equipment available and to adjust staff levels and work days so that they are commensurate with achieving a maximum degree of public safety.[7]

These comments in a signed letter by Reagan are not taken out of context and are not paraphrased summaries of what Reagan might have said. They are further bolstered by the concluding two paragraphs in his letter. Candidate Reagan said:

As in all other areas of the federal government where the President has the power of appointment, I fully intend to appoint highly qualified individuals who can work harmoniously with the Congress and the employees of the government agencies they oversee.

I pledge to you that my administration will work very closely with you to bring about a spirit of cooperation between the President and the air traffic controllers. Such harmony can and must exist if we are to restore the people's confidence in their government.[8]

There may be ways to twist or misconstrue what candidate Reagan had in mind when he signed the October 20 letter. However, any reasonable person reading the letter in its entirety would conclude that the individual writing the letter was firmly supportive of the air traffic controllers' plight. What other conclusion is possible?

Robert Poli certainly believed it. In fact, he found the letter so convincing that "he framed it and hung it on the wall behind his desk in Washington."[9] What, then, happened between October 20, 1980, and August 3, 1981? The PATCO, one of the few labor organizations to do so, endorsed the candidacy of Ronald Reagan. Ronald Reagan defeated Jimmy Carter in the general election and became president of the United States. President Reagan selected Drew Lewis as secretary of transportation and Lynn Helms as administrator of the Federal Aviation Administration. Into early 1981, the PATCO decision to support Ronald Reagan was viewed as a shrewd political move. The PATCO had a well-known cause, the president had acknowledged that he understood the problems, and now he was in a position to do something about them. Robert Poli felt that he had finessed a substantial political advantage, and now the controllers would receive their rightful rewards.

Poli knew that there would be some tough bargaining because the package he proposed contained a number of items that would make any administration gag. Nevertheless, he believed that when the chips were down, his new-found friend, Ronald Reagan, would intercede and ensure that the PATCO received substantially what it asked for. Poli knew there had to be considerable public posturing by both sides because of the stakes involved. He knew the new administration was struggling with tough economic problems, but in the grand scheme of things, the PATCO demands were lost in rounding error. With a trillion dollar federal budget, what could a few hundred million dollars amount to, especially when the needs of the controllers were so widely known and the solutions so easily attainable? While Secretary Lewis and FAA administrator Lynn Helms were tough bargainers, Poli always kept his "ace card," his friend Ronald Reagan, clearly in mind.

When little progress was made early in 1981, Poli knew he would have to rattle the war chest and begin talking strike. He knew strikes by federal employees were illegal, but he also believed that at the last minute there would be no strike because his new friend, President Reagan, would instruct the government negotiators to move toward settlement favorable to PATCO. Therefore, the bargaining strategy was to hang tough on a long list of major demands.

Early in the negotiation process, Secretary Lewis indicated that the maximum package that the administration would accept was one that did not exceed $40 million in new costs. The PATCO proposal had been variously estimated to cost about $700 to $800 million annually in new costs. There was no general disagreement by either side about what each package would cost, but the disparity between the two packages was monumental. A 50 or 100 percent difference was not unusual, but a twenty-fold difference was a sign that something was seriously wrong.

To Poli's dismay, the federal position did not change through many bargaining sessions. Federal negotiators were prepared to alter the configuration of the package, but they were not prepared to increase its size. However, without some movement on the size of the package, Poli realized that none of the PATCO objectives were possible. The $10,000 increase in the controller base salary, the thirty two-hour workweek, extensive retraining, and other elements would all breech the $40 million limit imposed by Lewis. The $10,000 base salary increase, alone, would have added $150 million to new costs.

The PATCO contract had expired, and therefore Poli had to reestablish urgency in the process by setting a strike date. He chose June 22, 1981, with the 7 A.M. shift, as the strike target. Setting this date was not easy for Poli. After months of negotiations, he was beginning to feel that the "understanding" he had with the new president was less firm than he had believed earlier. With the difference in positions so large and with no movement in the administration's package, setting a strike date raised the specter of an actual stoppage.

But, what to worry? Other federal employees had been involved in work stoppages over the years, and there had always been a way to resolve the impasse to everyone's satisfaction. Even if he had to take the union out on strike, he was confident that it would be a short one and that all controllers would end up with improved terms and conditions of employment. Poli believed that the critical nature of air traffic controllers in the aviation sector would ensure a strike of short duration. Then, too, always in the back of his mind was his "understanding" with the new president.

As the bargaining process wore on, Poli was not the only one concerned about a possible stoppage. The aviation industry was busily making contingency plans, as were the countless firms dependent on the movement of people and products by air. The new administration expressed concern about the possible disruption of the economy at the time in which economic renewal was needed. Secretary Lewis was particularly concerned because he understood clearly the role and importance of the aviation sector in myriad economic processes.

ROBERT POLI AND THE CONGRESS

A month before the general election that brought Ronald Reagan to office, Poli testified before the Congress about conditions in the air traffic control system. One can sense the frustration and irritation Poli felt about the protracted difficulties the union had experienced with the FAA. He noted, for example: "PATCO has in recent months been the target of repeated, scurrilous attacks which have questioned the integrity of our organization and this Nation's air traffic controllers."[10]

He attributed most of the operational and labor-management problems they were experiencing to FAA administrator Langhorn Bond (a Carter administration appointee). He observed specifically, "Unfortunately, it appears that Administrator Bond is attempting to divert attention from these deficiencies [in the air traffic control system] by confusing air safety and union relationship issues. He [Bond] has repeatedly attempted to trivialize safety problems by asserting that PATCO raises them as stalking horses for labor matters."[11]

The FAA had repeatedly alleged that the PATCO was using perceived problems in the air traffic control system as a vehicle to force concessions in the labor-management relations process. Poli took the opposite view. He asserted that the "cavalier attitude [of Administrator Bond] is an insult not only to our professional integrity, but to the flying public, and the facts lead one to an opposite and disturbing conclusion: The FAA uses labor/management relations to minimize or ignore deficiencies in their air traffic control system."[12]

As evidence of the types of concerns the PATCO had with the system, Poli observed, "These machines [computers used in the air traffic control system] experienced 6,651 failures in 1979 alone. Yet the FAA claimed that PATCO's concern with computer reliability was mere cordwood for the fueling of a labor dispute."[13] He then argued: "PATCO has always had, and will continue to have, a strong interest in aviation safety. We have made every attempt possible to keep safety issues completely separate from labor issues. It is the FAA which has commingled them in an apparent attempt to deflect criticism of its management of the air traffic system."[14]

In his statement to the committee, Poli summarized the current state of relationships between the PATCO and the FAA. He noted that "the state of labor relations between PATCO and the FAA is not at an ideal level. The FAA's strategies in dealing with its controller work force have been primitive, petty, unfortunate, and in conflict with the expressed intent of the Federal labor management relations statute."[15]

The congressional hearings occurred eleven months before the strike. At the hearings, Poli reiterated his position about a PATCO strike. Responding to a question from the committee chairman, Poli said, "I have stated on two separate occasions before the Congress that this organization is not going to strike next year. I have stated that on a television program in an interview with Mr. Bond. Mr. Bond constantly throws around documents which have come from our organization and states these are strike plans of PATCO."[16]

Congresswoman Gladys Spellman pressed Poli about the intent of the union in constructing and contributing to the National Controller Subsistence Fund, that is, the strike fund. Fifteen percent of the dues received by the national office of PATCO were allocated to the fund, which had been established in 1977. She asked, "You have said that the fund is to be saved for such a time as Federal employees are guaranteed the right to strike. Are you saying, then, that if some or all of your members should strike next March, not 1 cent of that fund would be used to assist those strikers?"[17]

Poli responded, "That is correct."[18] Since the congresswoman had tied the strike fund to the expiration of the current agreement in March 1981, Poli's statement was technically correct. The controllers did not strike in March; they struck in August.

It was during these hearings that Poli set the "money agenda" as the primary concern of the PATCO. His statements to the committee provided ammunition for those who argued that all Poli wanted was more money and nothing else. His comments in response to a question about bargaining goals was, "I think that any time you go into negotiations, any advancement in salary, any benefits that equate to salary, are certainly the No. 1 issue, and this isn't just our organization."[19] Importantly, he did not say that money was the only goal; rather, that it was the number-one goal. Nevertheless, these comments provided an opening for those who wanted to portray the PATCO agenda as simply money.

While the issue never gained much public acceptance during the period before the strike, Poli also argued the disparate treatment American controllers received in relation to controllers in Canada. Observing that Canadian controllers work a thirty-four-hour workweek, Poli inferred that American controllers were working an unreasonable workweek. Congresswoman Spellman challenged Poli about this issue. She observed: "I work 18 hours a day, so I don't have a lot of sympathy for folks who talk a 40-hour week as though it is overdemanding."[20]

Poli responded, "I hope I say this right and you take it right. I think that it is voluntary. In the case of air traffic controllers, it is forced. They are assigned to work. I understand to get your job done it takes that much time, a lot of times late into the night; to be here today, it took me that much time. In the case of air traffic controllers, in almost all cases, they don't have a choice. They are told they must work."[21]

Poli concluded his comments about work hours by comparing air traffic controllers in several countries with U.S. controllers.

In Canada, they work 34 hours a week and the busiest airport in Canada would be No. 31 in the United States. Chicago's O'Hare works more airplanes than the three busiest airports in Europe put together, if you took all of them; if you took Heathrow, Paris, and Frankfort, and put them together, they still don't work as many airplanes as they work at Chicago's O'Hare.[22]

Poli also addressed an issue that came back time after time to haunt the union. The specific allegation made by the FAA was that controllers in Chicago had instigated a demand for a salary supplement because of the stressful nature of their work. Poli argued that the manner in which this demand arose was different from what the FAA alleged.

The statements made by the FAA that we went in there with a cavalier attitude and asked for a $7,500 raise, which the Congress cannot give them, in their statement they made this morning, that didn't come from PATCO. That came from the FAA management who made that recommendation 2 years ago, that controllers in Chicago should be given a $7,500 tax-free raise.

That wasn't something that we pulled out of the air. That is something that the Regional Director of the Great Lakes region proposed to the controllers at O'Hare.

When you are dealing with people in that particular type of situation and that kind of stressful atmosphere, and you bait their appetite and pat them on the head and try to treat them like little boys and let them think something like that might be coming, certainly they will ask for it.[23]

While the FAA national office had not proposed the $7,500 supplement, it is clear that the PATCO had not done so either. Since a Regional FAA official considered this supplement appropriate, it is disingenuous, later in the process, to label demands for the supplement by PATCO as unreasonable.

THE NATIONAL ASSOCIATION OF AIR TRAFFIC SPECIALISTS SUPPORTING PATCO

While this entire discussion relates to the PATCO and its relationship with the FAA, there was another organization that also represented FAA employees. The head of that organization, the National Association of Air Traffic Specialists (NAATS), testified before the same committee that Poli addressed. Lawrence C. Cushing, president of the NAATS, generally supported the testimony by Poli but found several areas of disagreement. Supporting Poli, Cushing observed:

Talking on the subject of how the FAA treats its personnel, staffing, I cannot help but agree wholeheartedly with Mr. Poli that it is totally inadequate. They appear to have from top level management to the bottom, the feeling that the system runs on equipment and that people are only incidental to the system, and I will point out to you one more time that the FAA over the past several years, I think six to be precise, has requested not a single additional person for flight service. Only through the good graces of Congress have we had additional staffing during that period, although the record is adequate and perfectly clear that we still use, in the main, World War II and older equipment. [24]

Cushing continued:

I would point out to you, Mr. Chairman, that we have—the National Association of Air Traffic Specialists—have been negotiating with the FAA for over 2 years to renew our current agreement, and I can state unequivocally that they have used every delaying tactic known; they have used every means at their disposal to guarantee lengthy contract negotiations, and at this point if the FAA proceeds in the manner that they are now stating, we can still be another 18 months before we have a new contract.[25]

He continued, "I understand contract negotiations and I understand they can take time. I also understand that the present delay is—it has no real purpose. It serves no purpose except to alienate the work force."[26] In addition,

Mr. Chairman and Members, this Association has been negotiating with the FAA for a contract for two years (two years September 26, 1980) and the end is not even in sight. The FAA has used every delaying tactic known with their very large staff pitted against our very small one. We believe that the delay is unreasonable and capricious. It certainly is, at the very least, another contributor to low morale amongst our membership and yet another deterrent to aviation safety. It is also a reason why others might adopt a more militant approach to insure a more reasonable time frame for contract settlement and completion.[27]

In response to questions about how he would rate the stewardship of the current FAA administration, Cushing gave the current FAA administrator, Langhorn Bond, relatively high marks for his effort to automate the system's flight service stations. However, Cushing was less flattering about Bond's personnel prowess. Cushing noted, "As far as under his administration, the dealings with people, I would say that this is perhaps one of the worst we have had."[28]

The testimony turned to relationships between employees Cushing represented, that is, FSS personnel, and those represented by the PATCO, that is, air traffic controllers. FSS personnel do not directly control aircraft. Their functions relate more to communications between aircraft in flight,[29] weather briefings and reporting, and other types of activities related to the safe operation of the system. While both categories of employees enjoyed the same job title, that is, air traffic control specialists, Cushing argued that the FAA and Congress had treated them very differently. The reason for the differential treatment was, according to Cushing, because the FSS personnel did not push their needs as aggressively. Comparing how the FAA treats air traffic controllers as compared with flight service station personnel, Cushing noted, "Substandard working conditions, increased user demand, obsolete equipment, and neglect, coupled with lavish attention to other workers [air traffic controllers] in the same personnel category are excellent reasons for low morale [of FSS personnel]."[30]

Couching all of his comments in the context of air safety, Cushing observed:

My fourth point relating to dangers to aviation safety and low morale for the flight service controllers is Public Law 92-297. This law, while well intended by the Congress, has resulted in a *vicious* caste system within air traffic control. It is devastating to station controllers. The law provides early retirement and second career training to air traffic control specialists at centers/towers and denies like benefits to station controllers. This is a major threat to aviation safety.[31]

SUMMARY

The key person in the PATCO strike was clearly Robert Poli. He established the bargaining agenda, he was the primary spokesperson, and he knew the character and content of his "understanding" with the new president. However, there were signs that the understanding was not filtering down to lower levels of Department of Transportation and FAA management. These key bargainers were inflexible and persistent. What they brought to the bargaining table was at variance to what Poli had expected would, and should, be attained under the terms of his understanding. Nevertheless, Poli and the PATCO kept pushing their agenda and set a strike deadline for August 3, 1981.

NOTES

1. "PATCO Chief Robert Poli Resigns Post," *Washington Post*, January 1, 1982, p. D8.
2. Jonathan Fuerbringer, "Militant Controller Chief: Robert Edmond Poli," *New York Times*, August 4, 1981, p. B23.
3. Ibid.
4. Ibid.
5. Ibid.
6. Mike Causey, "The Federal Diary," *Washington Post*, October 24, 1980, p. C2.
7. Lindley H. Clark, Jr., "Reagan: Labor's Love Lost?" *Wall Street Journal*, June 30, 1981, p. 31.
8. Ibid.
9. Ibid.
10. House of Representatives, Committee on Post Office and Civil Service, Subcommittee on Investigations, *Air Traffic Control*, 96th Cong., 2d sess. (Washington, D.C.:

GPO, September 30, 1980), p. 16.
     11. Ibid., p. 16.
     12. Ibid.
     13. Ibid.
     14. Ibid., p. 17.
     15. Ibid.
     16. Ibid., p. 19.
     17. Ibid., p. 21.
     18. Ibid.
     19. Ibid., p. 23.
     20. Ibid., p. 25.
     21. Ibid.
     22. Ibid., p. 26.
     23. Ibid.
     24. Ibid., p. 29.
     25. Ibid.
     26. Ibid., p. 30.
     27. Ibid., p. 38.
     28. Ibid., p. 30.
     29. Flight service station personnel may relay clearances to aircraft in flight or awaiting takeoff instructions, and they may relay requests for clearance changes from pilots. However, the actual clearance must come from the controllers in the air traffic control system.
     30. House of Representatives, *Air Traffic Control*, p. 34.
     31. Ibid., p. 37.

Chapter 5

The Skies Will Be Silent

The escalation of animosity intensified in the four months preceding the August 3 strike. Kenneth Moffet, acting director of the Federal Mediation and Conciliation Service, convened meetings of the principals to keep the dialogue flowing. A federal judge in the federal district court in Brooklyn told the PATCO that an injunction against the union would not be lifted. The injunction that had gone into effect in 1970 enjoined the PATCO from engaging in any concerted actions. FAA officials offered a package addressing some of the union's demands but not others. The Justice Department warned controllers about the seriousness of striking against the federal government and warned that the government would be very tough on strikers.

In late April, Secretary Lewis and Robert Poli testified before the House Post Office and Civil Service Committee's Subcommittee on Compensation and Employee Benefits. The union proposal had been introduced by Congressman William Clay (D–Mo.) as HR 1576. The Secretary argued that the union's proposal would add $1.1 billion to FAA costs in the first year. Poli argued that the proposed package would cost an additional $1.7 billion over three years.

Since the PATCO/FAA collective bargaining agreement had expired on March 15, 1981, Poli told the committee that PATCO members were becoming angry and frustrated about the slow movement in the negotiation process. Poli hoped that the negotiations could begin moving forward so that the FAA could support a bill in the Congress providing for all or most of the "big-ticket items." In these hearings, Congresswoman Mary Rose Oakar (D–Ohio) read a letter into the record that indicated that even if the FAA were to agree with the PATCO on the big-ticket items, the position of the Reagan administration was one of opposition.

There was little chance that the FAA was going to agree to the PATCO proposals. At that point, the median annual salary for a journeyman controller at a busy airport was $32,000. At the air traffic control centers, it was $39,000.

With the inclusion of overtime, controllers at busier facilities were earning up to $56,000 per year. The PATCO proposal provided for, among other things, a separate pay scale for controllers, with a pay "cap" of $73,000 per year.

Both sides addressed the contentious overtime issue as well. The secretary argued that overtime was modest and well within reasonable limits for this type of work. He observed that the average overtime worked at the air traffic control centers was thirty-two hours per year and at other facilities only seventeen hours per year. These average amounts were less than one hour per week. Poli replied that the secretary's "averages" were misleading. He argued that "although most facilities do not work overtime, large amounts of mandatory overtime are forced on crews in the few busiest facilities, placing even more stress on already over-worked people."[1]

It was during these hearing that the strike issue was raised again. Poli commented on the extensive bargaining sessions they had with the FAA but in which no progress occurred. Since February 1981, there had been "no movement, no response that speaks to our demands. We are not planning a strike, but there is a certain unrest."[2]

While Poli was saying publicly that no strike was being planned, writers for the *Daily Labor Reporter* heard other sentiments in the audience. During the hearings, Congresswoman Oakar commented about how frequently she flew between Washington and Cleveland-Hopkins International Airport in her district. A controller said quietly in the hearing room, "[N]ot this summer, you won't." Three months before the strike, this "certain unrest" that Poli spoke about was becoming more focused than many realized, maybe even more than Poli realized.

After thirty-seven meetings with the FAA representatives, Poli was apparently told at the last meeting that there was no room for "substantive discussion" of any of the outstanding issues. Poli walked out.

After walking out of the negotiations, the PATCO set a June 22, 1981, date for a national controllers' strike. Poli told delegates at a New Orleans convention on May 22, "If it [an acceptable FAA offer] does not come, if they do not come to their senses, I vow to you that the skies will be silent."[3] In direct defiance of the strike ban, he told the convention, "The only illegal strike is an unsuccessful strike."[4]

All of the government's efforts were designed to put the union on notice and in the process garner public support for the administration's position. With the PATCO not offering a serious challenge to any of the allegations placed on the public platter by the government, there is little wonder that public sentiment was on the side of government. Controllers were pictured as highly paid, underworked crybabies who didn't know when they had it good.

Little progress was made at the bargaining table, but as the deadline for a strike approached, the FAA surfaced a package that attempted to address several major PATCO concerns. The package was estimated to cost the federal government about $40 million annually over its current air controller costs. Secretary

Drew Lewis told the PATCO that the total package of $40 million was the upper limit to the government's proposal but that the union could reallocate the $40 million to better address controller needs.

According to the secretary, there were five key elements in the FAA proposal. These elements were

(1) boost by 10 percent the basic pay of controllers who act as on-the-job training instructors; (2) provide for a paid half-hour lunch period daily, effectively reducing the controllers' workweek from forty hours to thirty-seven and one half; (3) grant certain controllers retiring on medical disability one year's severance pay as a supplement to the retirement program; (4) give PATCO the right to name members to operations advisory committees; and (5) impose a six and one half hour per day limit on the amount of time controllers in the busiest facilities would be required to spend at radar screens watching traffic.[5]

The PATCO was unimpressed. Poli observed that the FAA proposal attempted to address some of the controllers' concerns in a piecemeal, hit-and-miss fashion, but in some ways, it worked more to the advantage of supervisors than to bargaining unit controllers. For example, since most of the training was conducted by supervisors rather than controllers on the screen, supervisors would reap the benefits of the 10 percent on-the-job training pay.

Since all of the big-ticket items required legislation, the Congress was frequently in the middle of the negotiation process. Congressman William Clay (D–Mo.) was the primary member of the Subcommittee on Compensation and Employee Benefits who introduced legislation to accommodate the demands and proposals of both sides. Clay recognized that the PATCO proposal for $1.7 billion over three years was not going to make it through the Congress. Therefore, he restructured a bill that would reduce the first-year costs of the PATCO proposal from $1 billion to $250 million. He reduced the top two levels of the special controller pay schedule that provided for a cap of $73,000 to a cap of $59,950. Also, the revised bill would provide for controllers receiving the same salary comparability pay increases as other salaried federal employees. The original PATCO proposal provided for a 10 percent increase in addition to a 1.5 times the annual increase in the cost-of-living index.[6]

Just prior to the initial signing of the agreement by Poli on June 22, an interesting controversy arose in the House hearings. Poli provided the committee with copies of letters he had exchanged with candidate Reagan and letters that members of the Reagan Election Committee had sent to the union's general counsel, Richard J. Leighton. The presumed reason to release the letters was to show the committee that President Reagan had in fact committed to major improvements in the air traffic control system. Rather than finding the letters useful corroboration for the administration's support for the PATCO position, several committee members interpreted the letters as an improper "deal" between the union and the Reagan campaign team to elicit the union's endorsement.

Incredibly, the letters promised a number of specific changes that were consistent with the union's wishes. Included in the promises were (1) the replacement of FAA administrator Langhorn Bond with somebody "competent"; (2) replacement of outdated FAA air traffic control equipment as soon as feasible; and (3) "a promise to 'give air traffic controllers the right to strike in certain circumstances.'"[7] The specific "circumstances" were not described in the letter.

These and other "promises" were purportedly the basis of PATCO's agreement to endorse Ronald Reagan for president. If, in fact, these letters were what they appeared to be, they would be illegal. The agreement to replace Bond in exchange for PATCO's endorsement is contrary to federal law. Congressman Buddy Roemer (D–La.) called the letters "incredible" and "demonstrated incompetence on the part of the Reagan campaign team."[8] Committee members asked that the matter be referred to the Justice Department for investigation. Four members of the House of Representatives sent a letter to Attorney General William French Smith asking him to consider the appointment of a special prosecutor to investigate violations of the criminal code and possible abuse of the governmental processes.

The differences between the two sets of proposals were too great. PATCO members were pumped up over the prospect of finally being compensated for the real contribution they made to the aviation community and for being recognized as important parts of the decision-making process concern with improving the system's operating environment. Poli argued that controllers were different and that they were not part of a "union" but rather a "religion." PATCO members strongly believed in their invincibility, their strategic importance, and their cause. It may have been the fervor with which controllers viewed their situation that led to Poli's loss of control over PATCO members.

While certainly the package the government was offering was not in line with PATCO demands, three hours before the 7 A.M. EDT, June 22 strike deadline, tentative agreement was reached. Working under the auspices of the FMCS, the union and the FAA crafted an agreement that met the needs of both sides. Secretary Lewis said the package had the full support of the administration. He said, "We believe that the settlement represents a just, reasonable, and fair agreement. At a time when the President has called for reduced federal spending, and has asked all Americans to help control inflation, our proposal—we believe— represents an equitable package."[9]

The package contained considerable detailed language, but in general, in relation to wages, it provided that each controller would receive an additional $4,000 each year; it permitted time-and-a-half for work over thirty-six hours per week; each controller would receive fourteen weeks of salary if retraining for medical reasons was required; and it would provide increased differentials for night and overtime work. The *New York Times* indicated that the signed agreement on June 22, 1981, "would have provided forty-two hours of pay for forty hours of work; a 15 percent night differential, up from the current 10 percent; exemption of night, Sunday, and holiday premium pay from the rule limiting total annual wages to $50,112, and fourteen weeks of pay for retraining of many medically disqualified controllers."[10]

Poli was all smiles, too. He told reporters that he was satisfied with the contract and would recommend ratification. "I feel good about it," he told reporters outside the FMCS headquarters. Not only did he feel good about it, he went further and called the agreement "fair."

At this point, the scenario becomes rather murky. While Poli put on a happy public face and publicly urged ratification of the agreement, there was considerable evidence that a very different process had been worked out ahead of time. The presumed process that seems to have been developed was something like the following: Poli would sign the proposed contract; put on a happy face; urge ratification; and, then, the rank-and-file members would overwhelmingly reject the proposal. Rejection of the proposal would send Poli back to the bargaining table.

Under normal circumstances, membership ratification of a collective bargaining agreement is pro forma. Leadership in touch with the membership knows the issues members feel strongly about, and there are usually few surprises when ratification is called for. Poli undoubtedly knew the issues. Therefore, there are two possible explanations of what was to happen. Either the above referenced process of membership rejection was played out, or he didn't understand the depth of dissension in the controller ranks. The membership had been pumped up, and expectations were high. A charitable explanation is that Poli may have believed that once the reality of the government's proposal sank in, controllers would shift their expectations back into a more moderate range. This did not happen.

WHY DID POLI SIGN THE AGREEMENT?

There are several answers that may or may not clarify what happened. First, the union had a publicly reported provision in its operating requirements that 80 percent of bargaining unit employees must vote for a strike before the union could strike. The strike vote taken just prior to the June 22 action did not meet the 80 percent approval requirement. Union officials argued that the union rules requiring an 80 percent approval rate did not happen and therefore, presumably, Poli could not take the union out on strike. In this environment, he may have believed that the only thing left to do was to come to agreement and then let the membership voting process decide the next step.

The second possible answer is that Poli did in fact consider the package "fair" even though he knew that the PATCO membership would reject it. The FAA had given some concessions that were important to the PATCO, and these could have been the base upon which future negotiations were built. Poli may have recognized that the "climate" was not right for the all-or-nothing stance being pushed by union hard-liners. In an emotion-charged, dynamic situation such as eleventh-hour collective bargaining, "fair" packages do not necessarily mean that they will be accepted.

Soon after the structure and content of the proposed agreement reached the newspapers, the PATCO organization reported that there were a flurry of telephone calls, faxs, and other communications that were against the proposed contract. This activity occurred before the rank and file had received copies of the proposed agreement for review. The intensity of the reaction suggested that it may have been preplanned.

As spokespersons for the union provided pessimistic appraisals of the membership's views of the proposed agreement, the administration sought to turn up the heat to compel ratification. Secretary Lewis testified before the House Public Works Subcommittee on Oversight and Investigations that the government would not increase the total cost of the contract even if it was rejected by the membership. He placed the direct responsibility for ratification on Poli. He told the subcommittee, "I am counting on Mr. Poli and his people to get it ratified. Once they get the facts, that it's all we have to offer, then they'll accept it."[11]

Further evidence that all was not up front in the PATCO position on the proposed agreement occurred in the consideration of the agreement by the PATCO executive board. Robert Poli, who had indicated satisfaction with the agreement and indicated that he would seek ratification, was given a standing ovation at a meeting in Chicago a week after signing the proposal in Washington. However, at the same meeting, when the unanimous decision of the executive board was to reject ratification, 500 local union presidents cheered wildly and chanted, "Strike, strike, strike." [12]

The obvious disparity between the two positions was explained by spokeswoman Marcia Feldman as follows: Poli was confronted with circumstances on the morning of June 22 that prompted him to sign the agreement; these "circumstances" were apparently the failure of an informal poll of controllers to achieve 80 percent of those responding being in favor of a strike; now, with the exact terms of the agreement known, the executive board unanimously favored rejection of the contract. This is a most curious "explanation." If Poli was unhappy with the terms of the agreement, he had no need to publicly indicate that he was "happy" with the agreement. Nor did he have to call for ratification publicly. It would have been acceptable to indicate in the public forum that the agreement did not meet all of PATCO's demands and that the membership would have to make the final decision. Poli chose to put a very different face on the signed proposal.

The resolution of the nine-member PATCO board indicated support for Poli's actions under the circumstances existing on June 22 but called for rejection of the contract because it "does not address the fundamental issues important to the air traffic control process."[13] In fact, Poli served on the PATCO board, and "Poli was one of the nine executive board members to recommend rejection of the contract."[14] As the ballots were being distributed to PATCO members, Secretary Lewis continued to emphasize that the size of the package was the upper limit for the administration. He argued that the government didn't want a strike but that the administration couldn't "agree to an inflationary contract that would be patently unfair to the taxpayers and to other federal workers."[15]

A spokeswoman for the union observed that the agreement reached by the union and the administration was not selling well within the rank and file. She said, "I haven't heard of a single member who likes the contract, and I'd be amazed if it were approved."[16]

With the prospects of a union rejection of the agreement growing greater every day, there were signs in the Congress that the PATCO core of support was softening there as well. In a span of three days, significant numbers of senators and congressmen warned Poli that if the union rejected the contract and initiated a strike, there would be no backing for legislation to achieve their goals. In fact, these legislators indicated that they would seek government action against the controllers if a strike occurred. [17]

More than 9 out of 10 controllers—13,495 to 616—rejected the agreement and in the process ordered Poli back to the bargaining table. It would have been one thing if the vote had been close. Small modifications in the package could have produced enough votes to ensure ratification. With the controller package, there was no change in any of the major variables from the government's perspective. Drew Lewis was hanging tough and expressed dismay at the members' rejection of the package. After consulting with the president, Lewis reaffirmed that there was no more money for the controllers. Lewis and the president believed that the $40 million package was fair and that anything in excess would be inconsistent with the economic program initiated by the administration.

The union did not soften the rhetoric about striking. Patrick Doyle, PATCO legislative director, pointedly challenged the administration's hard-line position. He argued, "If Lewis is adamant about the amount, a strike is what they're going to get. I'm not talking about 10 days or 20 days, I'm talking imminent." [18] Dominic Torchia, a member of the union's executive board, argued that PATCO members "are impatient. They're mad there's absolutely nothing in that contract that addresses the issues important to them."[19] John Willoughby, a Kansas City PATCO official said that the controllers were "scared" to strike in June, but after the proposed contract, their attitudes had changed. He observed that "they've finally accepted the fact that the only way we'll get anything out of Congress and the administration is through a job action."[20]

These comments by senior union officials add further credence to the notion that the Poli signing, followed by membership rejection was a preplanned game plan. If, as Torchia said, there was "nothing" in the proposed contract that addressed the union's issues, how could Poli have been "happy" with the agreement?

The size of the rejection of the contract by PATCO members buoyed the resolve of the union leadership. Poli indicated that he had read the letter from the Congress and that he was impressed by it. However, he felt a duty to the membership, and that duty outweighed other considerations. Poli set a new ultimatum for 12:01 A.M. on Monday, August 3, 1981, for the production of a new settlement. He informed the administration that if a new agreement was not reached by that point, a strike vote would be taken immediately. If authorized by 80 percent or more of the PATCO membership, a strike would start with the 7 A.M. dayshift on August 3.

The Administration and the union were unable to find any areas to modify the contract that would be jointly acceptable to the controllers and the government. Secretary Lewis met several times with Poli, but no new positions arose. As the deadline for a new agreement approached, the secretary asked Poli to delay the strike vote for one week. Poli declined the request.

The media campaign by the administration continued in full force. Importantly, Poli and the PATCO did little to counterbalance what the administration was saying. Secretary Lewis argued that a strike could do "billions" of dollars of damage to the economy and he was adamant in his opposition to the "controllers' 'outrageous' economic demands and their 'unreasonable and irresponsible' use of the strike threat."[21] In a ploy of reasonableness, the secretary again indicated a willingness to restructure the $40 million package to help controllers achieve a sense of greater satisfaction, but he steadfastly refused to increase the size of the package.

Attorney General French appeared on NBC's *Meet the Press* to indicate how the legal system would be brought to bear if a strike occurred. He argued that the "full force" of the federal legal machinery would be used if the controllers struck and broke the law. Secretary of Defense Casper Weinberger told ABC's *Issues and Answers* that a contingent of military controllers would be assigned to civilian controlling to maintain reasonable levels of operation.

All through this barrage of administration statements, the only thing heard from the PATCO were statements that it was not happy with the administration package and that it wanted more. Regardless of the merits of the PATCO position, and it had merit, the ineffective communications campaign used by the union undoubtedly evoked little public understanding or sympathy. The public was concerned about the disruption of air traffic, costs to the airline industry and the economy, and possible safety issues, but there was little apparent sympathy for the controllers' plight.

WHAT DID PATCO REALLY WANT?

The demands of PATCO were characterized as one-dimensional by the FAA and multifaceted by the union itself. It may be useful to examine each issue and assess its relative importance in the bargaining process. As noted elsewhere in this study, the notion that the only PATCO demand was money is simply not sufficiently credible to pursue at length here. Suffice it to say, money was important to the PATCO, as it is important to virtually all workers, organized or not. However, as the following will show, there were a plethora of issues and problems, many spanning more than a decade without adequate attention or resolution, that contributed to the strike. There may be differences of opinion about the relative weight to assign to each issue or problem, but what cannot be refuted is that these issues and problems had a basis in fact.

After the strike was well under way, Poli attempted to simply describe the issues underlying the strike. In a letter to PATCO members, he said, "[T]he strike was called because of early burnout, because U.S. controllers work more hours than controllers in other free-world countries, because wages do not keep up with inflation and because of management attitudes that ridicule our profession and turn deaf ears to our input into aviation safety."[22]

Other analysts have attributed a much more global objective to PATCO leaders. Specifically, Herbert Northrup argued:

Under Leyden's leadership, PATCO had as an objective the establishment of a separate FAA corporation, modeled on the U.S. Postal Service, but providing for PATCO and other union participation on the board of directors and for the right to strike for its employees. PATCO hired a consultant to draw up this proposal, and a bill incorporating the idea was introduced in Congress. The objective, of course, was wage determination on a private sector model.[23]

The inference is that this goal was somehow at variance with how governmental functions should operate. Not many years later, the privatization of a vast array of federal functions, including air traffic control, has become a major initiative in government. Northrup also argued that the PATCO sought "the unionization of noncontroller employees of the FAA under PATCO's aegis and control and then expansion to other 'elite' groups of government employees."[24]

In support of his analysis of PATCO objectives, Northrup enlisted comments by former FMCS director Kenneth Moffett. Responding to Hurd and Kriesky's rejection of the global goal of PATCO, in a letter to Northrup, Kenneth E. Moffett, former director of the Federal Mediation and Conciliation Service, observed, "After having lived and worked through the entire PATCO debacle, I have to agree with you [Northrup] that the ultimate plan of PATCO was to become separated out from under the Civil Service Reform Act, similar to the U.S. Postal workers, but their nirvana would have been to become a private sector organization with all airport facilities and their employees falling under the Taft-Hartley Act, as amended."[25]

If this was the union's "nirvana," one must ask the question, So what? Obviously, Bonneville Power, the Tennessee Valley Authority, the U.S. Postal Service, and others had consummated a working relationship outside the traditional governmental "agency" system, and for the most part, these relationships worked. If the PATCO was not able to develop a relationship with the FAA that met the union's needs, there seems little reason to be surprised or critical of their efforts to engage a different "model" for labor-management relations.

While these goals or objectives may have motivated PATCO actions, the public debate focused on several other issues. The relative importance of each issue is difficult to determine, but one can see that they were not amenable to an easy solution. When one talks about "burnout" and "management attitudes" as being underlying problems, there is certain to be difficulty in crafting a settlement package. Nevertheless, each of the issues warrants review. The following discussion attempts to categorize the issues in a somewhat different manner from that used by Poli in order to draw explicit attention to the character of the problems being addressed.

Although it was not discussed at great length by the media and probably not effectively by the PATCO in negotiations, one of the major concerns of controllers in the 1970s and early 1980s was related to job stress and their inability to perform their jobs fully until normal retirement. The 1970 Corson Committee Report "was impressed with the fact that air traffic controllers constitute a unique group within the Federal establishment. While many other categories of Federal employees must possess some of the talents, and while their jobs impose some of the exacting responsibilities which make the controller's job difficult and demanding, few combine as many sustained demands upon the individual as does this job."[26]

Senator Daniel Fong on the Committee on Post Office and Civil Service argued in a committee report:

It is ironic, in the committee's judgment, that a blackjack card dealer at a gambling casino in Las Vegas is generally relieved from his duty after 40 minutes of dealing because of the monotony and mental stress of keeping up with a deck of cards, while an air traffic controller responsible for moving airplanes in and out of a busy airport will frequently remain on a radarscope for 4 hours without relief, and when relief comes after 4 hours or more, it will be so that he can go to the tower for visual control of takeoffs and landings.[27]

This work environment contributed to a variety of perceived problems including aviation safety and the inability of controllers to remain proficient into their later working years. Over a decade before the strike, the 1970 Corson Report observed, "A major cause of dissatisfaction among the controller work force is the deepseated and widely held belief that most individuals will be physically unable to continue to control air traffic (even while physically able to perform other kinds of work) well before they will have qualified under prevailing provisions for retirement."[28] As reported in the *AFL–CIO News*, "PATCO members claim that few of their number last long enough on the job, twenty-five years, to collect full retirement benefits. They point to FAA statistics, obtained by the union through the Freedom of Information Act, showing that between 1976 and 1979 about 89 percent of U.S. controllers who retired did so for medical reasons before they were eligible for full retirement benefits."[29] Thus, the problem recognized by the Corson Committee did not go away. The FAA had apparently done little to address a serious concern that every employee, in every occupation, must consider in assessing his or her employment relationship. Most employees do not work for retirement, but all employees want to be sure that they can work enough years to warrant full retirement. Air traffic controllers faced the prospects of leaving the workforce with substantial medical problems and a reduced retirement annuity.

Based on these conditions, "[t]he controllers feel that the FAA should provide the aging controller an opportunity to transfer to less arduous work at no loss in grade or pay, or to other positions within the FAA when they can no longer perform proficiently as a controller."[30] This issue, while possibly less attention-grabbing than safety, was an important one within the ranks of controllers. They simply looked around at their colleagues and pictured themselves in difficult emotional or physical crisis long before they were eligible for normal retirement. They knew that debilitating stress existed in this profession and were incensed when former FAA administrator Langhorn Bond argued that driving a bus in New York City was just as stressful as the functions performed by air traffic controllers.[31]

The lack of basic understanding and the insensitivity of a former senior FAA official are shocking confirmation that the leadership in the FAA was indeed out of touch with the workforce, and one might argue with the conditions under which they worked. FAA officials could point to a controller in the uncongested airspace of Idaho and Montana and say with assurance that controllers in those parts of the air traffic control were not overly stressed. That may have been true. However, as noted earlier, the assignment process within the air traffic control system provided that as a controller gained proficiency, he or she was transferred to increasingly demanding positions. One should not be surprised by this assignment process because it makes good sense, and it was a primary avenue for promotions. However, what the controllers saw happening was that as each controller gained proficiency, they would ultimately, in maybe eight to ten years, be assigned to an intense, high-volume, stress-producing sector or control tower. They would then stay in that assignment the remainder of their controlling career. This is where the problem arose. In those demanding positions, the relentless stress was so debilitating that many could not continue working to the time of normal retirement. In this sense, Bond's comments were gratuitous and largely off the mark.

Finally, in an editorial in the *Washington Post* on August 8, 1981, the issues relating to the money demands of PATCO, stress, and FAA management were brought into focus. The editorial argues that the huge money demands were simply surrogates for other deeply felt needs. The article then provides an important twist on the work stress issue. Specifically, the editor argued that air traffic controllers, operational stress was substantial but no more than the stress found in other occupations. However, "it's evident that this stress has been severely compounded by other tensions and frustrations generated less by the nature of the work than by the nature of the FAA."[32] This observation was more extensively reviewed in an article by David B. Bowers in *Organizational Dynamics* entitled "What Would Make 11,500 People Quit Their Jobs?"[33]

A second issue of importance to controllers related to work hours and the length of the workweek. Mandatory overtime, the inability to take vacations during normal vacation periods, six-day workweeks, rotating shift work, short lunch hours, long periods on the scope without relief, and other hours issues were important to air controllers. There was a sustained and widespread feeling that these conditions led to the problems noted in issue one, above. Controllers believed that the quality of their lives outside the work environment was diminished because of the long hours they were required to work. In poll after poll, controllers and, in most cases, supervisors and managers recognized the hours problem. However, in every survey, senior management believed that the hours were in a normal range and that controllers were basically happy in their jobs. Here, too, there was a wide gulf between the attitudes and preferences of employees and the attitudes of senior managers in the FAA.

A third issue related to the technical aspects of their jobs. The hardware and software controllers used were uniformly inadequate for the effective and safe control of aircraft. Mechanical system failures of old and worn-out hardware were a frequent occurrence. Nevertheless, senior management argued that while improvement in hardware was always desirable, what was used by the FAA was adequate to the task. Anybody who would talk openly about this problem was viewed as a troublemaker and not a "team player." As the Corson Committee said a decade earlier, the inability of the air traffic controller workforce to communicate upwards caused "great dissatisfaction." If employees expressed dissatisfaction with working conditions, they were characterized as disloyal to the agency. If they filed a grievance or made waves of any kind, they eliminated any chances for future promotions.[34] Eleven years later, similar conditions existed. As reported in the *Washington Post*, "There is a certain style of management that deals with lower echelon complaints by arranging never to hear about them. The word is passed down the ladder to shut up and get on with the job. It's pretty clear, not merely from the strikers but from congressional inquiry before the strike, that the Federal Aviation Administration has often managed the air control system in that spirit."[35]

Controllers were constantly told that the FAA was going to improve the hardware. While outsiders could interpret these kinds of comments as designed to alleviate some of the concern by controllers about hardware needs, the real intent was somewhat more sinister. The character of these pronouncements was more to suggest that hardware advances would *replace* controllers than it was to upgrade and enhance the operation of the system. Naturally, some controllers were apprehensive about the automation initiative, but those who thought carefully about the scheme recognized that job security was not threatened by machines. Rather, the vagaries and tedium of the work role could be much improved.

Then there was the "money" issue. Controllers are among the highest-paid employees of the federal government. Nevertheless, due to work conditions, early burnout, and other aspects of their jobs already noted, controllers believed that they deserved special pay consideration. The $10,000 increase, noted widely in the media, was an item on the bargaining agenda. Controllers in Chicago had attempted to obtain a $7,500 supplement in earlier negotiations but had failed. As described earlier, the last concerted action before the August 3 strike was a slowdown at Chicago's O'Hare International on August 15, 1980. The FAA had refused to provide O'Hare controllers with an annual tax-free bonus of $7,500.[36] There was sharp disagreement about the origin of the $7,500 pay enhancement proposal. The FAA made it sound as though the proposal originated in the PATCO. However, testifying under oath, Poli argued that the proposal had originated with the regional director of the FAA in the Great Lakes Region.[37]

In spite of this particular issue, there should be no ambiguity about the controllers' demand for higher salaries and special provisions for a separate pay system. In fact, the administration agreed with the controllers' demands. What they could not agree with was the size of the pay increase. The idea that controllers were special and performed in a unique segment of the American air traffic system was not disputed by any informed person, other possibly than former Administrator Bond. What was in dispute was how these differences translated into higher income levels.

A fourth concern by controllers that received little public attention related to fairness of work assignments. Controllers in similar occupations in other countries worked fewer hours than American controllers and enjoyed longer vacations. Canadian controllers, for example, worked an average workweek of thirty-four hours. Controllers in Britain, Spain, and France also worked shorter workweeks. Table 5.1 shows the hours worked, vacation days, and sick leave available to air traffic controllers in a number of countries and regions.

The U.S. controllers noted these differences and concluded two things. First, the shorter workweek must be evidence that officials in other countries recognized the stressfulness of these jobs—and therefore American officials should pay attention. Second, if American controllers were going to be required to work long workweeks, they deserved substantial income supplements to compensate for the additional stress and trauma.

There were other issues related to hardware improvements, complaints about management insensitivity, training programs, and a variety of other concerns. Nevertheless, the countdown to a strike was set in motion. Poli seemed to have personal confidence that the PATCO membership supported his overall bargaining strategy and positions. He was quoted in the *New York Times* as saying, "I believe I have the pulse of the members. It is legitimate to believe that they'll stay out under threats, intimidation, fines, and jailings."[38] Others suggested that he was held in such high regard within PATCO that "[y]ou can kiss the man's feet."[39] There is no question that Poli had energized the controller workforce and that they were ready to take on the union's "most difficult challenge." Northrup attributed comments to Poli during the hours before the strike that suggested a fanatical adherence to the goals that Northrup argued underlay PATCO actions. According to Northrup, Poli said that what the union was heading toward "will test our union as it has never been tested, namely, the 'definitive strike' aimed at achieving PATCO's basic aims of inducing Congress to establish an independent FAA, permitting wage bargaining, and legitimizing strikes."[40]

Table 5.1
Work Hours, Vacation Days, and Sick Leave
Provided to Air Traffic Controllers
in Selected Countries, 1981

Country	Work Hours per Week	Vacation Days	Paid Sick
Eurocontrol	29	24–30	Up to 180
New Zealand	32	23–28	Up to 275
Denmark	33–34	24	n.a.
Australia	35	30	15
Sweden	38	30	n.a.
Austria	38.5	37	Up to 7 months
France	32	56	90
West Germany	33	20–28	n.a.
Canada	34	36	15
Norway	36	28	Up to 1 year
Switzerland	38	30	Up to 1 year
United States	40	13–26	13

Source: FAA, PATCO reported in "Controllers Strike Shows Limits of Public Workers," *New York Times*, August 16, 1981, p. B3.
n.a. = not available.

Without concessions by the FAA on any of the major issues, Poli and the PATCO had extended themselves publicly beyond their ability to retreat. They still believed, of course, that a strike would bring the nation to its knees, and therefore the stoppage would be short. They had misjudged the resolve of the new administration and the American people—and it would cost them dearly.

SUMMARY

The period immediately preceding August 3, 1981, could be characterized as chaotic and intense. Neither side budged on its offers or demands, but the administration won the public relations battle. The administration's hard-line position on the compensation package simply mismatched the union's attempts to resolve longstanding problems by obtaining higher wage and salary increases. The issues of controller burnout, unreliable hardware, adverse working conditions, and other important union issues never became the focal point of public discussion. With the support of the Congress apparently on its side, the administration braced for a stoppage.

NOTES

1. "House Panel Hears Differences between FAA and Air Traffic Controllers," *Daily Labor Reporter* (Bureau of National Affairs), No. 84, May 1, 1981, p. A-10.

2. Ibid.

3. "Air Traffic Controllers Set a June 22 Strike Deadline," *New York Times*, May 24, 1981, p. 24.

4. Ibid.

5. "FAA, Airlines Bracing for Strike as Air Controller Talks Break Down," *Daily Labor Reporter* (Bureau of National Affairs), No. 117, June 18, 1981, p. A-10.

6. Ibid., p. A-11.

7. Ibid., p. A-8.

8. "Air Controller Strike Averted; Union Accepts Administration Offer," *Daily Labor Reporter* (Bureau of National Affairs), No. 119, June 22, 1981, p. A-8.

9. Ibid., p. A-7.

10. "Tentative Air Control Pact Is Rejected by 95% of Union," *New York Times*, July 30, 1981, p. A12.

11. "Air Controllers Threatening to Reject Tentative Contract," *Daily Labor Reporter* (Bureau of National Affairs), No. 123, June 26, 1981, p. A-6.

12. "PATCO Board Rejects Tentative Contract with FAA; Recommends Membership Rejection," *Daily Labor Reporter* (Bureau of National Affairs), No. 127, July 2, 1981, p. A-7.

13. Ibid.

14. John Burgess, "Union Officials Urge Controllers to Reject Pact," *Washington Post*, July 3, 1981, p. A1.

15. "Air Traffic Controllers May Reject Tentative Agreement with U.S.," *Wall Street Journal*, July 6, 1981, p. 7.

16. Ibid.

17. "Air Controllers Reject Tentative Accord; Strike Vote Next Week Is Threatened," *Wall Street Journal*, July 30, 1981, p. 23.

18. Ibid.

19. Ibid.

20. Ibid.

21. Warren Brown, "The Air Controllers: At First, Frustration, Then Risk," *Washington Post*, August 3, 1981, p. A4.

22. "PATCO Sees U.S. Waiting for Decertification Decision," *Washington Post*, October 13, 1981, p. A3.

23. Herbert K. Northrup, "The Rise and Demise of PATCO," *Industrial and Labor Relations Review*, Vol. 37, No. 2, January 1984, p. 171.

24. Ibid., p. 173.

25. Herbert K. Northrup, "Reply," *Industrial and Labor Relations Review*, Vol. 40, No. 1, October 1986, p. 124.

26. Senate, Committee on Post Office and Civil Service, *Air Traffic Controllers*, 91st Cong., 2d sess., Report to Accompany S. 3959, Report No. 91-1012 (Washington, D.C.: GPO, July 9, 1970), p. 9.

27. Ibid., p. 3.

28. Ibid., p. 110.

29. "Kirkland Blasts Attempt to Bust Air Controllers," *AFL–CIO News*, Vol. 26, No. 33, August 15, 1981, p. 12.

30. Senate, Committee on Post Office and Civil Service, *Air Traffic Controllers*, p. 49.

31. "Air Controllers' Strike Will Be Broken, Goals Failed, Analysts Say," *Wall Street Journal*, August 4, 1981, p. 16.

32. "After the Strike," *Washington Post*, August 8, 1981, p. A20.

33. David B. Bowers, "What Would Make 11,500 People Quit Their Jobs?" *Organizational Dynamics*, Winter 1983, pp. 5–19.

34. Senate, Committee on Post Office and Civil Service, *Air Traffic Controllers*, 91st Cong., 2d sess., Calendar No. 1016, Report No. 91-1012 (Washington, D.C.: GPO), July 9, 1970, p. 124.

35. "After the Strike," *Washington Post*, August 8, 1981, p. A20.

36. Northrup, "The Rise and Demise of PATCO," pp. 170–171.

37. House of Representatives, Committee on Post Office and Civil Service, Subcommittee on Investigations, *Air Traffic Control*, 96th Cong., 2d sess. (Washington, D.C.: GPO, September 30, 1980), p. 26.

38. "Threat of Air Strike Tomorrow Grows as Talks Fail," *New York Times*, August 2, 1981, p. 17.

39. Jonathan Fuerbringer, "Militant Controller Chief: Robert Edmond Poli," *New York Times*, August 4, 1981, p. B8.

40. Northrup, "The Rise and Demise of PATCO," p. 174.

Chapter 6

Bring the Nation to Its Knees

THE STRIKE

At 7 A.M. on August 3, 1981, the nation's air traffic controllers walked off their jobs at en route centers and towers across the nation. More than 13,000 controllers initially left their positions in support of the strike. The White House immediately issued a statement accusing the controllers of violating federal law and the oath they had taken when they joined the Federal workforce. The union indicated that about 80 percent of controllers were on strike, but the FAA argued that about 30 percent of controllers were ignoring the strike and reporting to work. The precise numbers didn't matter. What did matter was that the American air traffic system was abruptly disrupted by a relatively small number of highly skilled employees who chose to lay their economic future on the line to win concessions at the bargaining table.

As promised, the federal government began moving against the union through the legal system, the use of military controllers, supervisors, and recalled retirees. In courtrooms across the nation, government lawyers sought injunctions and restraining orders to force controllers back to work. In addition, private sector organizations such as the Air Transport Association went to court to seek injunctions against the PATCO and impose fines for violating earlier injunctions. U.S. marshals and Federal Bureau of Investigation agents began taking pictures and collecting names of striking controllers for use in future criminal actions. The Federal Labor Relations Authority issued a complaint charging the PATCO with an unfair labor practice for violation of federal law. In addition, the FLRA sought a temporary restraining order against the PATCO to terminate the strike. The FLRA publicly noted that Section 7116(b)(7) of the Civil Service Reform Act provides for the removal of a federal union from its representational responsibilities if the union participates in a strike against the federal government.

Almost immediately after the strike started, the administration played the "decertification card." As the *Wall Street Journal* reported, "The Reagan administration clearly hopes the decertification threat might be the tactic that ends the strike. 'I have a feeling we could drop the decertification move as a bargaining chip, as a sort of face saver,' said one White House official. 'Poli could decide that, rather than end the union, we better go back to work,' the official added."[1]

While the adrenaline flowing during the early hours of the strike may have clouded the judgment of striking controllers, comments by controllers indicated that they knew precisely what they were doing. The president of the Kennedy Airport Chapter of PATCO said, "He [Reagan] can put us in jail. We're fighting for a cause, if this is what it takes to get the Congress and the President to listen."[2]

The President then issued his forty-eight-hour ultimatum. In his statement, he outlined what had happened, what some of the consequences would be for the nation, and why he believed the government could not meet the PATCO's demands. He closed his statement by saying, "It is for this reason I must tell those who failed to report for duty this morning they are in violation of the law and if they do not report for work within 48 hours they have forfeited their jobs and will be terminated."[3]

The controllers scoffed at the president's ultimatum. A few controllers, numbering in the low hundreds, did cross the picket line and return to their duty stations. Whether they would have returned in the absence of the president's directive is unknown, but what is important is that it really didn't make any difference. The vast majority of controllers remained away from their jobs. While the apparent solidarity of the controllers stemmed from their belief in being able to flout the law with impunity, there was also support from other quarters. Lane Kirkland, president of the AFL–CIO, called the president's threat a "harsh and brutal" reaction to a situation precipitated by the "very serious problems" in the nation's air traffic control system. The executive council of the AFL–CIO also issued a statement of support and urged the government to "call off its punitive measure" and engage in "frank and open negotiations."[4]

The statement also said, in part: "The present situation will not be wisely resolved if the government goes ahead with its present plans of punishment and retribution against the air traffic controllers and their union. These punitive measures are no substitute for fair dealing with PATCO, and for joint and constructive efforts to work out a settlement that will be fair to the controllers, the government and the flying public."[5]

When asked whether he felt the controllers were justified in breaking the law, Kirkland responded, "I respect the law, but events here and elsewhere in the world have demonstrated that when working people feel a deep sense of grievance they will exercise what I think is a basic human right to withhold their services, not to work under conditions they no longer find tolerable."[6]

This theme of justifiable violation of the law was to be repeated often during the next several months. In the total review of this job action, it was the single factor that could be sighted as justification for the strike. There is precedent in federal and state law for workers to leave their work areas if they feel threatened by unsafe or unhealthy working conditions. In most cases, these threats are obvious and immediate—rising water in the workplace, a bare electric wire, or the presence of an explosive gas. The issue that relates to the PATCO strike is whether or not the conditions of employment and their purported impact on the controllers' health warranted a strike response.

While a variety of labor organizations made public statements of support, all were careful to avoid the appearance of sanctioning an illegal strike. They urged the administration to resume negotiations and call the controllers back to work, but they did not provide indications that they would financially support the strike.

In the early hours of the strike, the issues that served to focus both the union and the government melted away. Rather than the question of whether the union demanded too much or the government offered too little being the focal point, the new focus was on the ability of a union to violate the law. An editorial in the *Wall Street Journal* on the day after the strike began observed that "the issue has become a question of whether the union has the power to flout the law. The notion that it is illegal to strike the government might seem, at first blush, distasteful to some. America is, after all, a land in which a man is free to withhold his labor if he feels he's not being paid a fair wage."[7]

The editor went on to explain that there is a difference between public and private sector strikes because of the monopoly power the government holds in the provision of services. Since there are no viable alternatives to the government provision of services, certainly air traffic control services, the workers can exploit this position to extract greater concessions out of management.

The first hours of the strike were not pleasant for the government, the union, the airlines, or the traveling public. About 65 percent of the normal volume of air traffic flew during the first day of the strike. For those airplanes that did fly, everything was uneventful. There was no chaos or complete collapse of the system, as some had predicted. Partially responsible for the order in the system was that many air travelers simply canceled their flights or arranged for alternate forms of transportation. The union had warned the country that a controller strike would produce an unsafe system. Therefore, many passengers changed their plans and were more flexible in arriving on time. An AVIS rental agency in Atlanta reported a 75 percent increase in the demand for rental cars; Greyhound Bus Lines had to put on fifty additional buses on its departure schedule from New York City. These types of changes occurred nationwide.

While domestic flights were moving at a reduced volume, and for the most part moving on time, the same could not be said for international flights. There were delays of many hour's duration on both incoming and outgoing international flights. Foreign carriers were allocated fewer landing slots, in general, and there were differences between countries. Foreign carriers delayed or canceled flights rather than have them arrive in the United States without landing guarantees.

As the early hours wore on, federal judges issued contempt citations against the PATCO for ignoring back-to-work orders. Within hours after the strike, "[t]emporary restraining orders against the strike have been issued by 40 federal district courts around the country, and in at least 12 of these courts U.S. attorneys also have obtained contempt sanctions against union locals and their leaders."[8]

Federal officials obtained a court order freezing the controllers' strike fund, began proceedings to decertify the PATCO as the controllers' bargaining agent, and asked that the union's leaders be jailed. Courts levied stiff fines against the PATCO and against Robert Poli. Since the assets of the PATCO were estimated to be less than $4 million, it was clear that the fines would soon be moot. The fines imposed by Judge Harold Greene alone were designed to rise to $1 million per day over a several-day period. Once they exceeded the total assets of the union, there would be little additional pressure on the union to relent.

The president and Secretary Lewis adamantly refused to reenter negotiations with the PATCO. They characterized the strike as a "hostage situation" in which the union was holding the airlines, the government, and the traveling public hostage. A White House official said, "If you give in to a sort of hostage situation, it sets a precedent."[9]

As the hours dragged on, one could almost feel that participants on both sides were holding their breaths. When and where would the first midair collision occur? When would pilots refuse to enter the cockpit and fly in the reduced system? Nothing unusual happened. As the day neared its end, the administration cautiously ventured forward with a reaffirmation of its position. To put even more pressure on the union, the government announced that even if the controllers returned to work, the government would not increase a "very satisfactory" offer.

Day Two

On the second day of the strike, "President Reagan reiterated his threat to fire all strikers if they aren't back on the job today at 11 A.M. EDT, saying he hadn't any choice in the matter. 'They took an oath in writing that they would not strike,' he said. 'It's not a case of firing—they've quit.'"[10]

From the middle of the second day, confidence began rising on the administration side. The government began taking actions suggesting that the system was returning to normal. For example, late in the afternoon of day two, the FAA lifted restrictions on general aviation flights—restrictions that had canceled 50 percent of these flights a day earlier.

However, the president's ultimatum to the controllers had little impact. Both the union and the administration agreed that the number of strikers who returned to work on the second day of the strike was about the same as on the first day. PATCO said that only thirty-eight controllers who struck on Monday were on the job on Tuesday.

Lane Kirkland said in Chicago that he knew about a proposal to involve "high-level mediation" as a means to keep the two sides talking. Mediation by respected individuals who are knowledgeable about both public and private sector labor relations could provide a vehicle for the administration to move away from its "we won't talk to the union while the strike is on" position. Mediation is not negotiation unless the parties choose to accept it as negotiation. While Kirkland alluded to a mediation process, the principals who presumably would conduct the mediation claimed to know nothing about the proposal. Dr. John Dunlop of Harvard University and former Labor Secretary William Usery denied that the mediation proposal had been discussed with them.

The initial order by Judge Harold H. Greene, the first in the PATCO strike, stated, in part, "It is clear on this record that the harm threatened in this situation is of the highest magnitude. During the first day of the strike, commercial flights have been reduced by one-half, and private aviation has been shut down completely."[11] Nevertheless, the judge rejected the government's request for a large, immediate fine on the union. The judge reasoned: "It is of course somewhat speculative as to what sanction would or would not be effective. The Court has rejected the government's request for a large fine to be due immediately, essentially on the ground that the purpose of civil contempt is to cause future compliance rather than to punish for past acts, and that defendants must therefore be allowed a minimum amount of time to purge themselves of the contempt before a fine becomes effective."[12]

Day Three

In an effort to put additional pressure on controllers, the president reiterated his dismissal threat on the third full day of the strike. He told the public and the controllers that he was left no choice in the action he threatened to take. David Gergen, White House spokesman, tried to deflect charges that the president was deliberately trying to bust the union. Gergen argued, "We don't call it union busting. This union is in flagrant violation of the law. We're out to end an illegal strike."[13]

Turning up the heat on the controllers and the PATCO, the administration overstepped its legitimate authority. An administration spokesperson, Secretary Lewis, said, "Striking controllers who don't return will get one-week firing notices, and will be 'banned from employment with the federal government forever.' 'There will be no turning back, no second chance' for those who ignore the President's back-to-work call, he said. Controllers who do report for their scheduled workturns today won't face any civil or criminal charges, he added."[14] The secretary lacked the authority to ban strikers from federal employment forever.

The union began to sense that things were not going well. Massive fines were piling up by the hour, the decertification process was under way, the FAA was able to keep a semblance of order in the air traffic system, and other unions were not rushing to PATCO's defense or providing support. The AFL–CIO did gesture toward support, but Lane Kirkland said, "I'm not volunteering anything at the moment; but, we would respond to requests for help from these people to the extent our capabilities allowed."[15] In one glimmer of support, the Machinists Union indicated that they would honor the PATCO picket lines. William Wimpisinger, president of the Machinists, said, "I expect our people to act like trade unionists, I expect them not to cross a picket line if they confront it."[16]

There had been no contact between Poli and Kirkland during the first three days of the strike. Nevertheless, Robert Poli kept a stiff upper lip and stood steadfast in defiance of the law. Betty Griffith, a union official in Atlanta, argued that the presidential firing served to make the controllers' resolve stronger. In spite of the president's pledge that there would be "no amnesty" for strikers, Griffith asserted that "we're very optimistic that those fired would be rehired."[17]

Immediately after the 11 A.M. deadline on August 5, the government began sending controllers dismissal notices. The notices said that controllers would be dismissed from their job in seven days. Strikers would have the opportunity to respond to the dismissal notice during the seven-day period. At the end of seven days, each controller would receive a written termination decision including an effective date for the action. In a last-ditch effort to entice substantial numbers of controllers back to their jobs, Secretary Lewis announced that "the 11 A.M. deadline meant that strikers must return to work on the first shift beginning after that hour—thus giving morning shift employees until 7 A.M. on August 6 to return to work."[18] In addition, the secretary promised that no criminal charges would be lodged against those who returned to their jobs. While obviously the administration wanted the controllers back on the job, it is curious that government officials were prepared to sanction the violation of the law and oath that had already occurred. They apparently were prepared to overlook the violation of federal law with individual controllers but not with the controllers' union.

The president's ultimatum did not have the effect of compelling thousands of controllers back to work. However, the secretary reported that 471 additional controllers reported to their jobs on Wednesday and that 93 others indicated intent of returning to work. He felt that these actions were a "considerable improvement," and he was "gratified" by these employees' decisions.

As the court actions began taking effect, the first incarceration of a controller occurred in Alexandria, Virginia. Fines on the PATCO and individuals within the union began escalating as temporary restraining orders occurred in fifty-two federal district courts.

The AFL–CIO executive council was meeting in Chicago as the strike began. As the strike wore on, the more reasoned members of the council began suggesting that the PATCO strike may be in trouble and that the longer-term consequences of the strike could result in major damage to the entire labor movement. While members of the council joined PATCO picketers on the O'Hare International Airport picket line, Douglas Fraser, president of the United Auto Workers, painted a gloomy picture. Referring to discussions by the council, Fraser said, "There was no expression of optimism."[19] Council members were critical of Robert Poli and PATCO in terms of how they let the situation evolve into a course of action from which they could not retreat. The council's concerns stemmed from the recognition that the president was riding high in public opinion polls and that the public may not understand the intricate issues that formed the basis of the strike. Fraser noted that "unions are not popular" with the general public, "no matter how stressful" the job union members perform.[20]

In spite of the verbiage of support provided by some segments of the labor movement, the rift between the PATCO and the ALPA became increasingly apparent. While both the PATCO and the ALPA had endorsed Ronald Reagan for the presidency and both organizations must work closely together to ensure the safe movement of airplanes in controlled airspace, the coup that led Poli to the PATCO presidency left a bad taste in the mouth of John J. O'Donnell, president of the ALPA. O'Donnell said that he personally would not cross a picket line—presumably any picket line—but he would leave it up to each pilot's judgment as to whether or not he or she would honor PATCO's picket lines. When members of the AFL–CIO executive council joined the picketers at O'Hare Airport, O'Donnell was not among them.

As the positions of both sides stiffened, it became clearer that the administration was not going to back down easily. The *Wall Street Journal* reported, "Yesterday afternoon [August 5], President Reagan told reporters that he felt sorry for the fired strikers but that he had 'no other choice.' He said those dismissed are 'fine people . . . who don't quite understand our position has to be irreversible.' He expressed hope that more controllers would return to work."[21]

As the plight of the PATCO grew increasingly difficult, Robert Poli finally did something that he apparently had been unable to do earlier. He sent letters to all of the 102 AFL–CIO union presidents asking them for support. He asked them to "please instruct your members to honor our picket lines." He described what he believed was the administration's intent to "destroy organized labor." He characterized the government's tactics as "fascist" but asserted that union members were standing firm in "the face of this brutal repression."[22]

LEWIS: THE STRIKE IS OVER

One can sense in the tone and character of Poli's statements the frustrations he was feeling about the progress of the strike. As the dismissal letters began flowing into the system, the reality of defeat for the PATCO began setting in. Secretary Lewis indicated that he would have accepted suggestions by outsiders to turn the talks over to a neutral third party if Poli had ordered the controllers back to work before the president's deadline. Now that the deadline had passed, the secretary said, "It's too late now. As far as we are concerned . . . it's over with."[23]

The dismissal letters sent to controllers were hard-hitting. They notified the recipients that they were being dismissed from their jobs for their failure to report to work as the president had ordered. In addition, the letters indicated that the controller's actions gave "reasonable cause to believe that you have committed a crime for which a sentence of imprisonment can be imposed."[24] The letters spelled out the rights of controllers to respond to the dismissal and their right to legal representation.

As the notices began arriving in the hands of controllers, Lane Kirkland weighed in with his beliefs about the actions taken by the government and the character of the controller workforce. He observed that controllers are "decent, normal, typical Americans not revolutionaries. They represent a cross-section of what is best in this country." Further, "He said that the controllers are engaged in an 'unequal struggle' with a powerful government and have demonstrated 'remarkable' courage in the face of threats and harsh reprisals."[25]

Since the government repeatedly asserted that the strike did not represent a threat to public safety, Kirkland called the government action "out of all proportion," and the rationale for their actions was to deflect attention and "avoid examining the merits of the controllers' complaints."[26] In one of his few direct comments about the air traffic control system, Kirkland answered a question about whether the Executive Committee in Chicago would fly home by saying, "I think it would be highly imprudent for anyone to ride aircraft now."[27]

As the administration's actions indicated that large numbers of controllers would, indeed, be fired, the logical question surfaced: How long would it take to repair the system? Secretary Lewis admitted that there would be "serious problems" handling air traffic for some time into the future. Lynn Helms, administrator of the FAA, indicated that it would take twenty-one months for normalcy to return. As experience would show, there would be some problems in the system, but most problems were manageable. However, the time to repair the system was grossly optimistic. Six years after the strike, there would still be major shortages in the controller workforce.

During the third day of the strike, five more union officials were jailed for refusal to obey judicial back-to-work orders. These jailings followed the incarceration of the first union official, Steven L. Wallaert of PATCO Local 291, in Newport News, Virginia. While there were potentially hundreds of union members who could have been jailed for the failure to return to work, the government reconsidered its actions to continue pressing for contempt actions or criminal complaints. The controllers who had been fired were no longer federal employees staging an illegal strike. Therefore, it wasn't clear exactly what the government's position should be relating to back-to-work actions.

After the initial swirl of activity, thoughtful commentators began asking questions about how and why this action occurred and whether the president's response was appropriate. In relation to the latter question, an editorial in the

Wall Street Journal summarized the perspective offered by numerous writers. Arguing that the Reagan administration was trying to establish clarity and constancy in the role of the presidency after the "zigzags of the Carter Administration," "If the President backs off on what he said he would do—both respect for the law and his presidency will suffer."[28]

Day Four

By day four, the full magnitude of the dismissal action began setting in. Poli said that the union's resolve was as steady as it had been on day one and that the struggle would go on. However, the public began feeling that the imminent chaos of the strike was not going to materialize and therefore felt more positively about the president's actions. Congressman Morris Udall noted that "Reagan is clearly riding the popular mood and handling it very skillfully." Others, such as Congressman William Frenzel, observed that he detected "little sympathy for the strike and [substantial] support for Reagan's strong stand."[29]

Nevertheless, the shortage of controllers and the intense pressure on the administration to provide a semblance of stability and order in the system began taking its toll. Controllers who had remained on the job were working long hours, and the intensity of work increased. For many of those who had remained on the job, concerns were raised about burnout and system safety. Typical of these controllers was Evan Black at the regional control center in Hampton, Georgia. Black said a supervisor at the center warned controllers that they would be fired if they called in sick or failed to report to work. He said "he'd never seen the air traffic control system so unsafe."[30] The FAA denied Black's allegations.

On the fourth day, Secretary Lewis confirmed more directly his position on the strike that he had taken on the third day. He said that "as far as he is concerned, the strike 'is over' and he isn't interested in negotiating with current union management." However, he expressed interest in bargaining with the controllers who supported the President's back-to-work order and suggested that their benefits might be increased.[31]

Ironically, after the extensive efforts to portray the illegality of the PATCO strike, Secretary Lewis expressed his "opposition to the incarceration of striking PATCO members," because "nothing is gained by putting anyone in jail."[32] Much was made, of course, by the secretary and other administration officials of the fact that the strike could entail criminal penalties of fines and more than one year in prison. He sidestepped responsibility for the incarceration process by saying, "These decisions . . . are a matter for the Justice Department and the federal courts."[33]

By the sixth day of the strike, conditions inside the United States were slowly returning to normal. Even though the PATCO was not successful in obtaining explicit support from many American unions, the Canadian air traffic controllers weighed in by refusing handoffs of American flights into Canadian airspace. Canadian controllers were refusing to handle U.S. flights because of purported "unsafe flying conditions." Based on pressure from the Reagan administration, Canadian officials took a strong position that the determination of safety of air travel is not up to the individual Canadian controllers.

However, before the Canadian situation was stabilized, a new disruption to international air travel arose. Portuguese controllers notified the airline industry that they were going to quit handling flights over the North Atlantic. This action would effectively ground all flights between the United States and Europe. Portuguese controllers are responsible for a key sector of the North Atlantic air routes that is handled in the Azores. To complicate the problem further, Spanish controllers initiated a sympathy slowdown. Australian controllers, too, refused to handle some U.S. flights, but the impact was sporadic.

AIR CARRIER RESPONSES

While the American air carriers uniformly criticized the PATCO strike, the fact of the matter was that the strike permitted many carriers to take initiatives that would have been impossible without the strike. Specifically, many of the larger national and international carriers were burdened with aircraft, routes, and staffing that were breaking their backs. When the government imposed limitations on certain routes and other operational procedures, the carriers took advantage of these prescriptions to consolidate and downsize. They eliminated routes that were not profitable, tried to mothball old, inefficient airplanes, and reduce staffing in terminal facilities and flight personnel. Many industry analysts believed that the "retrenchment" would ultimately produce an aviation system that was stronger and economically more vigorous.

As these changes were initiated, the result was not necessarily to the benefit of the consumer. For most passengers it was believed that "it will still be possible to fly from one city to another, but it may be a little more difficult to get there, possibly requiring a one-stop trip instead of a nonstop. And travelers are probably going to have to pay more, on average, for their tickets."[34]

With reduced operational capacity, more seats would be filled. With more seats filled, the airlines would be in a position to withdraw the discounts used to lure passengers to air travel. This process, too, would result in higher fares for the traveling public. One airline official, Neil Effman of Trans World Airlines, compared the impact of the controller strike on the airline industry to the impacts from the 1973 Arab oil embargo. He observed that "the Arab oil embargo caused a jet-fuel shortage. The airlines grounded some planes, raised fares, and reported record profits."[35]

The government reduction of airline regulation was intended to, among other things, encourage carriers to extend routes into previously underserved markets. With the controller strike curtailing flights in the system, generally, it was feared that few airlines would extend service into new territory. This aspect of the process would work to the detriment of the flying public, too.

With the government notifying the public and the airlines that it would limit flights into most of the major airports to 50 percent of prestrike capacity, for a period of almost two years, the airlines moaned publicly but cheered privately. They would have an opportunity to ground smaller, less efficient airplanes without fear of undue competition from alternative carriers. Filling more seats on larger, more efficient airplanes could only push the bottom line profit upward.

Not every airline official saw the silver lining in the controller strike cloud. Some carriers, Braniff, for example, needed a strong third quarter to convince lenders that it could operate at a profit. The strike worked to this carrier's disadvantage. As a result, Braniff immediately laid off 1,500 of its employees. John Casey, Braniff chairman, called the strike a "tragedy for all airlines." Certainly, for carriers in a weak financial position, the strike was disastrous. But for the stronger carriers, there would be opportunities to consolidate operations, streamline the route structure, and improve overall operating efficiency. Airlines in a position to capitalize on these types of changes would almost certainly benefit from the strike in the long run.

PICKET LINES

One of the inviolable rules in the American labor movement is the recognition of a picket line. Union members have long recognized that there is strength in unity, and as a consequence, when one union is compelled to go on strike, other unionists will not cross the striking union's picket line. This action places additional pressure on the firm to settle, which, after all, is the purpose of the action. Union members who cross picket lines are viewed in the most negative terms by other union members. The sight of the picket line has been one of the primary places for violence in historical labor management relations. In most cases, the constitution of the union requires certain procedures before and during a strike. The general procedure is that the local union must consult with and in some cases be sanctioned by—the national union prior to the strike. Since the PATCO was a national union, it could proceed with strike activity without consulting with the AFL–CIO even though it may not have been prudent or political to do so.

Throughout history, there have been instances in which union members crossed picket lines of their own unions and those of other unions. Sometimes these actions have resulted in violence, threats, and intimidation. In the case of the PATCO, it was generally assumed that other unions would recognize the PATCO picket lines. Preeminent among those who could have a major impact on the process was the Air Line Pilots Association. If the PATCO picket lines kept ALPA pilots out of the cockpit, the strike would have maximum effect.

As noted earlier, the PATCO knew that about 2,000 controllers were not members of the union, and therefore these individuals would probably remain on duty during the strike. Managers and other employees outside the bargaining unit would probably cross the picket lines, as would any military personnel assigned to the process.

PATCO President Poli asked each of the AFL–CIO affiliates to "please instruct your members to honor our picket lines." Under most circumstances, such a request would have been unnecessary. However, the PATCO strike was a blatant violation of the law. Under these circumstances, it was less clear what the implications were for non-PATCO union members honoring—refusing to cross—the PATCO picket line. Several unions instructed their members to refuse to cross the picket line. Among those unions were the International Association of Machinists and the Brotherhood of Railway and Airline Clerks. However, neither the president of the AFL–CIO nor most of the remaining national union affiliates explicitly instructed their members to honor the PATCO picket lines. Various union leaders, including Lane Kirkland, president of the AFL–CIO, individually avoided air travel so that they would not have to cross the picket lines.

Union leaders pointed to the U.S. District Court for the Eastern District of New York's injunction in 1970 that prohibited PATCO or "'any other person acting in concert with it [PATCO],' from striking, encouraging a strike, or 'any other concerted, unlawful interference with or obstruction to the movement or operation of aircraft.'"[36] This injunction, still in effect, worried union leaders. They feared that they could be exposed to massive fines for defying the injunction and could be "charged with aiding or abetting a violation of federal law."[37]

Other union leaders continued to criticize the government's "despicable attack" on the PATCO while attempting to find some mechanisms to bring the impasse to an end. Roy Williams, president of the Teamsters, expressed great concern about public employee strikes and urged the development of a mechanism such as binding arbitration to resolve them.

With all of the uncertainty and fears of being drawn into a strike that appeared to be lost, union leaders sidestepped the issue of what position to take on the picket line question. What occurred was that most unions did not honor the picket lines or engaged in activities such as avoiding air travel so that the issue would not be confronted. Whatever the motivation or procedure used, the failure of other unions to honor the PATCO picket line explicitly was another aspect of the process that weakened PATCO's position.

EFFECTS OF THE STRIKE

As the impasse ground on, Poli and administration officials continued to exchange barbs about conditions in the airline industry and the effects the strike was having on the economy. Poli continued to claim that the strike was working and that the air traffic system was faltering. Secretary Lewis argued the contrary. He also reiterated the position that there was "no possibility at the present time that we will sit with Mr. Poli and negotiate with him."[38] In fact, the secretary flatly rejected any meetings with anybody who had been terminated. This, of course, meant every controller and Poli because they had all been fired by the president. Agreeing with the secretary, a White House official said that it is foolish "to think that the President is going to eat crow on the White House lawn."[39]

The secretary asserted that while the government was still looking at the possible effects of the strike on the economy, he believed that when the impact estimates were released, there would be "almost no impact" on the overall economy. Further, he said, "[T]he airways have never been safer."[40] However, responding to reporter's questions, the secretary said, "'I can't say there won't be any harm whatsoever' to such industries as airlines, hotels and restaurants. 'I'm saying it won't have a significant impact.'"[41] This position by the secretary seemed at variance with comments by Attorney General Smith. Speaking at an American Bar Association (ABA) meeting in New Orleans, Smith said that the strike was inflicting "some $35 million a day of injury upon the airlines alone— and perhaps ten times that injury upon the whole economy."[42]

The trauma and disruption the strike was causing in the economy were being studied carefully. However, there were other signs that the emotional impacts were similarly difficult. For example, on August 11, the American Bar Association, meeting in New Orleans, issued an endorsement of the manner in which President Reagan handled the strike and the discharge of the air controllers. Members of the ABA Section of Labor and Employment Law were angered by the endorsement. They threatened to leave the ABA and establish their own association. The basis of their threat stemmed from their belief that the ABA had "sullied and stained its professed adherence to fair and impartial justice for all Americans."[43] The attorneys in the Section of Labor and Employment Law said, "We are appalled by the precipitate actions of the Assembly and House of Delegates in condemning the striking air-controllers. These actions violate fundamental rights guaranteed by both constitutions [U.S. Constitution and the ABA Constitution and Rules]."[44] The statement continued:

There is no more basic right under the United States Constitution than the due process protections accorded defendants to fair and impartial trials of criminal and civil charges brought against them. Defendants are presumed to be innocent until found to be guilty by impartial judges and juries after trials conducted in a calm and reasoned atmosphere. However, defendants who are tried in an atmosphere of hysteria, and whose actions have been prejudged and condemned in advance of trial by the nation's professional association of lawyers [the ABA], are denied their rights to impartial justice. [45]

The statement concluded by saying, "Procedural due process within our organization and common sense itself have been sacrificed for the sake of partisan political expediency."[46]

On August 11, the PATCO was granted some relief from the stiff fines imposed by Judge Greene. The judge reduced the accrued fines against the union of $4.75 million to $750,000. He also reduced the accrued fine of $6,000 against Poli to $2,000. He denied the government's request to make the fines immediately payable. In addition, he denied the government's request for preliminary injunctions "against PATCO to prevent alleged interference by union members with air traffic and to guard against the possible disposal of the Controllers Benefit Fund [strike fund]."[47]

Noting that the government itself had repeatedly said that there was little disruption in air traffic and that economic impacts would be minimal, the judge reasoned that the irreparable harm rationale for injunctive relief had not been met by the government. The judge also denied PATCO's motion to dismiss all federal charges against the union and its request to "not be required to testify on matters concerning its strike fund."[48]

Judge Greene noted that once Secretary Lewis announced on August 5 that the strike was over, neither the union nor its president can be viewed as in violation of the court's return-to-work order "after that time." After the employer, the FAA, has effectively locked out the employees, "the employees, as well as the union and its officers, cannot purge themselves of the contempt of a no strike order when compliance with the order has been made impossible by the employer and, being unable to purge themselves, they can no longer be held in or punished for civil contempt."[49]

On August 12, the Canadian controllers began handling U.S. flights again, and normalcy returned to the northern air routes. However, the terms of the agreement between the Canadian government and the controllers did little to convince the flying public that air travel was safe. The agreement tended to bring more attention to the safety issue in that teams of observers were dispatched in both the United States and Canada to "scrutinize border air safety at locations across the country." The simple fact that these teams were needed to examine the system was enough to raise doubts in the minds of air travelers. Throughout this process, Secretary Lewis repeatedly argued that there were no safety problems. The secretary "repeatedly denied that such problems have cropped up, either along the Canadian border or in the United States since the strike began. The airline pilots flying the system have indicated [safety] is equal to, if not better than, before."[50] In this situation, as in many others, the secretary did not, as subsequent study showed, portray conditions in the system accurately.

However, with the threatened Portuguese strike, there were potential problems ahead. Late in the first week, other controller unions in several foreign countries other than those noted above also threatened actions. Dutch controllers were reportedly engaged in a slowdown and British controllers indicated that they would vote on some type of "job action" on August 14.

After a week in jail, Steven Wallaert, president of PATCO Local 291, was released on August 12. The four other controllers who had been jailed in Kansas had been released two days earlier. Wallaert agreed to comply with an order from Judge Oren Lewis that required members of Wallaert's local who were eligible to go back to work to do so. A spokesperson for the union noted that all of the local's members still on strike had been fired, and therefore there were no jobs for them to return to.

On August 13, the PATCO strike was dealt its most serious setback from the international sector. The International Federation of Air Traffic Controllers Associations recommended to member countries to delay the anticipated sympathy boycotting of U.S. flights. The Portuguese controllers immediately withdrew the walkout threat they had planned for August 17. The IFATCA set a meeting date of August 22 to consider the situation if the strike was still on. Without support by the International Federation and a week delay in consideration of what response was appropriate, the support of foreign controllers was fundamentally gone. Based on these events, the Atlantic air routes returned to normal operation. A spokesperson for the FAA noted, "The system is working absolutely normally, both domestically and across the North Atlantic."[51] In this case, too, PATCO's withdrawal from IFATCA left the union with little ability to garner international support.

In spite of the bad international news for the PATCO, Poli refused to back off on his recalcitrant rhetoric. Responding to reporters in Washington, D.C., he said, "We're not going to kneel; we're not going to crawl back; we're still on strike."[52] President Reagan responded similarly: "I just don't see any way that it could be expected that we could now just go back and pretend that they weren't breaking the law or breaking their oath."[53]

A variety of overtures occurred during the first two weeks of the strike concerning methods and reasons for resolving the impasse. Of particular note was a letter by Congressman William D. Ford to the president on August 14, 1981. Later reported in House documents:

On August 14, I [Congressman Ford] sent the President a telegram, which I would like to read at this point:

Mr. President: The strike of the nation's air traffic controllers is now in its 12th day with no resolution in sight. The walkout is costing the country millions of dollars a day, poses a threat to the safety of the airways, and is causing disruption and hardship in the lives of air travelers.

I strongly urge you to appoint a blue ribbon panel made up of leading citizens to recommend a solution to this collective bargaining impasse. Such a panel could include skilled negotiators from business and labor, as well as former Secretaries of Labor. Respectfully, William Ford, Chairman, Post Office and Civil Service Committee.

I didn't receive any response to that telegram. Then early in September I started receiving copies of a newspaper clipping from the Los Angeles Times—and I'll read it in part. This is from the Los Angeles Times of Wednesday, September 2:

Seeking to counter reports that have portrayed President Reagan as working short hours and being out of touch with important developments, the White House showed the Times' documents Tuesday that disclosed that he had, among other actions, personally rejected suggestions that he seek a solution to the air traffic controllers strike. Representative William D. Ford, Democrat of Michigan, wrote the President a letter urging him to appoint a blue ribbon panel made up of leading citizens to reach a solution. In the margin of a document summarizing Ford's letter, the President wrote, "no way."

That was the first notice I had of the action of the administration to our suggestion.

I called the White House to find out if that was the final word, and that caused me to receive on White House stationery under date of September 10 a letter signed by an Assistant to the President:

Dear Mr. Ford: On behalf of the President, I would like to thank you for your August 14 telegram suggesting that the President appoint a panel of private citizens to make recommendations concerning the situation of the air traffic controllers. We appreciate receiving your views on this matter.

The administration's position on this issue was made quite clear on August 7th in a statement by the President, and the question and answer period which followed with the Attorney General and the Secretary of Transportation. At that time the air traffic controllers were given notice of the illegality of their proposed actions and were informed— "proposed actions," you understand—on the 7th of August, whatever they proposed four days after the strike. I have no idea what that part of the letter refers to.

At that time the air traffic controllers were given notice of the illegality of their proposed actions and were informed of the steps which the Administration would take if they did not report back to work. In spite of these warnings, the members of PATCO insisted on breaking the no-strike oath they took as a condition of their employment.

As I am sure you know, the Administration feels very strongly that safety is of the highest priority with respect to our nation's air traffic. Therefore, every effort will be made to ensure that our air system is operating safely as we move to rebuild the system.

Thank you for your interest in writing. With cordial regard, I am, sincerely, Max L. Friedersdorf, Assistant to the President.

At that it became very clear that either we didn't say it properly or they completely missed the intent of the original communication, because if you note the formal response, while stated much more kindly than the President's own note "no way," really said "no way." It didn't address itself to the problem of resolving the dispute, but addressed itself to steps to be taken on the assumption that the dispute was not going to be resolved. Indeed, that's what happened.[54]

To no one's surprise, on August 14, Administrative Law Judge John H. Fenton recommended to the Federal Labor Relations Authority that the authority decertify the PATCO as the exclusive bargaining agent for the air traffic controllers. The recommendation was based on the provisions in the statute (Title VII of the 1978 Civil Service Reform Act) that made strikes, slowdowns, or other concerted actions against any federal agency an unfair labor practice. In addition, the statute removes any person or union who participates in a strike or concerted action from the definition of an "employee" or "labor organization."[55] Fenton gave the PATCO one month to appeal the ruling.

THE STRIKE WAS WRITTEN IN THE STARS

There was no levity in the strike or its aftermath. People's lives were being destroyed, and the nation teetered on the brink of disaster. Air safety was being compromised, and rhetoric flowed from both sides. In the midst of all this confusion, people looked for reasons and answers. There seemed to be few. However, Svetlana Godillo, a Washington astrologer, argued that the strike was "pressaged by the pattern of lunations and eclipses that fell on the chart of the United States, and that of the inauguration, as well as on the charts of the three main protagonists [Reagan, Lewis, and Poli]."[56] Godillo placed a heavy responsibility on Poli. She pointed out that Poli's chart is "the chart of a man incapable of negotiating anything, at any place, at any time."[57] If Poli had been born on any other day other than February 27, 1937, the outcome of the negotiations could have been decidedly different. After a contorted description of suns, moons, planets, and eclipses, the astrologer makes one interesting observation. She noted, "His [Poli's] Mercury without any aspects to his Moon (the population) indicates also an inability to communicate well with the public. His Mercury-Mars aspect can 'bulldoze through' but does not garner much good will since it is never diplomatic."[58]

There you have it. The strike was simply one of personality conflicts. Godillo concluded: "When I look at Poli's chart, so preoccupied with himself and the drive for power, and see his inflexible Mercury, I come to the conclusion that to send any person into complex negotiations with such a chart is to invite disaster. This is especially true if he has to negotiate with people whose charts are stronger than his and cannot be bulldozed. That is exactly what happened when he ran across the Scorpionic and Taurian charts of Lewis and Reagan."[59] In a subsequent article,[60] the astrologer elaborated on the astrological characteristics of all three major players. For those who rely on the moons and stars for their guidance, the astrological configuration of all three principal actors in this process ensured that a strike would occur.

Whether the same interpretation would have occurred in a prestrike reading of the charts is not known, but one cannot miss the important observation about the inability of Poli to communicate well with the public. There can be no question that Poli failed to "make the case" with the public about the concerns of the controllers. The public saw the controllers as focused on money and little else. Money was an important issue for certain, but it was only one of several issues. An editorial in the *Washington Post* on August 8, 1981, captured the notion completely. The editor suggested, "The gigantic claims for pay increases were hardly more than surrogates for other, and more deeply felt, claims."[61]

If it is written in the stars, there is a certain inevitableness about it. Whether one accepts the power and interpretation of astrology as an influence on worldly events, one must be impressed by the interpretation of Poli's chart as an explanation of disaster. The Reagan and Lewis charts were less fully interpreted except to note that they exemplified strong personalities that could not be "bulldozed" in Poli's drive for power. Obviously, the interpretations of astrologer Godillo would have been more useful prior to the strike than afterward.

ECONOMIC COSTS

As the system gained increased stability each day, attention began shifting to issues other than system safety. One of the most interesting concerns related to what the strike was costing the airlines and the related industries that service the industry. Secretary Lewis had argued that there was no substantial impact on the industry or the overall economy. Nevertheless, Table 6.1 provides one estimate of direct and indirect costs.

Table 6.1
Estimated Costs of the Air Traffic Controller Strike

Industry	Cost per Day (In millions)
Airlines	$35.
Fuel suppliers	$08.
Travel agents	$04.5
Striking air controllers salaries	$01.7
Airport landing fees	$01.4
On-board food caterers	$00.25
Total	$50.85

Source: U.S. News and World Report, August 17, 1981, p. 21.

The $50 million per day impact on the industry and related activities seems like a large impact. In terms of the overall economy, it probably didn't amount to much. There were still prophets of both gloom and doom and prosperity selling their wares to the public. Airlines in financial trouble before the strike were undoubtedly placed in even more precarious positions. Airlines that were healthy before the strike probably suffered some short-term financial setbacks but, as noted elsewhere, were probably positioned to rebound even stronger in the long term.

Two weeks after the strike, Secretary Lewis appointed a task force to study the employment conditions of air traffic controllers. The secretary indicated that the task force "will look into all 'people aspects' of the air traffic control system, including the requirements for air traffic control employment, promotional opportunities, retirement, and personnel practices."[62] As the task force was announced, the secretary said, "The American people have our assurance that we will fulfill [sic] our obligations to improve relations between the FAA and the air traffic controllers to see that the situation that troubles us all today hopefully will never happen again."[63] As the subsequent ten years of disruptive labor relations will show, the secretary's assurances were based more on political expediency than on a realistic attempt to improve employment conditions.

When asked why the issues the task force was charged to address were not effectively addressed in discussion with the PATCO prior to the strike, the secretary made a gratuitous comment that shifted the entire blame for the strike to the controllers. Observing that Robert Poli had not remained at the bargaining table, the secretary said, "He [Poli] decided he would violate his oath and go on strike and therefore we have to do an independent study."[64]

The secretary failed to mention, however, that the negotiations "at the bargaining table" had been going nowhere for several months; that prior task forces had identified severe problems in the personnel and management processes in the FAA that remained unresolved by the Secretary; that Poli was told at the last formal meeting that there were no more resources available; and that hardware and working conditions were contributors to the stress and frustration felt by large numbers of controllers. Ironically, the secretary noted in his comments that "as we proceed with the rebuilding of our air traffic control system, we want to be certain that we provide every possible support to the men and women working in the system." In addition, "Our objective is to be responsive to the controllers and their supervisors, and to provide them all the tools available to assure the continued safe and effective operation of our air traffic control system in a suitable work environment."[65]

Arguably, if the FAA had provided "every possible support" to the controllers prior to the strike, there may never have been a strike. The provision of "tools"—which must have meant physical tools such as improved computers—remains an important question a decade and a half after the strike.

This task force, soon to be known as the "Jones Task Force" after its chairman Lawrence M. Jones, was joined in its investigation by the Flight Safety Foundation. The foundation, a nonprofit, international organization, was asked to assess safety conditions in the air traffic system in the aftermath of the PATCO strike. In addition, concurrent with the secretary's task force study, the National Transportation Safety Board initiated an eight-week study of air system safety. The board planned to examine the full range of issues related to air safety including controller qualifications, air traffic density, work schedules, and so forth.

Both sets of studies were announced soon after a report by Poli that "systems errors" and "near misses" had increased early in the strike. Lynn Helms, FAA administrator, kept saying that there were no signs of deterioration of the system. However, the Aviation Safety Institute reported that there was an average of one systems error *each hour* between 6 A.M. and 10 P.M. during the first week of the strike. This compared with one and a half systems errors *per day* prior to the strike. The institute also reported that there were more near misses after the strike than prior to the strike.[66]

Whether the information being provided by either the union or the FAA was accurate may never be known. Both sides had public relations reasons for providing their "information." The volume of air travel was slowly beginning to increase, which suggested that the flying public believed the statements by the FAA more than those by the controllers. Nevertheless, the president continued to be accused of union-busting, and reporters continued to raise the system safety questions. On August 18, speaking to a group of California Republicans in Los Angeles, the president reiterated that he had no choice in what he did. Seeking to tie himself to prior presidents who rejected public employee strikers, the president argued that both Franklin D. Roosevelt and Calvin Coolidge detested these actions. President Reagan then argued, "I have seen myself heralded as setting out to union-bust." However, "I am the first union president that ever got elected President of the United States."[67]

Throughout the early days of the strike, one of the most important dimensions of the environment was the lack of support by organized labor for the PATCO. There were several aspects of this lack of support that have been discussed elsewhere: the anger of O'Donnell of ALPA about how Poli assumed the PATCO presidency; the fear that direct support may expose other unions to fines and lawsuits; Poli's inability to communicate effectively with other union leaders; Poli's "shoot from the hip" approach to the strike; among others. As conditions stabilized, questions about what impact, if any, the strike may have on the labor movement and organized labor began to be asked.

On the one hand, it was clear that an already weakened labor movement did not respond as it would have thirty or forty years earlier. Most of the support was rhetorical rather than substantial. As Audrey Freedman of the Conference Board noted, "[T]he American Labor Movement doesn't have the muscle and solidarity it might have shown in the 1940s."[68]

Representatives of organized labor didn't share this dismal view. They argued that the labor movement and organized labor will not be substantially weakened and certainly not destroyed "because a bad strike has been held." Not all strikes succeed, of course. However, very few strikes are as visible as the PATCO strike, and few affected the public more directly. In this sense, it was not just another strike, one among many. It was not an ordinary strike that could be expected to slide easily from the public psyche.

Since it was a public sector strike, there were fears that other levels of government—particularly state, county, and municipal—would emulate the stance taken by the president when their employees struck. There were over 500 strikes by public employees in subnational unions in 1980. There had been an average of over 400 strikes by state, county, and municipal employees for all of the 1970s.

The clear message from the way the president handled the controllers was that "we can replace you," no matter how irreplaceable you may feel you are. As work stoppage data indicate, the fears of unionists about the consequences of the PATCO strike may in fact be coming true. Indicative of those fears was a statement by a union spokesman that "now we will have thousands of little Ronald Reagans across the country in every town saying 'Fire them,' whenever public employees confronted them in a labor dispute."[69]

Even a staunch unionist like Douglas Fraser, president of the United Auto Workers, sang a dreary song. He argued that the PATCO strike may spill over into private sector labor relations as well. He argued, "It's a fair warning to all unions that if they get into a struggle and look to the government for some kind of comfort, they aren't going to get it."[70]

There were some who saw a silver lining in the president's approach. They thought that the severe union-busting approach of the administration could have a backlash effect. If union members felt sufficiently besieged, they would band together in greater solidarity and support one another's effort even more vigorously. Union leaders prognosticated that the upcoming Solidarity Day rally scheduled for September 19 in Washington would turn out to be a huge, militant reaction to the president's actions. Even John Leyden, former president of the PATCO, and now head of the AFL–CIO Public Employees Department, believed that the reaction of the president to the PATCO strike could bring employees into the unions. According to Leyden, employees outside unions are going to say, "I can't fight this thing myself. I need the Labor Movement."[71]

The Solidarity Day rally was one of the largest gatherings of unionists in many decades. One saw considerable rhetoric and chest-beating—but little else. While union representatives were angry about the government's handling of the PATCO strike, few knew what to do about it. The rally ended without a feeling of increased solidarity; in fact, there was heightened frustration and uncertainty about the future.

The short-term and long-term impacts of the PATCO strike are certain to provide the fodder for heated discussion far into the future. The complexity of the issues and problems that precipitated the strike, the legal implications of the strike for air traffic controllers and other workers, the motivation of the administration in it's response to the strike, and a dozen other factors make a clear assessment difficult.

Throughout the first two weeks of the strike, John J. O'Donnell, president of the Air Line Pilots Association, had attempted to support the individual controllers by asking that the president consider them as decent, conscientious Americans with families. However, he was always careful not to provide support for Robert Poli. In fact, he carefully contradicted Poli's assessment of air safety. On August 18, he declared the air traffic control system as "safe" and called a press conference to dispute claims by the air controllers that public safety was at stake in the strike. He said, "I can say without equivocation that the air traffic control system in this country is safe. If it were not safe, we would be the first to speak out."[72] Earlier in the week the PATCO had released a list of "near misses" and "systems errors" that suggested problems in the system. O'Donnell's statements refuted the PATCO list.

Three weeks after the strike began, the question of striker amnesty arose again. When the president issued his ultimatum to strikers immediately after the strike started, he pledged that "there will be no amnesty" for those who did not return to work in the forty-eight-hour time period he provided. Nevertheless, there were those who believed that some form of amnesty was warranted when the full set of conditions was considered. The *U.S. News and World Report* asked two prominent Americans to provide the "pros and cons" of granting amnesty. For the unions, Moe Biller, president of the American Postal Workers Union, provided his views. Secretary Lewis argued the administration's position.

Biller argued that strikers should be given amnesty because of several important factors. First, he argued that the United States is the only democratic county in the world that imposes economic capital punishment on government workers by firing them if they strike.[73] He said that the causes of the strike were not one-dimensional. He felt strongly that the government should acknowledge all factors causing the strike—many of them within the purview of government control.[74]

Second, Biller noted that the rhetoric used in the early weeks of the strike suggested that the controllers were advocating a revolution or staging a mutiny against the federal government. This perception, he felt, was nonsense. Rather, "What we have is a labor dispute, pure and simple—a reaction against an employer that has been too repressive and acts as if it can escape its responsibility by waving around a no-strike law."[75] In Biller's view, the government made its point. It had demonstrated its power. The objective of government policies and actions should not be to bring free Americans to their knees. Rather, it should be to resolve problems and create an environment in which the needs of all parties—the American people, the government, and the air traffic controllers—can be addressed.

Third, while it is clear that President Reagan was sending a signal to organized labor throughout the nation, Biller argued that the dampening effect of busting the union would only be temporary. He pointed to the 200 postal workers who had been fired three years earlier for an unauthorized strike. Half of them were still trying to get their jobs back. Their example did not discourage other public sector unions from engaging in strike activity. Biller argued that the PATCO strike can have a short-term impact on strikes by federal workers.[76] When the problems of a group of workers are real enough and are not addressed by the employer, they will boil over eventually.[77]

Finally, Biller noted that as a strong nation public policy should be tempered by understanding and compassion. He referenced the admiration all Americans had for the Polish Solidarity trade union who did the same thing that the air controllers did—strike against the government. He concluded, "The U.S.

does not have a dictatorial government, but in a very real sense the controllers felt repressed by an agency that would not treat them fairly."[78] Based on all of these conditions and relationships, Biller argued that amnesty for the controllers was an appropriate, humane, and reasonable public policy response.

Secretary Lewis opposed amnesty. He argued that the controllers signed an oath to uphold the United States Constitution and not to strike against the U.S. government. He suggested that this oath was doubly important because the functions controllers performed affected the health and safety of the public. He felt that strike amnesty would place the core of our democracy in jeopardy.[79] Everybody, including the president, was to support the Constitution, and the president cannot permit a relatively few people to violate the law knowingly while expecting everybody else to respect and uphold the law.[80]

Second, Lewis argued that amnesty was not needed because the striking controllers are not needed to keep the air traffic control system functioning effectively. Lewis argued that in the third week of the strike the air traffic control system was running safely and would continue to operate safely.[81] He pointed to the reduction in scheduled flights, the elimination of smaller towers, the utilization of military controllers and supervisors, and the accelerated training of controllers as important factors in maintaining system safety. This argument by Lewis is particularly interesting. If striking controllers were not needed to keep the system operating safely, how can one argue that striking jeopardized safety in the air traffic control system?

Third, while acknowledging that there were problems within the FAA in terms of its relationships with the controllers, Lewis argued that all the union wanted was more money. He observed, "This thing has festered for 10 years. I asked Robert Poli of PATCO to sit down and talk about the difficulties his people have with the FAA, but all he wanted to talk about was money. He talks of idealism when he gets on television, but when it comes down to real negotiations, all he talks about is money."[82]

Based on these activities and conditions, Secretary Lewis adamantly opposed granting amnesty to striking controllers. He went further by flatly opposing any discussion with strikers. He said there was no possibility of negotiating with the "people who are on strike, who have walked off the job, who are out there picketing, tearing up their termination notices and violating statutes and orders of the federal courts. We cannot do it."[83]

The strength of the pros and cons for amnesty can be debated without end. The fact is that the government was not inclined to grant amnesty, and therefore the arguments supporting this action were moot. A final observation about this set of issues that may serve to clarify how the secretary felt about controllers relates to who becomes a controller. Secretary Lewis acknowledged the communications problems between the FAA and its employees. He suggested, "We may even be hiring the wrong people to be controllers—we don't know. This is the thing that we have to get into and get into very deeply."[84]

Certainly the secretary has the right to his views about who the controllers are and that the FAA may be hiring the "wrong people." However, the opposing view that arose in every independent study of the FAA was not that the FAA was hiring the wrong people as controllers but, rather, that the "wrong people" were escalated to management positions. This difference may seem subtle, but the problems most frequently raised by controllers were the inability to communicate well within the FAA and the dictatorial nature of the management process. One long-term controller described the "military model that ruled rather than a cooperative one." Describing conditions in the FAA when he started his career, this controller noted, "The day I reported [for duty with the FAA], we were taken up to the roof and given a tongue-lashing, as if we were going into basic training."[85]

Two weeks after the strike, Secretary Lewis was talking about the need to improve communications and working conditions within the FAA, as though these were new revelations. He responded to reporters, questions about employment conditions within the FAA. In response to these questions, "[t]he Transportation Secretary described plans to improve working conditions for the 5,000 controllers currently on the job. Using surveys and outside consultants, the FAA will 'try to identify their needs and aspirations, to establish some kind of communications and to improve the work environment,' he said. 'Maybe we haven't done a good job in the past.'"[86]

Nowhere, of course, did the secretary suggest that management problems in the FAA could have contributed to the problem and in that sense be a condition upon which a compromise could be developed. By this stage of the process, the FAA was again, in total control. Rather than use this control to respond to controller concerns, the FAA and DOT suggested that surveys, consultants, and committees would be used to study these problems. There was no need to study the needs and aspirations of the controllers. They were obvious and immediate. It takes time and money to reconfigure the computer hardware in a system as large and complex as the American air traffic control system. However, it takes little time and little money to begin attacking inept, insensitive management. With the situation unfolding on the FAA's terms, the transportation secretary chose to do little.

SUMMARY

The U.S. government destroyed, for the first time, a union that represented its employees. There were many reasons cited by the government for its actions, but one has to conclude that a combination of events and factors permitted the union-busting process to work. First, the government was lucky because there was no chaos in the first days and weeks of the strike. System disruption was significant but manageable. Second, due to shortcomings of Robert Poli and other PATCO leaders, the case for the union was articulated poorly. The public simply did not understand conditions in the air traffic control system or what issues the union believed were important. Third, the new president effectively communicated with the public and was able to shift public opinion against the union. Fourth, there was little support either domestic or foreign for the strike.

Therefore, the government took some risks with its political future and the safety of the flying public. These risks were managed well by the administration and as a consequence the impacts from firing the controllers were minimal. Late in the process, after the union was effectively broken, others began to realize that the picture was not as one-sided as many had observed. The next chapter begins with the late support of the AFL–CIO for the strikers.

NOTES

1. "Air Controllers Found in Contempt of Court; Dismissals Threatened," *Wall Street Journal*, August 4, 1981, p. 17.

2. "Reagan Says Striking Air Controllers Have Until Wednesday to Avoid Discharge," *Daily Labor Reporter* (Bureau of National Affairs), No. 148, August 3, 1981, p. AA-3.

3. Ibid., p. AA-4.

4. Ibid.

5. "Massive Fines and Criminal Sanctions Threatened if Air Traffic Controllers' Walkout Continues," *Daily Labor Reporter* (Bureau of National Affairs), No. 149, August 4, 1981, p. AA-3.

6. "Kirkland Blasts Attempt to Bust Air Controllers," *AFL–CIO News*, Vol. 26, No. 33, August 15, 1981, p. 2.

7. "The Sky's Not the Limit," *Wall Street Journal*, August 4, 1981, p. 30.

8. "Massive Fines and Criminal Sanctions Threatened if Air Traffic Controllers' Walkout Continues," p. AA-1.

9. "Air Controllers Found in Contempt of Court; Dismissals Threatened," p. 17.

10. "Air Controllers Union Holds Line on Strike Despite Threats of Massive Fines, Firings," *Wall Street Journal*, August 5, 1981, p. 2.

11. "Decision of U.S. District Court for District of Columbia in United States v. Professional Air Traffic Controllers Organization," *Daily Labor Reporter* (Bureau of National Affairs), No. 149, August 4, 1981, p. E-1.

12. Ibid.

13. "Air Controllers Union Holds Line on Strike Despite Threats of Massive Fines, Firings," p. 2.

14. Ibid.

15. Ibid., p. 20.

16. Ibid.

17. Ibid., p. 20.

18. "Government Begins Sending Dismissal Notices to Striking Air Controllers," *Daily Labor Reporter* (Bureau of National Affairs), No. 150, August 5, 1981, p. AA-1.

19. "AFL–CIO Council Members Join PATCO Pickets, Privately Expressing Concern," *Daily Labor Reporter* (Bureau of National Affairs), No. 150, August 5, 1981, p. A-22.

20. Ibid.

21. "Firing of Air Controllers Begins as Efforts to Resume Talks Stalls," *Wall Street*

Journal, August 6, 1981, p. 3.

22. "PATCO Asks AFL–CIO Unions to Honor Picket Lines, Government Proceeds with Plans to Fire 12,000," *Daily Labor Reporter* (Bureau of National Affairs), No. 151, August 6, 1981, p. AA-1.

23. Ibid.

24. Ibid.

25. Ibid., p. A-11.

26. Ibid., p. A-12.

27. Ibid.

28. "No Room for Compromise," *Wall Street Journal*, August 6, 1981, p. 22.

29. "Washington Wire: A Special Weekly Report from *The Wall Street Journal's* Capital Bureau," *Wall Street Journal*, August 7, 1981, p. 1.

30. Ibid., p. 2.

31. Ibid., p. 2.

32. "Unions Wary of Legal Risks in Honoring PATCO Picket Lines," *Daily Labor Reporter* (Bureau of National Affairs), No. 152, August 7, 1981, p. A-11.

33. Ibid.

34. William M. Carley, "Cutback in Flights, Higher Fares Seen," *Wall Street Journal*, August 7, 1981, p. 21.

35. Ibid.

36. "Unions Wary of Legal Risks in Honoring PATCO Picket Lines," p. A-11.

37. Ibid.

38. "Sympathy Action by Canadian Controllers Shuts Down U.S.-Canada Air Traffic Flows," *Daily Labor Reporter* (Bureau of National Affairs), No. 153, August 10, 1981, p. A-8.

39. "Airlines Face Cuts in Number of Flights to Allow Training of New Controllers," *Wall Street Journal*, August 10, 1981, p. 3.

40. Ibid.

41. Ibid.

42. "Sympathy Action by Canadian Controllers Shuts Down U.S.-Canadian Air Traffic Flows," p. A-9.

43. "ABA's Endorsement of President's Stance on Traffic Controllers Angers Union Lawyers," *Daily Labor Reporter* (Bureau of National Affairs), No, 155, August 12, 1981, p. A-8.

44. Ibid.

45. Ibid.

46. Ibid.

47. "Preliminary Injunction against PATCO on Picket Lines, Strike Fund Denied," *Daily Labor Reporter* (Bureau of National Affairs), No. 155, August 12, 1981, p. A-15.

48. Ibid.

49. Ibid., p. A-16.

50. "Atlantic Flights Begin Returning to Near Normal," *Wall Street Journal*, August 13, 1981, p. 3.

51. Ibid.

52. "Foreign Air Controllers Postpone Plans for Boycott, but Industry Remains Wary," *Wall Street Journal*, August 14, 1981, p. 3.

53. Ibid.

54. House of Representatives, Committee on Post Office and Civil Service, Subcommittee on Investigations, *Federal Labor-Management Relations and Impasses Pro-*

cedures, 97th Cong., 2nd sess., Serial No. 97-50 (Washington, D.C.: GPO, February 24, April 29, May 4, July 22, 1982), pp. 24–25.

55. "Federal Labor Relations Authority Advised by ALJ to Decertify PATCO," *Daily Labor Reporter* (Bureau of National Affairs), No. 157, August 14, 1981, p. A-16.

56. "The Air Traffic Controllers: A Strike Written in the Stars?" *Washington Post*, August 16, 1981, p. F6.

57. Ibid.

58. Ibid.

59. Ibid.

60. Ibid.

61. "After the Strike," *Washington Post*, August 8, 1981, p. A-20.

62. "Task Force Named to Study Air Controller Job Pressures," *Daily Labor Reporter* (Bureau of National Affairs), No. 159, August 18, 1981, p. A-9.

63. Ibid., p. A-10.

64. Ibid.

65. Ibid.

66. Ibid., p. A-11.

67. Ibid.

68. "The Air Strike's Effect on Organized Labor," *Wall Street Journal*, August 18, 1981, p. 32.

69. "Air Controllers' Strike," *Facts on File*, Vol. 41, No. 2136, October 23, 1981, p. 772.

70. Ibid.

71. Ibid.

72. "Air Line Pilot's O'Donnell Declares U.S. Air Traffic Situation 'Is Safe,'" *Daily Labor Reporter* (Bureau of National Affairs), No. 160, August 19, 1981, p. A-6.

73. "Should the U.S. Grant Amnesty to Air Controllers?" *U.S. News and World Report*, August 24, 1981, p. 18.

74. Ibid.

75. Ibid.

76. Ibid.

77. Ibid.

78. Ibid.

79. Ibid., p. 19.

80. Ibid.

81. Ibid.

82. Ibid.

83. Ibid.

84. Ibid.

85. Suzanne Garment, "PATCO Strike: Trying to Find Out the Reasons," *Wall Street Journal*, August 14, 1981, p. 22.

86. "Boycott by Portuguese Controllers Causes Only Minor Delays in U.S.-Europe Flights," *Wall Street Journal*, August 18, 1981, p. 2.

Chapter 7

Slamming the Door on PATCO

LABOR SUPPORT AT LAST

As the third week of the strike drew to a close, the timidity of American unions began dissolving. The realization that the destruction of PATCO was at hand prompted the AFL–CIO and affiliated national unions to begin providing monetary support. The AFL–CIO established a "Family Assistance Fund" for discharged controllers and their families. The federation was careful not to characterize the initiative as support for the strike. One of the first large contributions to the fund came from the Communications Workers of America (CWA) union. The CWA committed $100,000 to the fund for aid to controllers, and the executive board authorized "up to $1 million from CWA's defense fund to be used to aid the controllers 'in defense of unionism and the process of collective bargaining in the public sector.'"[1]

In providing the CWA's contribution to the fund, Glenn Watts, president of the CWA, observed that the firing of the controllers and the move to decertify PATCO "[set] an alarming precedent which can only be viewed as an attack on public sector unionism at all levels."[2]

Watts continued, "It is time for the labor movement in this country to recognize that its enemies are rallying to turn back the clock in the files of labor relations. Those who would destroy organized labor can only draw encouragement from the Reagan Administration's brutal attempt to crush PATCO."[3]

ADMINISTRATIVE AND JUDICIAL REVIEW OF THE STRIKE

On August 25, the FLRA rejected PATCO's petition to find that the FAA committed an unfair labor practice for not negotiating in good faith prior to the

August 3 strike. Alexander T. Graham, director of FLRA Region III, ruled, "There is no basis to support the allegation that [the FAA] failed to negotiate a new tentative agreement in good faith."[4]

Graham argued that the PATCO established unreasonable deadlines for agreement on a new contract that could not have been met by the FAA. Specifically, he observed the disparity between the $40 million FAA offer and the $490 million PATCO demand. When PATCO set a three-day time interval for agreement, Graham argued that a time interval of this length "must be considered unreasonable as there was no justification for the union's argument that this radical change could be negotiated in 3 days."[5]

Graham summarized the timetable that unfolded in the negotiation process shown in Table 7.1.

Table 7.1
Graham's Summary of the 1981 PATCO-FAA Negotiation Timetable

Date	Event
February 1981	Bargaining began.
June 22	Tentative agreement reached.
July 29	Lewis informed by Poli that the contract had been rejected by the members.
July 29	Poli requested resumption of negotiations.
July 31	Prior to resumption of talks, Poli announced an August 3 strike if no agreement was reached by then.
July 31	Lewis agreed to resumption of talks.
July 31	New PATCO demands; Lewis indicated he needed time to cost proposals; Lewis asked Poli to call off strike deadline; Poli refused.
August 1	Lewis rejected union proposal as excessive and unreasonable; again asked Poli to call off strike deadline; Poli refused.
August 2	Parties met again; Poli asked for FAA counterproposal; Lewis increased $40 million package to $50 million—on "certain conditions."
August 2	Poli rejected the counterproposal.
August 3	Controller strike began.

Based on this summary chronology, Graham concluded that the FAA had bargained in good faith by agreeing to meet and confer with the union, by proposing alternative packages for consideration, and by requesting time to consider and respond to PATCO proposals. He faulted PATCO for imposing arbitrary and unreasonable time frames for agreement that effectively precluded agreement. Graham also said that the FAA's duty "to bargain was suspended on Aug. 3 after the rank-and-file overwhelmingly rejected a $40 million-a-year contract offer the government made in late June."[6] What the union had hoped would be a finding against the government turned into a finding against the union.

On August 26, the joint observation team of government and union officials in Canada issued their first report. The team was established to monitor air safety in flights between Canada and the United States as a condition of settling the two-day boycott of U.S. flights by Canadian controllers. A spokesperson for the team indicated that the report would show a higher-than-normal number of errors was occurring. Bill Robertson, president of the Canadian Air Traffic Controllers, indicated that "the definite conclusion is being reached that it's because of untrained personnel operating in the U.S."[7] The Reagan administration refused to comment on the report. However, Secretary Lewis indicated willingness to meet with representatives of the International Federation of Air Traffic Controllers Associations to discuss safety issues.

The Commerce Department's Bureau of Industrial Economics issued its report on August 27 on the economic impact of the strike. The report indicated that there would be relatively minor long-run adverse impact but that specific sectors of the economy may be hit harder. Specifically hard hit would be the commuter airlines, financially weak major carriers, and state and local governments. The last category of participants experienced losses because the costs related to airport maintenance continued, but landing fees and collateral revenues were substantially reduced. Benefiting from the strike would be major carriers that are in a sound financial condition, buses and trains, rental car agencies, small suburban airports, and manufacturers of executive aircraft.[8]

At the beginning of the fourth week of the strike, a Harris Survey found Americans less supportive of the administration's handling of the strike. A bare majority of 51 percent of respondents agreed with the administration's position. There was strong support for the president in terms of his firing the controllers to uphold the law, but there was equally strong support for the controllers' claims of job stress.

Nevertheless, the government hardline against rehiring controllers continued in full force. As part of their strategy, "the Department of Housing and Urban Development announced that it would deny to fired controllers the standard federal aid offered to people behind in home-mortgage payments."[9] Arguing on the other side, John J. O'Donnell, president of ALPA, urged consideration for the controllers. He said, "No one disputes the fact that the strike is illegal. But I would hope President Reagan could find compassion to respond to the needs of a greater majority of the controllers who are family men—to try to take those steps to get the system going again."[10]

Addressing a convention of the Seafarers International Union, Lane Kirkland, president of the AFL–CIO, enlisted comments by former President

Eisenhower in which the former president said a man would have to be a "fool" to break a union and that "the right of men to leave their jobs is a test of freedom."[11] Kirkland then used President Reagan's campaign pledges as a reminder of how the President felt before the strike. The president had criticized the Carter administration for its handling of the air traffic control system. Candidate Reagan had criticized the "deplorable state" of the system in which there were "too few people working unreasonable hours" on "obsolete equipment." Now, Kirkland observed, the administration continues to declare the skies safe when it is "operating with less than half the normal work force and using 'less skilled strikebreakers.'"[12]

Adhering to the deadline to submit formal exceptions to administrative law judge (ALJ) John H. Fenton's recommendation that PATCO be decertified as the controllers' exclusive representative, the union responded on September 1 with an extensive list of exceptions. The exceptions addressed concerns about the "undue haste" with which the recommendations were made, questions about ex parte contacts between the ALJ and the FAA and the FLRA general counsel, and the absence of due process. The PATCO brief argued that controllers remaining on the job needed representation for pending issues that were unrelated to the strike. The union argued that there were appropriate remedies that fell short of decertification that would achieve the intent of the law. These remedies could "range from mild sanctions to very severe penalties just short of revocation of representation status."[13]

The union then took the astounding position that the PATCO National union may not have been involved in the alleged strike. The union argued that "even assuming that a strike took place, the evidence is insufficient to support the conclusion that PATCO National—the only respondent in this case—called it or participated in it."[14]

On September 8, the International Confederation of Free Trade Unions (ICFTU) filed a formal complaint against the U.S. government with the International Labor Organization (ILO). The complaint charged the U.S. government with the "infringement of basic trade union rights." In addition, the complaint alleged violation of three specific ILO conventions, that is, Nos. 87, 98, and 151. The complaint "contends that the U.S. government failed to bargain with the union, did not provide adequate safeguards in the absence of the right to strike, and discriminated against PATCO in several ways—urging workers to disassociate from the union, prosecuting the union, pursuing criminal indictments, imprisoning controllers, and levying excessive fines."[15]

While the specifications in the complaint are lengthy and detailed, one aspect of the submission warrants brief review. Under the section entitled "Failure to Bargain," the complaint alleges that FAA Administrator Helms refused to attend bargaining sessions with the PATCO. Specifically, the complaint alleges:

The Administration of the FAA, the only person authorized by United States law to bargain on certain safety issues presented by the union to the government, refused to attend any bargaining session both before and after June 22. This position, together with the government's refusal to bargain at all after August 3, is clear violation of the requirement to negotiate and obtain collective agreements.[16]

One might argue that since Secretary Drew Lewis was intimately involved in the negotiations, a subordinate, Helms, need not be present. If the ICFTU's contention is accurate, however, it is perplexing to understand why a key official with the day-to-day knowledge of FAA operations would not participate in the negotiation process. No one would be in a better position to discuss current issues important to the controllers than the administrator of the agency.

Throughout the early weeks of the strike, various estimates were made of the cost the strike imposed on the economy. Another important cost that was infrequently discussed was the direct cost of training and retraining the thousands of controllers needed to replace the strikers. While a precise estimate was difficult, Tom Donahue, secretary-treasurer of the AFL–CIO, said, "[I]t will cost in excess of $2 billion to train replacements for the striking members of the Professional Air Traffic Controllers Organization and to return the system to its former level of operation."[17] The source of his estimate was not provided, but he noted, "The nation is paying an enormous cost for the PATCO strike."[18]

On September 15, the PATCO appealed to the FLRA to order the agency and the union back to the bargaining table rather than decertify the union. Attorneys for the FAA rejected the proposed remedy on the grounds that such an order would in effect sanction strikes by government employees. The FAA representatives said that the PATCO had violated a federal law and under the statute decertification was the appropriate remedy. Ironically, the government attorneys argued that during the process prior to oral arguments in the case the union had provided "not a scintilla of evidence" that it did not engage in the August 3 strike. The union had argued earlier that there was no proof of its participation. One would suggest that if the presumption of innocence is basic to the system of jurisprudence, then, the burden relies on the government and not on the union.

The union argued for a thirty-day negotiation period. If that period failed to bring agreement, the proposal called for the use of an arbitrator to make recommendations to the FLRA before it made its final decision. Richard Leighton, representing the PATCO, asked for an "interim order" that would force the parties to resume collective bargaining. He argued that "the 'most qualified' parties to resolve the dispute are the parties themselves."[19] Arguing that the FLRA's main purpose is to help the parties find solutions to their problems, he noted that the course of action he proposed "could lead to a 'solution that benefits the public.'"[20]

FLRA member Henry Frazier III asked Leighton whether the PATCO had sought the involvement of a federal mediator or the Federal Services Impasses Panel before the strike. Leighton indicated that there was no indication in the record that such overtures had occurred. Frazier indicated that he had checked the evidentiary record and the records of the FSIP and had found no indication that the PATCO had sought those services prior to the strike. While not saying it explicitly, Frazier was asking the PATCO why these types of intervention were so critical now but had not been considered important prior to the strike.

In October, the House of Representatives held hearings on the strike. Little new ground was broken. However, Administrator Helms told the Post Office and Civil Service Committee that the agency had received over 125,000 applications for the controller positions and therefore had a pool of extremely qualified applicants to choose from. He also told the committee, "The agency estimates that it costs $160,000 to train a fully qualified controller, so the training bill for 12,000 replacements could be slightly under $2 billion."[21] However, since the agency did not have to pay the salaries of the displaced controllers, the government would have a net savings of about $200 million each year.

Counselor to the president Edwin Meese, too, reaffirmed the administration's position. With a semblance of stability in the industry and the belief that they had won, Meese told reporters, "'There's no way . . . and no reason' to rehire the 11,438 controllers who were fired for walking off their jobs Aug. 3. I can't imagine that happening,' because the PATCO strike 'is so clearly a violation' of federal law."[22]

Testimony continued over the next several weeks as witness after witness urged the president to reinstate negotiations and seek settlement of the strike. Increasingly, other sectors of the economy such as trucking, aircraft production and repair, and others were adversely affected by the cutbacks in the aviation sector. John Leyden, former PATCO president, argued that a decision to take the strikers back would not be viewed as a sign of weakness but rather as a sign of strength and compassion. He noted, "History measures a man or a president not only on his ability to be firm and resolute during times of challenge but in the charity displayed after the battle. The quality of mercy is not strained and I sincerely hope our President is equal to the task."[23]

As expected, on October 22, 1981, the Federal Labor Relations Authority voted to decertify PATCO as the exclusive bargaining agent for the controllers. The vote was two to one in favor of immediate decertification. Chairman Ronald Haughton dissented on immediate decertification and indicated that a more appropriate remedy would be remand of the case to the Authority's chief administrative law judge to hold further hearings and determine an appropriate remedy. None of the Authority members disagreed that the PATCO had committed an unfair labor practice by its strike action, but Haughton didn't believe that immediate decertification was the appropriate remedy. The chairman suggested that the remand motion was appropriate *if* the union ceased its strike within five days of the order and agreed to abide by the law's no-strike provisions in the future.[24]

Predictably, Robert Poli denounced the FLRA decision. He argued that the Authority had not investigated all the circumstances surrounding the strike. He told reporters that he would seek a court order to stay the FLRA decision and appeal the decision to the courts. He argued further that the public was beginning to see the controllers' conditions that led to the strike. Attempting to recast the nature of the strike, he blamed the situation on the administration's "lock-out" and argued that the administration had spurned all of the union's efforts to compromise. He then said, "'I'm as proud of my members today as I was of them on Aug. 3.' He said the only mistake he made 'was naivete in believing the promises' of candidate Ronald Reagan."[25]

Administration officials labeled the FLRA ruling a "sound and responsible decision." Secretary Lewis told reporters that he would be proposing to the Congress a pay and benefit package almost identical to the one rejected by the PATCO. He also noted that the FLRA decision "affirms a basic principle of our democracy, that no person or organization is above the law and that the citizens of this country cannot be allowed to pick and choose the laws they will obey."[26]

In a minor victory, the PATCO obtained a court order to temporarily stay the FLRA decision. The union told the court that implementation of the FLRA order would cause major harm to the union because the 2,000 controllers who remained on the job would not have their dues automatically paid to the PATCO through the checkoff. The court of appeals agreed to stay the FLRA action until the government responded to the union's concerns.

With a government motion opposing the Ccurt-ordered stay of the FLRA decision, the U.S. Court of Appeals for the District of Columbia Circuit lifted the stay on October 27, 1981. The government argued that the PATCO had received sufficient time to defend its case before the FLRA and that the decision to decertify the union was in the public interest. The court agreed with the government's position.

After the court of appeals lifted the injunction, the FLRA moved forward with decertification. The Authority noted in its written order:

With respect to the appropriate remedy, a majority of the Authority, member Applewhaite and I, held that section 7120(f) of the statute gave the Authority discretion to revoke PATCO's exclusive recognition status, or take any other appropriate action. Member Frazier was of the view that such discretion was extremely limited. Applying that section to this case, Frazier and Applewhaite, for the Authority, ordered exclusive recognition status be revoked.[27]

Haughton deferred his support of the order giving the PATCO a chance to order its members back to work. The overture by the chairman was gratuitous and rang hollow because the chairman knew that the PATCO had no ability to return to work, and further, the government had declared the strike "over" before the first week had expired. Haughton noted that if the union did not comply with his suggestions, he would concur with the Authority's decertification order. The PATCO responded to this position by saying:

As PATCO understands Chairman Haughton's decision, the only way that we could comply would be to order our members to return to work. However, PATCO's members have been locked out by their former employer and could not return to work even if so ordered.

The preceding notwithstanding, however, in an effort to comply with Chairman Haughton's decision, and to the extent of our ability to comply, when the FAA ends its lockout, PATCO would immediately order all of its members to return to work.[28]

This response by the PATCO was insufficient, and a formal decision decertifying the PATCO was issued by the FLRA on November 3, 1981. Thus, exactly three months after the strike began, the PATCO was no longer the exclusive bargaining agent for the air traffic controllers. This action effectively cut off all sources of direct funding for the PATCO and precluded the union from performing representational duties for the controllers.

The decertification decision had particular significance in public sector labor relations. "The decision to revoke the union's right to represent its members was a 2-1 vote of the three-member board. It was the first time the agency [the Federal Labor Relations Authority] had decertified a union."[29] This action, twelve weeks after the strike, sent chills through the ranks of all organized labor. Many could not believe that the federal government would break a union representing federal employees.

In a last desperate attempt to save the union, Robert Poli made a public statement in which he said he would call off the strike if the government would rehire the fired controllers. However, he made clear that the controllers had been "locked out" by the FAA since August 5, and therefore he did not have unilateral authority to end the stoppage. "'We're in a situation now where our people have been on strike for three months.' Poli said. 'The public is suffering, the economy is suffering. I think in the best interests of everybody; at this time, it would be my position I would tell the people to return to work.'"[30]

The FAA was under continued pressure to begin bringing the U.S. air traffic control system up to prestrike strength. The FAA plans called for the training of over 8,000 new controllers to replace the 11,438 who had been fired. The initial training program used by the FAA provided for seventeen to twenty weeks of classroom training, followed by progressively responsible on-the-job training at control facilities. As noted earlier, it can take as long as four years for a new controller to attain full proficiency.

In early November, a consortium of labor union officials and public interest groups filed suit in U.S. District Court to compel the Reagan administration to rehire the fired controllers. Consumer advocate Ralph Nader and Douglas Fraser, president of the United Auto Workers, announced the suit. They argued that the refusal of the administration to rehire the controllers jeopardized public health and safety. Fraser also noted that the August 3 strike "for all practical purposes, has been lost. The union's been destroyed. . . . He [President Reagan] has not only won the battle. He's won the whole goddamned war. The Administration has gotten its pound of flesh and now should exhibit an ounce of compassion."[31]

The plaintiffs were quick to point out that their suit was not taken on behalf of the air traffic controllers or the decertified PATCO. They argued that their suit took no position on the correctness of the administration's actions relative to the August 3 strike. Rather, the suit aimed at the harm the continued reliance on inexperienced controllers was having on the economy and the traveling public. The administration snubbed its nose at the lawsuit and argued that it was "groundless."

In late November, allegations of training problems began to circulate. Specifically, there were allegations that the FAA had manipulated test scores at the Oklahoma City training center to give the impression that a larger number of controllers were passing the test than were in fact passing it. Representative William Ford wrote to FAA Administrator Helms complaining about what Ford's staff had found concerning altered test scores. He alleged that test scores had been altered so that the number of students passing the November 19 examination had increased from seventy-nine to ninety-five to give the impression that all was working well in the retraining program. The FAA vehemently denied any test tampering. It argued that the changed scores were a result of technical corrections that had no bearing on the students' overall performance in their new profession.

Unconvinced by the FAA's explanation, Congressman Ford asked the inspector general of the Transportation Department to investigate the allegations. In addition, the congressman told the FAA that he would send two staff members to the training academy to investigate the charges.

As the impasse moved into the fall months, the administration submitted a proposal to the Congress to increase the pay of air traffic controllers. The proposal, according to Congressman Ford, "is about $17.5 million more than the $40 million which reportedly was offered by the government in negotiations with the Professional Air Traffic Controllers Organization."[32]

An important question now was, How and why did the government come up with an additional $17.5 million (almost 50 percent more than the government's final offer) for the controllers less than four months after the strike? If these resources were available, but not used, then the administration may have been bargaining in bad faith. The administration argued that the "upper limit" of their wage offer was $40 million because of the economic conditions in the country. It let a strike occur that jeopardized safety in the air traffic system, that resulted in the firing of over 11,000 controllers, and that disrupted segments of the economy in substantial ways. One must wonder how these additional resources suddenly became available after the union had been destroyed. It is not sufficient evidence that the administration was determined to destroy the union, but it does provide evidence that supports the position of those who argue that the administration had, in fact, established a course of action that led to union-busting.

The lawsuit initiated by Douglas Fraser and Ralph Nader not only was spurned by the FAA; members of Congress filed a countersuit designed to neutralize any efforts to rehire the controllers. Fifteen members of the House of Representatives filed a petition in U.S. District Court because they believed that the law "clearly intended that the federal workers who violate their oaths to refrain from illegal strikes would no longer enjoy employment."[33]

Congressman Edwards (R–Okla.) argued that the strikers were lucky that the government had lenience and only fired them. If the government had chosen, it could have sought to fine the strikers in amounts up to $1,000 and imprisonment for their offenses. The congressman argued, "The air controllers knew what they were getting into when they failed to report to work. They all agreed not to strike when they were hired, and the law said that they would lose their jobs if they did. A government job is not a right, and it is not a lifetime position. Those who break the agreement under which they were hired must suffer the consequences of their actions."[34]

In spite of congressional resistance, in early December, the president issued a statement that suggested a more conciliatory stance on the rehiring of the fired air traffic controllers. In a meeting with Teamsters officials, the president said in passing that he was "considering" rescinding the order that precludes hiring fired controllers for "any" federal job for a period of three years. This comment was heralded as a major breakthrough in the impasse between the president and the now-defunct PATCO. Administration spokesman David Gergen quickly pointed out that the president's overtures were not to be construed as a signal that fired controllers would be returning to the centers and towers. Gergen argued, "There has been no change in the president's fundamental position regarding air traffic controllers."[35]

The literal meaning of Gergen's comments was that the president was considering lifting the three-year ban on federal employment for positions *other than* those from which the controllers had been fired. This gesture by the president signaled an apparent thaw in relations between some segments of organized labor and the administration. However, Kenneth Blaylock, president of the American Federation of Government Employees, labeled the president's gesture a "smoke screen." He observed that "between 100,000 and 150,000 federal workers are likely to lose their jobs over the next 12 months due to federal budget cuts, and that there would be few job opportunities for controllers."[36]

While the president was apparently willing to relax restrictions on future employment opportunities, he continued to press controllers in other aspects of their lives by denying applications for unemployment insurance benefits, ordering controllers into court for alleged illegal acts after the administration declared the strike over, and denying controllers access to the Department of Housing and Urban Development assistance programs for individuals behind on their mortgage payments.[37] Since most of these programs are federally funded or federally controlled, several states with large numbers of controllers refused benefits to striking controllers in support of the federal process.[38] While state agencies establish their own regulations and procedures for awarding unemployment compensation benefits, the umbrella organization determining the structure and operational requirements for the entire system is the U.S. Department of Labor or the U.S. Department of Housing and Urban Development. One need not stretch far to see how the state agencies felt compelled to support the federal action.

On Pearl Harbor Day in 1981, columnist William Raspberry of the *Washington Post* joined the chorus of those who believed the president should reconsider amnesty for the strikers. Raspberry acknowledged the illegality of the strike. However, he believed that five months of punishment was enough. Speaking to what he called a "long American tradition of being uncompromising in war and generous in victory," Raspberry drew parallels to the wartime activities of Japan and Germany. He noted, "If America could restore its relations with Germany and Japan, elevating those vanquished countries to the status of allies and helping to lift their economies to unprecedented heights, surely it can muster enough compassion to help the defeated air traffic controllers to go back to supporting their families."[39]

Whether the analogy between the PATCO strike and the vagaries of the postwar are appropriate, Raspberry had a point. However, nobody in the administration seemed to understand or appreciate the point. Raspberry summarized his feelings by appealing to the president's earlier union activities. Raspberry argued that

as a former union president, Reagan ought to understand that the necessity for solidarity sometimes can lead workers to do foolish things, especially when they are certain that they are right on the basic issues. The air traffic controllers clearly thought they were right to demand some relief from the stress of their jobs; the tough hours; the deteriorating equipment; the pressures that led to an uncommon number of medical retirements. Indeed, candidate Reagan agreed with them and pledged, as president, to do something to help. Obviously, they miscalculated in assuming that his pledge of support meant that they would not be punished for their illegal strike.[40]

In mid-December, the International Labor Organization convened its annual meeting in Geneva, Switzerland. The ILO's Freedom of Association Committee discussed the character and outcome of the air traffic controller strike and the manner in which the U.S. government handled the strike. Grasping the opportunity to criticize the United States, Soviet Union delegate Vladimir I. Prokhorov lambasted the actions taken by the administration. He argued, "The controllers have become, since the strike, the subject of repression: they have been arrested: there have been dismissals: they have been brought before the courts: and in order to break the strike the government decided to deprive the trade union of the right to represent the interests of its members."[41] Prokhorov concluded that the response of the U.S. government to the strike was "a violation of the elementary rights of trade unions." He continued, "It seems to me this is an unprecedented case in the whole history of trade unions, not only in America but in the world."[42]

Robert Searby, deputy under secretary of labor and chief delegate to the ILO meeting, defended the U.S. actions as being in accordance with the law and appropriate under the circumstances. He argued that most countries place restrictions on the right of public employees to strike, but the United States provides a number of mechanisms such as mediation and arbitration to resolve differences that arise between public sector unions and their employers. He expressed frustration that the PATCO had not availed itself to those dispute resolution mechanisms.

On December 8, the National Transportation Safety Board released its independent review of safety in the aviation sector. The report was generally positive but raised possible concerns about the safety implications of tired and stressed controllers who work long hours. The report indicated that the investigation found no instances of unqualified controllers manning the system, as the PATCO had charged repeatedly. The report did question the ability of the FAA to train sufficient controllers to bring the system up to prestrike levels of performance by 1984. The report characterized this projection by the administration as "extremely optimistic."

The one area of FAA-controller interaction that the report was most critical about was that of labor-management relations within the FAA. The National Transportation Safety Board "also strongly criticized the FAA's handing [sic] of employee relations. Unless you improve, King said, 'we'll be faced with another labor dispute downstream.' Staff members said that many of the causes of the poor relations had not been corrected."[43] Since the study only covered the two-month period immediately after the strike, one must conclude that what they found was a reflection of problems by employed controllers who were fully sensitized by the ongoing calamity. Nevertheless, the several thousand employed controllers strongly criticized the labor-management relations processes and procedures used by the FAA. If conditions were not as the PATCO alleged, one would think that controllers who did not go on strike would not be critical of conditions. Since they were sharply critical suggests that the PATCO's allegations had some merit.

On December 9, the formal decision of the president concerning the employment rights of fired controllers was released. The decision provided that controllers could apply for and hold other positions in federal service, but they could not return to their former controller positions. In fact, the instructions sent to the Office of Personnel Management (OPM) explicitly directed that striking controllers "should not be deemed suitable for employment in the Federal Aviation Administration." In modifying the three-year ban on federal employment, the White House statement noted that the president embraced "another principle we honor in America—the tradition that individuals deserve to be treated with compassion. I do not believe that those who forfeited their jobs as controllers should be foreclosed from other federal employment. I am sure that many of those who were misled or badly advised regret their action and would welcome an opportunity to return to federal service."[44]

Representatives of the AFL–CIO who had met with the president a week earlier were not thrilled by the decision. They argued that their position with the president had been one of restoring controllers to the jobs they had been trained to perform. PATCO representative Marcia Feldman called the directive a "cruel hoax" because there were no jobs to be had in federal service by the controllers or anybody else, with the possible exception, of course, of the FAA. Therefore, the decision by the president was less than it appeared. Donald Devine, OPM director, acknowledged that there were few job openings in the federal government other than in the Defense Department. William Raspberry called the presidential action "more symbolic and psychological than practical."[45]

Two days after the president's directive was issued, three former controllers were sentenced to jail for violating a federal judge's order to return to work. The three men were shackled and handcuffed as they were led by U.S. marshals out of the federal courtroom. The graphic pictures of these three men, all in business suits and ties, as they were led away for incarceration, stands as a spectacle of a system that spun out of control. In "Letters to the Editor" of the *Washington Post*, a Hyattsville, Maryland, reader characterized the sentiment related to that picture. He argued that something is wrong in the country when

union officials are shackled and led off to prison, and criminals are routinely released on personal recognizance after being arrested for rape, murder, bank robbery, assault and just about any other crime you can name.

The government under President Reagan seems to have its priorities mixed up. A Post [*Washington Post*] story on Dec. 11 reported that the Justice Department is considering not prosecuting the thousands of young men who did not register for the draft, because the president is not sure that he agrees with the law requiring registration. I would like to ask if this country is to enforce only the laws that Mr. Reagan agrees with. I hope not. The country may have voted for a change, but it didn't vote for one-man rule.[46]

The earlier alleged problem with grade changes at the FAA Training Academy took on a more serious note in late December. Congressman Ford indicated that a congressional investigation had uncovered evidence that grades of controller trainees were manipulated to improve the public image of the academy. Ford released a committee staff report indicating that the staff was "persuaded that the grade changes were to improve the academy's sagging public image."[47] In addition, Congressman Ford alleged that testimony by FAA administrator J. Lynn Helms and academy director Benjamin Demps, Jr., were "less than candid." These government officials had testified that while there was no question that grade changes had occurred, they had occurred to "correct computer errors in grading."[48] The committee report indicated that when they testified, "Demps knew and Helms should have known that 26 scores had been altered and some of the changes had nothing to do with computer errors."[49]

Further damage to the government's position occurred in the form of a court order dismissing criminal indictments against PATCO leaders in Colorado. The U.S. District Court for Colorado said that the government selected PATCO leaders and placed them on a "hit list" for prosecution in the event that a strike occurred. This "prosecutive targets" list had been developed by the FAA as early as February 1981. Judge John L. Kane, Jr., found these facts to be significant "because not only had the previous FAA-PATCO collective bargaining agreement not expired at that time but also because the FAA and the union were supposed to be negotiating in good faith on a successor [contract]."[50]

In addition, the Justice Department had deviated from normal procedures in which local U.S. attorneys are given discretion to choose prosecutorial targets. The Justice Department had communicated the "hit list" to the field structure before any criminal activity had occurred. The list contained the names of union leaders, known as "choir boys," who were believed to be those who would whip the local union members into adopting a hard-line strike position. The government was unable, however, to show that those who had been targeted were the strike leaders or that they performed contrary to other activities protected by the statute. Therefore, Judge Kane concluded "that the defendants were selectively prosecuted on the basis of their protected activities in connection with their positions as union presidents and representatives."[51] Three months later, Judge Thomas C. Platt, of the U.S. District Court for the Eastern District of New York, issued an order that rejected the union's contention of selective prosecution. This decision stood in sharp contrast to the decision by Judge Kane that dismissed the indictments against strikers in Colorado.

At year's end, the lawsuit filed by five unions and two consumer advocacy groups was dismissed by the U.S. Court for the District of Columbia. The presiding judge, Judge Oberdorfer, reasoned that the plaintiffs had not exhausted all of their administrative remedies prior to seeking judicial intervention. Specifically, the judge noted the failure of the plaintiffs to voice their complaints about the contingency plan the FAA had published in March 1981. The plan contained the provisions for curtailment of air service under certain conditions. Because the plaintiffs failed to raise objections about the plan during the comment period, they could not petition the court to intervene after implementation, five months later. The court ruled that the plaintiffs could seek relief in an appropriate district or appeals court if they were denied relief from a petition to the FAA. The plaintiffs indicated that they would exhaust the administrative remedies first and then consider a judicial challenge if needed.

To kick off the New Year, Administrator Helms unveiled his plans for restructuring the nation's air traffic control system. Named the National Airspace System Plan, his proposal called for automating the air traffic control functions to the maximum extent possible. He planned to merge airport radar rooms and enroute centers; automate some of the weather information routinely transmitted to pilots in flight; eliminate ground-based radio, radar, and other facilities as new technology permitted; establish collision avoidance hardware; install advanced computers with more reliable backup capabilities; and so forth. The plan released on January 1, 1982, did not contain cost estimates, but those close to the industry believed that it would approach $10 billion over the life of the development program.

Also on January 1, 1982, Robert Poli resigned as president of the PATCO. Stating that his continued presence as PATCO president posed a stumbling block in the process of controllers' regaining their jobs, he decided to step aside. However, in leaving his position, Poli refused to acknowledge that the strike was unwarranted or unnecessary. He told reporters, "I will never, as long as I have a breath left in me, say that the issues for which we struck were incorrect, that we did not have a good reason for going on strike."[52] As he departed the presidency, Poli said that the only thing he would have done differently would have been to tell the union story better. He said he "goofed" by letting the administration convince the media and the public that the only issue of concern to air controllers was money.

Two days later, the only executive board member of the PATCO who had been jailed during the strike, Gary Eads, was named as Poli's replacement. Eads had been a controller in the Kansas City Air Route Traffic Control Center for over ten years. He had served as the Central Region vice president for the PATCO for three years preceding the strike.

While expressing no support for the striking controllers, on January 1, PATCO members who had not gone on strike indicated their intentions of forming another union and initiating legal action to secure union funds that had been lost as a result of the strike. Attorneys representing nonstriking controllers petitioned the U.S. District Court for the District of Columbia "to order an election among nonstriking controllers and direct the Federal Aviation Administration to bargain collectively with the new union officials."[53]

Ironically, four PATCO staff members had been terminated for trying to form a staff union within the PATCO. An administrative law judge for the NLRB ruled that the terminations were illegal because the plaintiffs "were terminated solely for their union and concerted activities" and therefore should be rehired by the PATCO and awarded back pay. However, since the PATCO had been decertified as the exclusive bargaining agent for the controllers, there were no jobs to return to. PATCO still existed as a union, but without bargaining responsibilities and without the inflow of dues, its days were numbered. The union was in bankruptcy with over $150 million in fines and other penalties outstanding. The four former staff members would have a long wait to collect their back pay as well.

EX PARTE DISCUSSIONS BY GOVERNMENT OFFICIALS

Throughout the first six months of the strike, the PATCO's major defensive action was an effort to retain exclusive bargaining rights for the air traffic controllers. As the PATCO attempted to have the courts overturn the FLRA decertification order, a new issue surfaced. Sometime prior to the vote for decertification by the FLRA, a member of the Authority had dinner with a prominent labor leader. At some point late in the dinner meeting, the subject of discussion turned to the PATCO case pending before the Authority. The two individuals discussed the case.

The exact character and content of the discussion will never be known, but what is clear is that a government official who had the responsibility to decide the certification issue had an ex parte discussion with another interested party. It was finally revealed that the union official was Albert Shanker, president of the American Federation of Teachers Union. He had dinner with FLRA member Leon B. Applewhaite in September, prior to the vote by the FLRA on PATCO certification.

There was no question about where Shanker stood on the PATCO issue. He argued strongly and publicly for the rehiring of the fired controllers. In his public statements and prominent position in the labor movement, Applewhaite had to have known Shanker's position on this issue. Nevertheless, Applewhaite accepted a dinner invitation by Shanker, who Applewhaite called a longtime friend and professional colleague.

The troubling aspect of this encounter was not the meeting itself but the fact that when the issue of the PATCO arose, Applewhaite did not terminate the discussion. Becoming an FLRA member does not preclude an individual from retaining prior friendships, but it does impose an ethical code that precludes entering into ex parte discussions about issues pending decision.

The issue in question goes to motivation. Shanker's dinner invitation undoubtedly was motivated, at least in part, by an interest to share his strongly held views with Applewhaite. Shanker certainly knew who Applewhaite was and what his role was in the PATCO situation. In fact, Shanker candidly admitted that he wanted to share his feelings with Applewhaite directly rather than through the press. Applewhaite, knowing Shanker's beliefs, should probably not have accepted the dinner invitation. He argued, however, that he did not know what Shanker wanted to talk about, which may be a reasonable position. Applewhaite accepted the dinner invitation of an old friend.

Up to this point, Applewhaite may have been motivated by the simple desire to have dinner with an old colleague and friend. However, where the story gets into trouble is at the point at which the discussion turned to the PATCO. Testimony by both individuals indicates that the PATCO situation did not come up for discussion until late in the meeting. When this occurred, regardless of his prior affiliation with Shanker, Applewhaite had a moral and ethical responsibility to terminate the discussion. He chose not to end the discussion.

Applewhaite ultimately voted for decertification of the PATCO. In that sense, one may infer that the Shanker overture was not effective. However, that isn't the point. While Applewhaite and Shanker met privately and discussed the PATCO, there is also evidence that other administration officials, including Secretary Lewis, called FLRA members to inquire about the "status" of the case. These discussions, regardless of their substance, gave the appearance that high-level officials had access to FLRA members, on a private basis, to discuss this case. When these types of interactions occur, one cannot know how they influenced, if they did influence, the final decision in the case. That is the problem. Decisions by individuals such as Applewhaite are supposed to be based on an impartial review of all the evidence in the case. They are not supposed to be tainted by private discussions with other individuals who have an interest in the outcome of the case. Once these discussions have occurred, no one can determine what, if any, influence affected the final decision.

There were allegations that Applewhaite, a Republican, was concerned about being reappointed to the FLRA by the Reagan administration and about his work opportunities after his tenure on the Authority. There was some evidence that he discussed these issues with Shanker and at meetings with various administration officials. Whether or not there was substantial discussion about his current and postprofessional activities is somewhat beyond the point. The public could reasonably infer that some types of discussion took place, and if that was the case, the impartiality of the decision was drawn into question. These allegations were not resolved quickly, but other events occurred during the same interval that require discussion.

The Air Florida Crash

On January 13, 1982, a major air disaster occurred in Washington, D.C. An Air Florida Boeing 737 crashed into the Potomac River shortly after takeoff from Washington's National Airport. Seventy-eight people died in the crash. It was snowing in Washington, and there were delays in arrivals and departures at National Airport. The conjunction of bad weather and inexperienced controllers may have created a situation in which Air Florida Flight 90 was cleared for takeoff without being adequately deiced for departure.

Surrounding the tragedy were several questions that required attention. First, due to system delays, Flight 90 was on the ground at National Airport for an extended period of time—probably for about one and a half hours—prior to its takeoff clearance. The question to be resolved is whether the heavy snow accumulated on the wings of the Boeing 737 in sufficient amounts to disturb the air flow over the wings and therefore reduce lift. In addition, accumulated snow may have added appreciable weight to the airplane and therefore made it difficult to climb. Second, since Flight 90 had a difficult time accelerating as it started its takeoff roll, there may have been two aircraft on the main runway at National Airport at the same time. An Eastern flight was on final approach to the airport as Flight 90 was given clearance to takeoff. Radar information indicated that the two airplanes came within 0.9 miles of each other. If these data are accurate, both airplanes were apparently on the runway at the same time.

Were it not for the horrifying tragedy of the crash, one could have expected the PATCO to argue strongly that the crash was caused by controller inexperience. Soon after the crash and the dramatic rescues that made several instant heroes, questions by the National Transportation Safety Board began arising about why Flight 90 was given permission to depart under the conditions that existed. The controller who actually gave Flight 90 its clearance was Stanley Gromelski. He was a supervisor in the National Airport tower who had taken more control responsibilities after the PATCO strike. Under questioning, he discounted the suggestion that he had let the two airplanes get too close together. Concerning "separation rules," Gromelski argued that he used what "I was taught 20 years ago. I've been using it for 20 years and it's never failed."[54]

What Gromelski was talking about were the separation standards controllers used in the departure and approach sequences. To facilitate traffic flows, controllers may vector aircraft closer to one another than what is provided in the published FAA standards. Under normal circumstances, with experienced controllers, these operations are routine and safe. Under less-than-normal conditions, prudence may have suggested a more conservative spacing process. It is easy in hindsight to second-guess the decision process of the National Airport controllers, but due to weather conditions and the limitations of recorded radar data, the true relationship between the Air Florida and Eastern flight will never be known. In addition, the spacing between the two flights did not cause the Flight 90 crash. In fact, the pilots of the two airplanes never saw one another. The Eastern pilot said he saw Air Florida's tracks on the runway as Eastern touched down, but he never saw the Air Florida Boeing 737 on the runway or in flight.

POSTSTRIKE CONTROLLER ATTITUDES

In late January, in an apparent attempt to convince themselves that they had acted in the interest of the membership, the PATCO conducted a survey of its membership. While the survey had several parts, of most interest was that the vast majority of striking controllers supported the strike action. In fact, "[d]espite the failure of their strike against the Federal Aviation Administration, nearly two-thirds of air traffic controllers who walked out last August would do it again under the same conditions."[55] Significantly, only one third of the surveyed controllers felt they had violated the law. One fourth of respondents felt the union had led them "down the primrose path." While virtually all surveyed controllers indicated that they would return to work if the government offered them their jobs back, many—about 40 percent—said they would only go back if the government addressed some of their grievances. Of the respondents, only about 5 percent said they would not go back to work for the FAA under any conditions.

Only 2 percent of the surveyed controllers said they could not work with individuals who had not gone out on strike. The remaining 98 percent of respondents said they could work effectively with any competent controller.[56]

However, survey results showed that striking controllers harbored deep-felt animosity against many of their colleagues who did not honor the picket lines. The strikers labeled most of those who remained on the job as "not having the fortitude to follow their convictions" or as "scabs." Only about 10 percent of the nonstrikers were characterized as following their convictions that "they did not have the right or privilege to strike against the government."[57]

A month after the PATCO survey, the Roper organization released a report showing that 58 percent of the *working* controllers opposed, unconditionally, the rehiring of any of the fired controllers.[58] Even though the working controllers believed the system was severely undermanned and that there was a limit on how long they could function under those conditions, a significant majority wanted no amnesty for striking controllers. About 31 percent of working controllers indicated that they would accept striking controllers back under certain conditions. Ten percent said that the controllers had paid "the price" and should be returned with no strings attached.[59]

The crosscurrents within these survey results make it difficult to assess how a return of the striking controllers would have affected the air traffic control system. There were bitterness, remorse, anxiety, frustration, and a variety of other sentiments about what happened and what role the various players assumed. It's likely that the vast majority of fired controllers could have resumed their professions with little or no animosity toward the nonstriking controllers or the FAA. However, it is also clear that there were a number of striking controllers who harbored extreme resentment and hatred toward those who did not strike. A major problem was that there was no way to differentiate the two factions.

THE JONES COMMITTEE REPORT

In mid-March, the Jones Committee submitted its report. Appointed by Secretary Lewis to study labor-management conditions in the FAA, the Jones Committee found a variety of poor management practices that contributed to the strike. In addition to the generally low morale found at "almost all levels" of the FAA, the task force blamed many of the agency's "people-problems" on incompetent managers and supervisors who were poorly trained for their jobs. The highly autocratic management style created tension between managers and controllers and led to the belief by controllers that management didn't care about them and was unconcerned about working conditions. The Jones Committee argued that factors that contributed to problems in the past were "reasserting themselves, and the FAA seems headed toward more people-related problems in the future."[60]

The 145-page Jones Commission Report "concluded that despite the strike and firing of 11,500 controllers, the FAA had made little effort to change its management approach and 'morale of most employees at almost all levels in the FAA is poor.'"[61] While there are no magic formulas for improving conditions in an agency with decades-long problems with its employees, the context within which these statements are made is one of a relatively small agency operating within a very narrow range of the aviation industry. One would think that in even six months there would be concrete management changes that at least had the possibility of improving working conditions.

Secretary Lewis acknowledged that relationships between management and labor had been deteriorating "over a period of years." He suggested that the FAA should implement the task force's recommendations over a several-year period so that "10 years from now the same problems do not occur again."[62] Ten years from now? Clearly, the secretary had no intention of implementing any of the Jones Committee recommendations. Rather, more rhetoric seemed appropriate to give the impression that decisive actions were being taken. "Transportation Secretary Drew Lewis, who ordered the outside study after the strike, told reporters that he expects no 'immediate solution' to the FAA's management problems but promised 'to begin as soon as possible the job of improving the working environment' for controllers."[63] One may reasonably ask why there would be no "immediate solution" to these problems of long duration. Managers in every organization, particularly top managers, set the tone for labor-management relations in the organization. If the secretary really believed the Jones Commission Report and the conclusions that it reached, why wouldn't there have been decisive changes in top FAA management immediately after the submission of the report?

Report after report showed the disparity between senior FAA managers and controllers and their immediate supervisors. Controllers and their immediate supervisors agreed concerning the problems of work hours, equipment condition, morale, stress, and the litany of other problems. Senior officials consistently argued that everything was in a "normal range" or that there was no problem. This disparity should have suggested to the secretary where to focus the change process. It's likely that the replacement of a relatively small number of senior managers would have gone a long way toward improving attitudes and conditions within the agency. To suggest that it would take many years to accomplish the change is simply not credible.

Clearly, the secretary did not take the report seriously. Rather, he indicated the intentions of beginning "as soon as possible" the task of improving working conditions for controllers. What this means is that there was no timetable for any type of improvement in management, programs, policies, or procedures. Rhetoric of this type is a delaying tactic that is premised on the belief that the public will tire of these issues and in a relatively short period of time forget about them. With the PATCO gone from the scene, the secretary was taking small risks that anybody would call his bluff.

As confirmation that the Jones Commission Report recommendations were not taken seriously, eight years after the strike, the General Accounting Office examined conditions in the air traffic control system. The shocking similarities between how controllers and supervisors felt about the system and what senior management felt about conditions in the system in the period before the strike and *eight* years later are almost beyond belief. The GAO reported, "Controllers and supervisors are troubled by working conditions and other aspects of today's [1989] air traffic control system that affect their ability to maintain the safety of the air traffic system. In contrast, facility managers viewed conditions much more favorably."[64] After eight years of efforts to improve conditions in the agency, the disparities between controllers and senior management persisted.

Importantly, committee chairman Lawrence M. Jones, president of the Coleman Company of Wichita, Kansas, reported that factors other than higher salaries were the primary motivation of the controller strike. He noted that economic considerations "did not seem to be a driving motive in any way."[65] This study result is in direct opposition to the position of the FAA stated publicly before and during the strike—namely, that money was the only issue of interest to the PATCO.

While the Jones Committee Report seemed to corroborate many of the concerns and problems the PATCO alluded to as causal factors in the strike, the next major event set back the union's cause. Special administrative law judge John M. Vittone ruled that the contacts between Albert Shanker, members of the administration, and members of the FLRA, described earlier, did not influence the final decision by the FLRA. There had been sharp differences between what Leon Applewhaite said transpired at the Shanker meeting and what Applewhaite apparently told his colleague Henry B. Frazier III had transpired. Frazier reported his feelings to the Justice Department, which set in motion an FBI investigation of the matter. Frazier said, "Applewhaite told him that Shanker said Applewhaite never could be appointed arbitrator in a grievance proceeding after leaving the Authority if he voted to decertify PATCO. Applewhaite maintained that no pressure was ever exerted."[66] Significantly, Applewhaite did not deny that Shanker had made the comment; he just maintained that no pressure was exerted.

Vittone resolved the apparent inconsistency between Frazier and Applewhaite by concluding that Frazier may have misunderstood what Applewhaite told him about the meeting. The ALJ also placed considerable weight on the testimony of the only other individual who knew what actually took place—Albert Shanker. Shanker maintained that there were no promises or threats made at the September 22 dinner. What could Shanker have told the ALJ? "I threatened Mr. Applewhaite and promised him cases as a labor arbitrator after his term at the FLRA." Obviously, Shanker would have indicated that there were no threats or promises because any other answer would have resulted in a direct violation of the law.

While the ALJ ruled in favor of the Authority, Vittone found some of Applewhaite's testimony "incredible in some respects and 'confusing and contradictory' in others."[67] He specifically noted conversations that Applewhaite had with the third Authority member, Chairman Ronald W. Haughton. Apparently, Applewhaite had told the chairman that the FBI agents praised Applewhaite for his courage relating to the Shanker dinner. The FBI agents contradicted Applewhaite's testimony, and the ALJ, too, suggested that it is "extremely doubtful that FBI agents praise the people they are investigating."[68]

While the Applewhaite-Shanker dinner was the most celebrated ex parte contacts relating to this case, there were other contacts between Authority members and other interested parties. These contacts occurred within the Authority, between Authority members and administration officials, several union officials and Authority members, and possibly members of the Congress and Authority members. In spite of all these contacts, ALJ Vittone ruled that none of them affected the decertification decision of the FLRA.

On June 11, 1982, the U.S. Circuit Court of Appeals upheld the FLRA decision to decertify the PATCO. The court noted, "We have carefully examined the alleged indiscretions and improprieties. Although we have found one (or possibly two) statutory infringements, we conclude that no parties have been prejudiced by the flaws in the proceedings."[69]

The court decision was unanimous. However, the court was less than kind to the several individuals who had engaged in ex parte discussions about the case. The judges were most critical of Albert Shanker's contacts with Leon Applewhaite. Shanker had attempted to convince the court that he was not an "interested" party, and therefore his contacts with Applewhaite were not forbidden by the FLRA rules. The court observed:

Even if we were to adopt Mr. Shanker's position that he was not an interested person, we are astonished at his claim that he did nothing wrong. Mr. Shanker frankly concedes that he "desired to have dinner with Member Applewhaite because he felt strongly about the PATCO case and wished to communicate directly to Member Applewhaite sentiments he had previously expressed in public."

While we appreciate Mr. Shanker's forthright admission, we must wonder whether it is a product of candor or a failure to comprehend that his conduct was improper.[70]

Since there were two sides to the dinner meeting, Applewhaite, too, bore some responsibility for not terminating the ex parte discussion. The court indicated that as the discussion turned to PATCO, "Member Applewhaite should have informed him [Shanker] in no uncertain terms that such behavior was inappropriate. Unfortunately, he did not do so."[71]

Chief Judge Robinson, while concurring in the court's decision, authored a separate opinion relating to ex parte communications. He observed that Vittone's investigation uncovered "an appalling chronicle of attorneys, high government officials, and interested outsiders apparently without compunction about intervening in the course of FLRA's decision making by means of private communications with those charged with resolving the case on its merits."[72]

The chief judge was particularly critical of the telephone calls by Secretary Lewis to Applewhaite and Frazier. He found the calls "extremely troubling" because of the nature of the position Lewis held.

For a high government officer to bypass established procedures and approach, directly and privately, members of an independent decision making body about a case in which he had official interest and on which they will be called to rule suggests, at the minimum, a deplorable indifference toward safeguarding the purity of the formal adjudicatory process. Regardless of the officer's actual intent, such a call could be felt by the recipient as political pressure; regardless could be perceived by the public as political pressure. Either way, the integrity of the process is dealt a sore blow.[73]

Gary Eads termed the court decision "disappointing" and indicated that the union might appeal the decision to the U.S. Supreme Court. Nevertheless, he suggested that the most important issue before the nation should be how to return the air traffic control system to a safer and more efficient operation. In addition, he observed, "Now that much of the debate as to what penalties should be imposed against PATCO is over, the attention of all of us, in labor and in the government, should be directed towards returning thousands of highly skilled, professional air traffic controllers to their jobs."[74] He indicated that the PATCO, while no longer the exclusive bargaining representative of the controllers, stood ready to help in any way possible.

With the adverse court decision, the PATCO's days were truly numbered. The millions of dollars of outstanding fines in conjunction with no source of dues or fees spelled a short life for the union. On July 1, 1982, the PATCO indicated that a motion would be filed for liquidation under Chapter 7 of the Federal Bankruptcy Act. This process generally results in the appointment of a trustee by the court to distribute the union's assets among its creditors.

Gary Eads personally filed the necessary bankruptcy papers with the court. Afterward, he asked the rhetorical question: "President Reagan has proven his point to everyone. It is logical to ask, what more can be gained by a policy which lacks understanding and flexibility and appears to be designed only to prove a point?"[75] After making the customary plea for the return of the striking controllers to their jobs, Eads observed:

For almost 14 years PATCO has virtually been the only group that was able to effectively monitor the FAA, insure that the Congress was informed about FAA operations, and keep the public educated on matters pertaining to the country's air traffic control system. If one were to examine the strides and gains made by the FAA with respect to equipment, manpower, procedures and other improvements to the ATC system, a direct line can be traced back to PATCO and the dedicated air traffic controllers that comprise its membership. Unfortunately, PATCO's watchful eye will now be gone.[76]

ONE YEAR LATER

The first anniversary of the PATCO strike produced the predicted good cheer by the administration and the forecast gloom and doom by the union. J. Lynn Helms, FAA administrator, provided the following observations about the current and future condition of the system. When questioned about the ongoing disruptions of air traffic, he responded, "Except for a 20 or 30-minute delay once in a while, air travel is back to normal. The number of flights is at 83 percent of prestrike capacity now. I expect it to be at 90 percent by the end of September and to 100 percent by next April."[77]

The irony of this assessment is that it took approximately one full year to move the system up from 75 percent of capacity to 83 percent of capacity—an 8 percent increase. As everybody knows, moving increasingly closer to full capacity takes much more effort than moving the first few percentages. To suggest that the system would be at 90 percent two months after the interview was wishful thinking, at best.

When asked about what the FAA was doing to improve working conditions that contributed to the strike, including stress and poor labor-management relations, Helms referred to a vague "four-year university program in airway sciences" to train supervisors. The problem, of course, was not that supervisors lacked training in "airway sciences" but rather that they lacked fundamental skills in working with people. In addition, he alluded to the old bureaucratic ploy of forming a "human-relations policy committee," which he would chair personally, of course, and a "massive communications program." These types of initiatives are used by bureaucrats when they want to make inaction sound like action.

As a follow-on to this line of questions, the administrator expressed how shocked he was to find that prestrike controllers only directed planes for four and a half hours each day. He then downplayed the allegations of stress experienced by controllers. He attributed most of the stress to "episodic stress," which occurs in sporadic events but is not sustained over time. Then, to go one further than his predecessor, he apparently agreed with a report that air controlling is "nowhere near as stressful as those of window washers in New York skyscrapers. If you want to see stress, join a policeman in the Bronx from 8 o'clock at night until 3 o'clock in the morning, or watch a deckhand on a gasoline barge on a foggy night in New Orleans harbor."[78]

When asked whether or not he detected much sentiment among controllers to join another union, Helms again demonstrated that he was out of touch with the controllers and that the "massive communications program" wasn't working. Less than four months after the strike, controllers in several centers, including the one closest to Washington (Washington Center in Leesburg, Virginia), were attempting to form a new union or take over the PATCO so that they could begin addressing ongoing problems. Then he made a gratuitous statement: "I think they [the controllers] see us making progress in improving the system."[79]

It is difficult to determine exactly what "improvements" the administrator was referring to, but they clearly could not have related to improving employee conditions within the FAA. In fact, in hearings five years and eight years after these statements by Helms, labor-management conditions in the FAA were as bad or worse than they had been the day of the strike and a new union to represent controllers had been formed.

One year after the strike, individual controllers were struggling with the government, with their families, and with themselves. Many of them had taken new jobs, virtually always at a fraction of the salary of their controller job. There was still camaraderie between the controllers that led to frequent meetings, shared work activities, and personal support when possible. Several hundred controllers were reported to have moved overseas to controlling jobs in Australia, Saudi

Arabia, and other foreign countries. Most controllers were simply struggling to change their lifestyles to fit a substantially lower income. College for the children and frequent evenings out were considered dreams of the past.

There were reported cases of family breakups, probably due to money problems. However, there were also cases in which families grew closer together and fathers found more time for their children. All in all, most Americans felt little sympathy for the strikers, and most probably felt that the controllers got what they deserved. The controllers felt that the public didn't understand and apparently didn't care about conditions within the air traffic control system. Controllers blamed the administration for distorting the truth, and they blamed the media for not providing a balanced commentary on system conditions.

With their union gone and there being no pullback by the administration, most controllers knew that the first anniversary marked the real end to their controlling careers. They had rolled the dice and lost. Virtually every controller wanted his or her job back, but virtually every one also said that under similar conditions they would strike again. While some controllers felt badly about breaking the law, most of them believed that conditions in the system warranted these actions. They were not proud that they had violated their oath or broke federal law, but they also believed that the penalty did not fit the crime. Most of them knew that violating the law required a penalty of some type, but in a historical context and in relation to other types of crimes, the penalty they received seemed out of line.

As the climatic temperature in Washington rose during August, the frustration of working controllers increased as well. The administration had promised the controllers a substantial pay raise, over and above what was proposed for other federal employees. However, both the Senate and House passed a bill as part of a continuing resolution that would have increased controller pay by 5 percent. President Reagan vetoed the bill. Congressman Ford then had the pay raise provision removed on procedural grounds from a later version of the continuing resolution. At this point, the controllers saw their long-promised pay raise evaporate before their eyes. Secretary Lewis knew that tempers were short, and he sought to calm the waters with a "Dear Colleague" letter to controllers. Ironically, the secretary indicated that he was working to obtain pay increases for the working controllers that they "so richly deserve[d]." The irony is that the working controllers richly deserved a $57 million pay raise, but one year earlier the administration couldn't find resources approaching this level that could have averted the entire debacle.

As the months wore on, the Merit Systems Protection Board (MSPB) heard each of the controllers' cases individually. The board had determined that each controller appeal was unique and therefore would have to be heard separately. A few controllers were able to convince the MSPB judges that they warranted their jobs back, but the number returning to work was small. Almost fourteen months after the strike, only 6 of the original 11,400 had won their jobs back under the MSPB hearing procedures. The FAA appealed every back-to-work order by a judge to the full MSPB for hearing. The first case appealed to the board resulted in a ruling sustaining the discharge of the controller. Roy L. Schapansky had sought reinstatement before an MSPB judge, but the judge ruled against him. On appeal to the full MSPB, the judge's decision was upheld, and Schapansky's discharge was sustained.

SUMMARY

After fourteen months of trauma, disruption, and turmoil, the rebuilding process of the air traffic control system began in earnest. The prognostications by federal officials were unrealistic; there were continued problems in the training program; air-lines were getting impatient about government intervention in the aviation sector; the touted automation program for the ATC moved glacially; and the public kept on tolerating delays, cancellations, and overbooked flights. Nevertheless, a semblance of normalcy was returning to the industry. Those on the outside watched the adjustment processes unfold. The problems that had contributed to the strike were not being resolved even though there was considerable rhetoric about improving the system. It would take many years for the system to return to prestrike levels of performance.

However, the lives of the controllers were disrupted and difficult. Many controllers believed that they had not been treated fairly by the FAA during the strike and in its aftermath. As a consequence, they started appealing their termination notices. Very few controllers were able to overturn the decisions made by the FAA, but a handful did return to work. Out of the appeal process, a singularly troubling situation arose. In the Chicago Region, a process was set in motion to sustain the discharge of controllers. This process led to what may be called the "Chicago Debacle." The next chapter addresses this troubled and troubling process by a federal agency that was unwilling to apply the legal system on a level playing field. No one can read the chronology of the Chicago Debacle without feeling shocked and outraged by a system out of control.

NOTES

1. "CWA Gives $100,000 toward Aid of Striking Air Controllers," *Daily Labor Reporter* (Bureau of National Affairs), No. 163, August 24, 1981, p. A-11.

2. Ibid.

3. Ibid.

4. "Government Bargained in Good Faith with PATCO, FLRA Director Concludes," *Daily Labor Reporter* (Bureau of National Affairs), No. 165, August 26, 1981, p. A-2.

5. Ibid., p. A-3.

6. "Official Dismisses Air Controller Charge of Unfair Labor Practices against U.S.," *Wall Street Journal*, August 26, 1981, p. 5.

7. Ibid.

8. "Air Controller Strike Not Likely to Cause Great Economic Harm, Commerce Study Says," *Daily Labor Reporter* (Bureau of National Affairs), No. 166, August 27, 1981, pp. A-10–A-11.

9. "Air Strike Starts to Wear Down All Sides," *U.S. News and World Report*, August 31, 1981, p. 22.

10. Ibid., p. 23.

11. "Administration Should Resume Talks with PATCO, Kirkland Tells Delegates to Seafarers Convention," *Daily Labor Reporter* (Bureau of National Affairs), No. 168, August 31, 1981, p. A-6.

12. Ibid., p. A-7.

13. "PATCO Unleashes Barrage of Exceptions to Recommendation That It Be Decertified," *Daily Labor Reporter* (Bureau of National Affairs), No. 170, September 2, 1981, p. A-9.

14. Ibid.

15. "ILO Urged to Examine U.S. Conduct toward Strikes by Controllers," *Daily Labor Reporter* (Bureau of National Affairs), No. 174, September 9, 1981, p. A-2.

16. Ibid., p. A-3.

17. "Donahue Predicts Public Managers Not Likely to Copy Administration's Style in PATCO Strike," *Daily Labor Reporter* (Bureau of National Affairs), No. 179, September 16, 1981, p. A-11.

18. Ibid.

19. Ibid., p. A-13.

20. Ibid.

21. "House Committee Questions FAA Chief on Labor Policies During Air Strike," *Daily Labor Reporter* (Bureau of National Affairs), No. 195, October 8, 1981, p. A-6.

22. "Concern Mounts on Controllers," *Washington Post*, October 15, 1981, p. D12.

23. "PATCO President Poli Appears Before House Panel; Defends Strike Action," *Daily Labor Reporter* (Bureau of National Affairs), No. 202, October 20, 1981, p. A-15.

24. "FLRA Agrees that PATCO Broke Law but Splits over Decertification," *Daily Labor Reporter* (Bureau of National Affairs), No. AA-1, October 22, 1981, p. A-1.

25. "U.S. Court Stays Decertifying of Air Controllers," *Washington Post*, October 23, 1981, p. A18.

26. "PATCO Leader Denounces FLRA Decision, DOT Proposes Controller Pay Package," *Daily Labor Reporter* (Bureau of National Affairs), No. 204, October 22, 1981, p. AA-3.

27. House of Representatives, Committee on Post Office and Civil Service, Subcommittee on Investigations, *Federal Labor-Management Relations and Impasses Procedures*, 97th Cong., 2d sess., Serial No. 97-50 (Washington, D.C.: GPO, February 24, April 29, May 4, July 22, 1982), p. 5.

28. Ibid., p. 6.

29. "Air Controllers' Strike," *Facts on File*, Vol. 41, No. 2136, October 23, 1981, p. 772.

30. "Rehiring of Members Sought; Controllers Would End Strike," *Washington Post*, October 30, 1981, p. A14.

31. "Suit Challenges Controller Firings," *Washington Post*, November 12, 1981, p. D13.

32. "House Panel to Hold Air Controller Pay Hearings," *Daily Labor Reporter* (Bureau of National Affairs), No. 228, November 27, 1981, p. A-3.

33. Ibid.

34. Ibid.

35. "Reagan Acts to Improve Labor Ties," *Washington Post*, December 2, 1981, p. A1.

36. "White House Softens Position on Air Controllers: May Return to Government," *Daily Labor Reporter*, (Bureau of National Affairs), No. 231, December 2, 1981, p. A-9.

37. "Reagan Administration May Allow Controllers' Return to Federal Employment," *Washington Post*, December 3, 1981, p. A18.

38. Ibid., p. B9.

39. William Raspberry, "PATCO Deserves a Gift," *Washington Post*, December 7, 1981, p. A15.

40. Ibid.

41. "Soviet Delegate Attacks U.S. Handling of Air Traffic Controllers' Dispute," *Daily Labor Reporter* (Bureau of National Affairs), No. 235, December 8, 1981, p. A-3.

42. Ibid.

43. "Air Travel Is Found Safe, with a Caveat," *Washington Post*, December 9, 1981, p. A2.

44. Ibid.

45. William Raspberry, "Fairness and the Air Controllers," *Washington Post*, December 11, 1981, p. A23.

46. "The Return of PATCO's People," *Washington Post*, December 18, 1981, p. A22.

47. "Grades Altered for Controllers, House Staff Says," *Washington Post*, December 23, 1981, p. A6.

48. Ibid.

49. "Ford Asks Probe on Allegations that Air Controller Grades Were Manipulated," *Daily Labor Reporter* (Bureau of National Affairs), No. 246, December 23, 1981, p. A-9.

50. "Court Voids PATCO Indictments, Charges Selective Prosecution," *Daily Labor Reporter* (Bureau of National Affairs), No. 251, December 31, 1981, p. A-1.

51. Ibid., A-2.

52. "Robert E. Poli Resigns as President of PATCO," *Washington Post*, January 1, 1982, p. D6a.

53. "Nonstriking PATCO Members Seek Right to Represent Controllers," *Daily Labor Reporter* (Bureau of National Affairs), No. 15, January 20, 1982, p. A-4.

54. "Controller Defends Handling of 2nd Jet and Doomed Plane," *Washington Post*, March 3, 1982, p. A2.

55. "Two-thirds of Fired PATCO Members Would Still Strike Under Same Conditions," *Daily Labor Reporter* (Bureau of National Affairs), No. 36, February 23, 1982, pp. A-6–A-7.

56. Ibid., p. A-7.

57. Ibid.

58. "Should Air Controllers Get Their Jobs Back?" *Washington Post*, March 26, 1982, p. A29.

59. Ibid.

60. "Air Controller Problems Resurfacing," *Washington Post*, March 18, 1982, p. A7.

61. Ibid.

62. "Incompetent Management Found to be Factor in Low Morale among Controllers," *Daily Labor Reporter* (Bureau of National Affairs), No. 52, March 17, 1982, p. A-1.

63. Ibid.

64. U.S. General Accounting Office, *Aviation Safety: Serious Problems Continue to Trouble the Air Traffic Control Work Force*, GAO/RCED-89-112 (Washington, D.C.: GPO, April 1989), p. 1.

65. "Incompetent Management Found to Be Factor in Low Morale among Controllers," p. A-1.

66. "ALJ Says Shanker Dinner, Other Contacts Did Not Affect FLRA Decision on PATCO," *Daily Labor Reporter* (Bureau of National Affairs), No. 63, April 1, 1982, p. A-1.

67. Ibid.

68. Ibid.

69. "Appeals Court Upholds Decertification of PATCO," *Daily Labor Reporter* (Bureau of National Affairs), No. 114, June 14, 1982, p. A-11.

70. Ibid.

71. Ibid.

72. Ibid., p. A-12.

73. Ibid.

74. "PATCO Declares 'The Union Is Gone,' Files for Bankruptcy," *Daily Labor Reporter* (Bureau of National Affairs), No. 128, July 2, 1982, p. A-5.

75. Ibid.

76. Ibid., p. A-6.

77. "How Air Travel Stands One Year after Strike," *U.S. News and World Report*, August 3, 1982, p. 51.

78. Ibid.

79. Ibid.

Chapter 8

The Chicago Debacle

While it may never be known precisely what motivated the Reagan Administration to destroy the PATCO through the mass firing of air traffic controllers, the procedural activities in at least one major FAA facility raised serious questions about motivation and adherence to process and law. The events described here indicate less-than-pristine motivation in the firing of the controllers but, more important, the apparent violation of federal law that went unpunished. Remember, the controllers were fired from their federal jobs because they violated a federal law and their oath of office. What follows is a description of federal employees who, according to members of Congress, also violated federal law and their oath to uphold the Constitution of the United States but went unscathed. In fact, it is likely that some controllers lost their jobs permanently because of the illegal activities of individuals within the FAA who altered official government records, created records where they did not exist, and obfuscated the process intentionally so that justice could not occur. As the following material shows, there was plenty of blame to go around, but due to the unbalanced nature of the judicial process, the legal system was unable to place the locus of responsibility on specific individuals.

The issues involved in the "Chicago Debacle" are reasonably clear. Every air traffic controller was given a notice of termination for his or her participation in the strike. That notice explained the reason for the action and provided the controller with appeal rights. One step in the process was appeal to the Merit Systems Protection Board. In the MSPB hearings in which individual controllers were given opportunities to argue against dismissal, it became clear that personnel records and other evidence had been "modified" to sustain the FAA's position. There is evidence that the modification took place not once but on several occasions during the process. What is most astounding is not that material evidence was modified but that the scope and volume of modification indicated that this activity could rank among the largest document alteration processes ever found in the federal system.

One need not be sympathetic to the plight of the controllers to be outraged at the cavalier attitude and demeanor of federal officials and the apparent inability or unwillingness of the MSPB to bring the clear violations of due process and violation of federal law to closure. The record shows that the MSPB vigorously moved forward to sustain the firing of the controllers who had violated the law but took a less vigorous approach to seeking out and punishing others who had similarly violated the law. Admittedly, the MSPB may be unable to prosecute criminal acts, but reason suggests that the board had the responsibility to bring these types of acts before the appropriate judicial forum. As noted, it is possible that individual controllers may have been denied due process and, based on that outcome, lost their jobs and their livelihoods because of the disparate application of justice.

The Chicago Debacle did not come to light immediately after the 1981 strike. In fact, only when individual controllers began attempting to understand how and why they had been fired—when they had legitimate reasons for not being at their assigned jobs—did the nature of the problem evolve. Out of nowhere, records seemed to appear and reappear in altered form as individual controllers pursued their cases. Controllers on approved leave found their time and attendance records showing AWOL (absent without leave). Controllers who had attempted to return to work but were locked out found their records similarly marked. As individual controllers pursued their claims, significant alterations or record creation appeared in significant numbers of cases. Eventually, the patterns and prevalence of alterations or modifications became clearly apparent. Attorneys for the controllers attempted to identify how and why these conditions existed.

One may reasonably believe that most controllers were fired because they broke federal law and their signed oath. It may even be reasonable to argue that a large proportion of the controllers were fired for supportable reasons. However, that misses the point. The one element in American jurisprudence that separates it, more than any other, from other systems is the existence of due process. Regardless of how heinous the crime, how obvious the guilt is believed to be, how odious the purported criminals, the one dimension that is most compelling is that due process must be followed. If even one controller was denied due process, then the system has failed. Nobody will ever know how many controllers lost their jobs and livelihood in the Chicago Debacle because due process was not observed. What should be apparent in what follows is that the American judicial system let emotion and haste override one of the most basic of our protections as Americans.

After extensive oral hearings before agency hearing officers, the vast majority of controllers remained dissatisfied with the decisions relating to their cases. Through two MSPB hearings, it became increasingly clear that something had happened to the personnel records in the Chicago Center that raised serious questions about motivation, procedure, and law. Controllers and their

representatives found no satisfaction through the MSPB process either and therefore sought relief in federal court and before the Congress of the United States.
To this day, the full scope of the alteration and fabrication process has not been
defined, and no federal officials lost their jobs or were punished for their participation in the process.

THE CASES WERE FULLY LITIGATED

When the House of Representatives initiated hearings on the Chicago situation, then FAA administrator Donald Engen wrote a letter to Committee Chairman James Oberstar, criticizing the Congress for holding hearings on these
issues. Engen said, "I am deeply troubled by the fact that the Subcommittee
intends to explore matters which not only occurred 5½ years ago, but which
have been litigated fully before the Merit Systems Protection Board."[1] While
one may argue that the MSPB "fully litigated" these matters, as will be shown
below, the MSPB, a politically derived organization, was less than diligent in its
consideration of evidence provided by the controllers in open hearings. In fact,
after promising to consider certain evidence and testimony, the board summarily
ignored it.

Engen then said:

The allegation that records were falsified to substantiate the firing of strikers at the
Chicago Center is not new. To the contrary, as the Subcommittee is aware, that specific
issue was addressed in a hearing in 1984 before a presiding official of the MSPB, who,
in short, concluded that, while records had been amended at the Center, these amend-
ments did not form the basis for the removal decisions of the affected controllers. Subsequently, on appeal to the full MSPB, the decision of the presiding official was upheld.
That same issue is now pending before the U.S. Court of Appeals for the Federal Circuit.[2]

What the administrator did not say, however, is that something more than
records being "amended" had occurred. Documents had been destroyed to prevent disclosure, entire new documents had been created where none existed
before, and apparently individuals who were not FAA employees and who were
not knowledgeable about these matters were permitted to perform these changes.
In addition, since these documents were the evidence the FAA used not only to
discharge the controllers but also to sustain these actions on appeal, these records
did form the basis for the FAA removal decisions.

Engen then attempted to argue that the motivation behind this massive document change process was pristine and relatively unimportant. Noting that counsel for the controllers would appear before the subcommittee and raise the "motives issue," Engen argued that the MSPB had found that "the FAA had not
evidenced any improper motives in the record changes that were made during
the processing of the removal cases."[3]

Here, too, one must consider the entire role of the MSPB in the hearing process, how the board was constituted, how hearing officers handled evidence before the board, and relationships between hearing officers and board members. The issue for consideration is whether or not the board and its constituent parts acted objectively and independently in the hearing and decision process. Each reader will have to decide for themselves whether political considerations entered this critical deliberative process that affected the lives of thousands of Federal employees.

Attorney Gary Ethan Klein, representing the controllers, testified before the Congress that the manner in which the cases of controller dismissal at the Chicago Center were handled should "shock the conscience." The United States is a nation of laws and not men. As noted earlier, the single aspect of the legal system that is most important is that of due process. When due process is denied, justice is denied. The Chicago Debacle argues strongly that due process was denied to many of the fired controllers. However, each reader can form his or her own judgment about this conclusion.

Testifying in 1987, Klein described to the Congress the parts of this situation that he believed were most egregious. He testified, "First, these controllers have been barred from their profession for 5-1/2 years, and yet to this very day not one of them has been given the identity of the FAA official who accused them of participation in the strike or of being absent without leave during the strike."[4] The purpose of the hearings before the MSPB was to determine whether individual controllers had not participated in the illegal strike due to illness, absence from the country or area, fear of retaliation, or other factors that might warrant reinstatement.

Second, "[o]ver the course of two MSPB hearings, one in 1982 and the other in 1984, during months of investigation, including the taking of depositions of approximately 25 FAA supervisors, managers, and others, the FAA did not identify a single witness who even claimed to have personal knowledge of the facts necessary to support the charges against any of these controllers."[5] As will be shown later, the FAA's entire case was based on personnel records that purportedly documented absence from the job by individual controllers. As will also be shown, these documents were altered, modified, created, or destroyed in such a manner that it became impossible to verify the authenticity of these documents and further demonstrate that they supported the dismissal of the controllers. Nevertheless, the MSPB ignored these "minor" problems and plunged forward with sustaining the dismissals.

Klein testified, "We have discovered that the documents used to fire the controllers are the product of what we allege may be the largest and most systematic evidence alteration scheme in the history of American jurisprudence. The perpetrators of that scheme and its coverup are government officials."[6] As testimony and evidence will show, not only was there document alteration and fabrication, but testimony suggests that government officials may have worked together to cover up their illegal actions. As described later, there were tens of thousands of altered records supplied to the MSPB. It is simply impossible to believe that one person could have conducted alterations, fabrications, or document creations of this number of documents without anybody else being involved or knowledgeable about the activity.

Fourth, "[c]opies of these fabricated business records were ultimately assembled, officially certified as true and accurate by the FAA's Director of Employee and Labor Relations, and submitted to the MSPB as evidence. These documents formed the sole evidence introduced against these controllers."[7] As noted in his statement, earlier, Engen argued that these documents were not the basis for removal of the controllers. As all the evidence shows, not only were they the basis for removal, they were the sole basis for these actions.

Finally, Klein argued, "At the first MSPB hearing on these cases in November of 1982, the Chicago Center chief, George Gunter, testified under oath that copies of the time-and-attendance records of the Center which had been submitted as evidence represented records compiled in the ordinary course of business."[8] As will be shown, where a single record should have been "compiled in the ordinary course of business," there were, in fact, five, ten, or more records provided to the MSPB alleging to show a specific controller's activities.

These allegations of wrongdoing by federal officials were substantiated by a bewildering scheme of fabrication, alteration, and falsification that covered a several-year period and involved a variety of federal employees. For example:

Even after Gunter was initially confronted with documents which demonstrated that the Chicago Center records had been altered, he persisted in being less than candid about the evidence-tampering scheme.

For example, Gunter initially attributed the change in the records to some sort of "updating" process which was performed by the personnel department under the direction of one Mr. Richard Pender. The agency was asked to produce the personnel specialists who had altered the records.[9]

They couldn't find them even though only two people reportedly worked in that function during the time period involved.

Klein testified:

Gunter made several other conflicting statements about the records at the first hearing [in 1982]. At one point he suggested that the differing versions of the records represented simple "mistakes." At another point, he suggested that the Center had maintained records which had to be "revised" within a few days after the dates shown. Then, when confronted with evidence that the records were changed after the controllers had made oral reply to the charges, Gunter stated that the Chicago Center had not even maintained the records originally [sic] prior to that time.

Most significantly, Gunter never disclosed his knowledge that Robert Miller, Chicago Center evaluation officer, was in charge of the alteration scheme and never identified persons he knew were involved with Mr. Miller's work. The first MSPB hearing ended with the Chicago Center's altered records, which were the sole evidence introduced against controllers, in an unexplained state.[10]

Not to be deterred, the MSPB hearing officer overlooked the charges of fabrication and alteration of federal documents and sustained the dismissal charges against the controllers.

The MSPB initial decision was appealed to the three-member MSPB panel in Washington, D.C. The full Board reversed the decision but not the removal actions. After noting that Gunter had contradicted himself, that the altered documents were insufficient, and that the FAA had failed to explain the alterations after being given numerous opportunities to do so, the Board remanded the case for a second hearing on the issue of the altered documents, thereby giving the FAA a second opportunity to explain their records.[11]

At this point, there was little chance that the FAA could "explain" the altered and fabricated documents. Counsel for the controllers had hard evidence in its possession that alterations and fabrications had occurred, and therefore, the FAA plunged down a different road. Preparing for the remand hearing, the FAA changed their position on a number of issues. First, "although the Chicago Center chief, George Gunter, was the only witness put on the stand at the first hearing to 'authenticate' altered documents as business records, the FAA took the position on remand that Gunter had so little knowledge of these records and the alterations made to them that it did not even intend to call him as a witness at the second hearing."[12]

Second, "[t]he FAA submitted an affidavit from Miller which claimed that Miller was responsible for the alteration process. The FAA pleadings specifically represented that Gunter had no knowledge of the alterations and that only Miller could explain them. The Board accepted these representations, and Miller testified at the second hearing, whereas Gunter did not."[13]

Third, "[t]wo years later, Miller would submit another affidavit in another case which asserted that Gunter not only knew about the alteration of the records; he specifically directed Miller to take charge of it and told him how he wanted it done."[14]

Fourth, "[a]nother affidavit, signed by the former deputy chief of the Chicago Center, Henry French, asserted that French personally observed Gunter tell Miller to alter these records. French served as the FAA's technical advisor in the remand hearing."[15]

The FAA was now implicated in a serious violation of federal law and individual federal officials were identified as being responsible for these violations. Gunter, Miller, and French were the only ones who could have been responsible because the circle of finger-pointing involved only them. Then, in a classic case of obfuscation, the FAA embarked on a process to either eliminate the records or prevent the identification of the "real" records. When the MSPB ordered the FAA to produce original, nonidentical documents, Klein testified, "The number of non-identical copies of these supposedly identical records is truly startling. There were supposed to be 175 pages of watch schedules. The agency produced 22,811 pages of nonidentical copies of the original 175. For what were supposed to be a total of 1,239 sign-in logs, the agency produced a total of 20,657 non-identical copies of what should have been 1,239."[16]

Klein testified:

Although many of the differences in these nonidentical copies were insignificant, there were numerous instances of material differences which resulted in there being as many as six materially differing versions of what was supposed to be a single business record. Of even greater importance, the agency never produced, in any form, originals or photocopies of any record which would have shown what the evidence looked like prior to the 4-month alteration process.[17]

Miller was challenged several times to distinguish the original entries from the altered ones. In frustration, after admitting that he could not tell the difference, he agreed, "No one, with the possible exception of God, could look at these evidence files and tell whether or not they are accurate." The attorneys then noted, "That is the evidence on which these controllers were 'convicted.' I guess the only possibility is that someone thought they were God."[18]

To determine what role, if any, individual FAA supervisors played in the fabrication-alteration process, "Depositions were taken of 25 supervisors prior to the hearing. The supervisors uniformly expressed surprise at what had happened to these records. They universally testified that they had not made the key 'AWOL' entries on the logs for their areas."[19] In addition, "[t]he supervisors universally disclaimed any knowledge of the identity of the individuals who altered the records. They all said that they were not consulted about alterations, even when the alterations involved the obliteration of original information and annual leave status and the substitution of AWOL status after the controllers were fired."[20]

However, while the official(s) who ordered the alteration-fabrication may never be known, what is known is that of the people involved in the actual alteration process, several were not FAA officials. In fact, Miller's wife was enlisted in the process, as were one or more of Miller's social friends. These individuals were paid by the FAA, and therefore the regional FAA officials considered them "federal employees." This is most curious in that the regulations controlling how a personnel record can be changed require that the person changing the record have personal knowledge about the required change and that this individual initial and date the change. Could Miller's wife and social friends have *any* knowledge about who was in attendance or absent from the center when none of these individuals were present during this period? Gunter later testified that he believed Miller's wife only performed record-copying activities and did not participate in changing or creating records. Since he had little, if any, firsthand knowledge of the activities occurring in the "war room," it is unlikely that he would have known what activities Miller's wife actually performed.

The locus of responsibility was tightly focused on several senior FAA officials in the Chicago Center. While Klein observed earlier that no controller had been permitted to confront a single individual (accuser) who had firsthand knowledge substantiating the involvement of individual controllers in the strike, the remand hearing served to clarify several relationships.

It [the remand hearing] did apparently demonstrate conclusively who were not the accusers or who were not the declarants. The area supervisors—the only ones having the requisite personal knowledge of their subordinates' schedules and leave status and a variety of other things that go to that status—these supervisors universally disclaimed making the key entries, as they had in the depositions, and no FAA witness challenged their testimony.[21]

Further,

[d]uring cross-examination of "War Room General" Miller, it was uncovered that, after controllers had responded to the charges that were in the original material relied upon to propose their termination, this material relied upon was altered, and in some cases completely manufactured where none existed before, and sent up to the MSPB as evidence of why the employee was fired. And, of course, from there it would have to be used as trial evidence. None of the controllers knew this. They responded to one set of charges and one set of material . . . in the informal pre-termination hearing, and when they appealed it, they had another set to contend with.[22]

Ironically, the Chicago Center "war room" that was used to alter and create documents that led to the firing of hundreds of controllers was the former "PATCO union office" in the center facility. David Erickson testified before the subcommittee, "During the seven or so weeks which followed, I worked in what had formerly been the PATCO office, which was called the war room, and which was the office we used to compile and review the necessary documents regarding the adverse actions being processed within the facility."[23]

Chairman Oberstar asked Gunter why the room was called the "war room." Gunter indicated that he didn't know where the term originated, but he believed it came about because of the fortress-type situation the center was in during the strike and the picketing. Oberstar suggested that the term may have arisen because of the mental set or attitude of the FAA officials about their dealings with the union.

In any case, after all of these machinations of the evidence, the FAA took a second classic evasive move. Klein testified:

After this substitution process was uncovered, the agency was requested in open hearing to produce the original evidence which had been removed from the MSPB files so that everyone could look at what was originally suggested as material relied upon to fire these controllers. Without hesitation, when this happened in open court or open hearing, the FAA attorney replied that the agency no longer had the original evidence. It had been destroyed.[24]

In addition, when counsel for the controllers asked for the time-and-attendance records for the fired controllers, "the agency claimed that the original documents were in Kansas City and that it would be burdensome to require the agency to produce them. After the MSPB ordered the agency to produce them, the agency claimed that the originals had been destroyed."[25]

There were similar inconsistencies between testimony by FAA supervisors and higher-level FAA officials concerning the center's "swap books," the "spot leave binders," and other documents needed to make sense of the watch schedules. Supervisors testified that the documents did exist, but Miller testified at the subsequent hearing that they had been destroyed.

At the second MSPB hearing, attorneys for the controllers found themselves in the enviable legal position of having determined that all of the evidence supporting the opposition's case had been destroyed. Klein testified, "Having established that the original facility records, the 'material relied upon' by the FAA to fire the controllers, was destroyed—and this is supposed to be the critical evidence at the trial—the controllers moved for immediate dismissal of the agency's case; FAA had no evidence."[26]

One would think that the MSPB would at least pause in the processing of the case to determine what, if any, reconsideration was warranted. This did not happen. "The MSPB presiding official issued his decision to affirm the removal actions on December 17, 1984." Klein testified, "The decision did not refer to the record transcript on the altered document issue in a single instance. It is a very slim opinion, as you can see."

Finally, nowhere in the MSPB's presiding official's statement

is the fact that the decision was made under very questionable circumstances. While this presiding official was considering the case, he was transferred to Washington at the MSPB in what was then called a secretary's position—I think it is now called a legal clerk—working directly for the chairman, I believe, on that. This [occurred] while he supposedly was writing one of the most critical MSPB decisions and perhaps the most critical air traffic controller decision at that time, and he came out with a decision that is highly unusual.

On July 5, 1985, the full Board denied the controllers' petition for review of the unusual presiding official remand decision.[27]

The July 5 decision brought to an end the controllers' case before the MSPB relating to a fair hearing on their dismissal appeals. Whether or not every controller who was fired warranted to be fired is an arguable issue. The purpose of describing the Chicago Debacle in some detail is not to make judgments about the controllers being fired, but rather to point to another example of actions by the FAA relating to this unfortunate situation that suggests something other than aboveboard, honest dealings with its employees. The agency apparently had no reluctance to take whatever action it deemed necessary, legal or illegal, to substantiate its actions. When confronted in open court, the agency resorted to the age-old ploys of obfuscation, amnesia, and destruction of documents to prevent revealing the truth.

Then, too, the role of the Merit Systems Protection Board is not above criticism. In spite of evidence relating to illegal acts by federal officials and the inability of the agency to substantiate its dismissal of the controllers with original documents, over which the agency had exclusive control, the MSPB ignored these facts and denied the controllers' petition for review.

All of these troubling actions by the FAA raise an important question: What motivated the agency and its managers to engage in actions that could led to criminal penalties and could have lead to reversal of the firing decisions? The answer may never be known, but one can speculate, as did Phillip S. Wood, attorney for the controllers, about motivation. He argued:

I think the simple answer is, what motivates anybody who engages in evidence tampering? They want to win their case.

I think there came a point in time when they had to make the decision—the other centers apparently were relying on the documents as business records. Their [the Chicago Center] records were in disarray. And, other than tell the truth about that, they decided, well, we are—they were arrogant enough to think that they could get away with manufacturing records and entries, and if they kept it secret enough, that they would get away with it.[28]

Concerned about the actions or inactions of the MSPB, Congressman Norman Mineta asked the question: "What about the MSPB? Why did they not want to get to the bottom of this whole thing to find out where the truth was in terms of what went on?" Woods responded to that question as well. He noted that the presiding officer (Mr. Manrose) had tried to persuade the government to settle the case and that this individual was under a lot of pressure. Woods did not say "political pressure." However, he concluded his remarks by saying, "I think that we have to understand that the head of the Merit Systems Protection Board, Mr. Ellingwood, who took office in December of 1981, was White House attorney, counsel to the President, advising him how to handle the controllers in August of 1981. I don't know how more plain I could put that."[29]

After listening to testimony before his subcommittee, Congressman Oberstar noted, "It does appear, in light of evidence the committee has obtained and the statements of witnesses, that [the] FAA has, in these instant cases, turned a fundamental principle of American jurisprudence on its head: instead of being innocent until proven guilty, controllers were presumed guilty—i.e., AWOL—until they could prove otherwise."[30]

To demonstrate how pervasive and complete the disregard was for controller rights, the committee heard testimony that controllers who were on approved leave lost their jobs before they had a chance to defend their actions. If a controller was not at his or her workstation, for whatever reason, the presumption was that he or she was guilty of violating the no-strike law and the president's directive to return to work. Based on this presumption, they received notices of removal. Even controllers who tried to return to work were denied access to the facility until they appeared for their oral hearing.

As the first round of congressional hearings ended, Congressman Molinari summarized the sentiment of the committee.

I am terribly distressed by what took place at the Chicago Center. Yes, a lot of people through the appeals process got back into the system, but they suffered enormously for something that was not their fault. The fault was on the part of the FAA.

They proved their case and got reinstated, but it cost them a lot of time, a lot of money, a lot of distress, and some of them still are suffering from the trauma today. I have very deep and abiding concern with the fact that others who may have had a justifiable case and didn't pursue their remedies properly, like some of these gentlemen that were reinstated, never got back in who should have been reinstated.

I am terribly bothered. I think this is a sad chapter, and I would hope that we can do something to change the record—and perhaps the law—so that we don't see a repeat of what transpired here.[31]

On September 14, 1987, the committee reconvened its hearings at O'Hare Airport in Chicago, Illinois. Chairman Oberstar opened the hearings on a somber note. Referring to the earlier hearings on March 10 and 11, 1987, he said, "Unfortunately, at that hearing, we were not told the whole truth. When asked to explain certain key documents or recall specific incidents, FAA witnesses, under oath, misled the subcommittee and did not tell the whole truth."[32] In his opening statement, he continued, "To suggest that the patience of the subcommittee is wearing thin is an understatement."[33]

The committee questioned many of the same witnesses that had testified in the March hearings. The degree of amnesia displayed by the respondents was truly astounding. They seemed not to remember anything about who did what, when. Throughout the testimony, there were inconsistencies and blatant contradictions of fact and procedure. The committee sought to clarify these events and establish a complete, accurate record. With none of the respondents able to recall even the most basic information about what happened, the committee did not succeed in its task.

Congressman Oberstar finally closed the hearings with observations about what had happened. He observed that "something occurred here that was more than accidental, a series of misadventures, a series of inappropriate bumbling, but perhaps well-intentioned actions. It does stretch one's credibility."[34] Further, "it raises questions in our minds as to what was really going on, what was the purpose of affixing stamps and changing records after oral replies and attempting to pass them off as contemporaneous records."[35]

Congressman Oberstar displayed frustration, and one can sense feelings of despair. He clearly did not believe what he heard in the formal testimony. The congressman concluded the hearings by observing, "If there is a lesson to be learned, then it is that the fundamental principles of American law, and our Constitution, and our government is that we are innocent until proven guilty, that a procedure must be followed, that procedure sometimes determines substance, and that in this case there was a rather overwhelming failure to adhere to fairness, and thoroughness, and accuracy."[36]

SUMMARY

Maybe the Chicago situation was unique in the FAA, and maybe the individuals involved in the debacle did not represent the FAA's official position on the dismissal question. What is significant is that the top officials in the FAA, DOT, and for that matter, the administration must have known exactly what was happening in Chicago. In fact, during the MSPB hearings, the FAA officials involved in the hearings had to "clear" the agency's positions on several aspects of the case with officials in Washington. To know and not do something or to not know is equally damning. None of these officials took any actions to address these problems, and therefore these officials must absorb some of the responsibility for what occurred. In a story of ironies, double standards, and unfair play, on both sides, the Chicago Debacle is perhaps the last vestige of conditions related to the air traffic controllers' strike. The Chicago Debacle represents a sad episode in the aftermath of a disastrous strike, specifically, and American jurisprudence, generally, that tarnishes the integrity of our system of law.

NOTES

1. House of Representatives, Committee on Public Works and Transportation, Subcommittee on Investigations and Oversight, *Examining Circumstances Surrounding the 1981 Firings of Air Traffic Controllers at the Chicago Air Route Traffic Control Center* No. 100-35, 100th Cong., 1st sess. (Washington, D.C.: GPO, March 10, 11, September 14, 1987), p. 16.
2. Ibid.
3. Ibid.
4. Ibid., p. 6.
5. Ibid.
6. Ibid.
7. Ibid.
8. Ibid.
9. Ibid., p. 7.
10. Ibid.
11. Ibid., p. 8.
12. Ibid.
13. Ibid.
14. Ibid.
15. Ibid.
16. Ibid., p. 9.
17. Ibid.
18. Ibid., p. 12.
19. Ibid., p. 9.
20. Ibid.
21. Ibid., p. 10.
22. Ibid., p. 11.
23. Ibid., p. 81.

24. Ibid., p. 11.
25. Ibid., p. 9.
26. Ibid., p. 11.
27. Ibid., p. 15.
28. Ibid., p. 26.
29. Ibid., p. 27.
30. Ibid., p. 28.
31. Ibid., p. 165.
32. Ibid., p. 171.
33. Ibid.
34. Ibid., p. 290.
35. Ibid.
36. Ibid.

Chapter 9

The Air Traffic Control System in the 1980s and 1990s

Officials in the FAA expressed complete confidence that the nation's air traffic control system would be returned to normal operations within two or three years after the PATCO strike. Secretary Lewis talked about the "excess capacity" or "overstaffing" they found *after* the controllers had been fired—the inference being that the nation's air traffic control system didn't need as many controllers as existed at the time of the strike. There was no discussion of excess capacity before the strike. Rather, there was repeated reference by Secretary Lewis, President Reagan, and many other "knowledgeable" officials to the fact that controllers were overworked. One of several conclusions can be drawn. Either the FAA management and other senior officials did not know what was happening in the air traffic control system, or if they did know, they were misleading the public about the process. What other conclusions are possible? Either they knew or they didn't know. Either conclusion is equally damning.

Eight months after the strike, as previously described, the Jones Commission submitted their report. The report provided yet another indictment of the FAA's labor-management policies and programs. As reported in the *Washington Post*, "An independent task force [the Jones Commission] concluded yesterday that many of the factors that led to the air traffic controllers strike are resurfacing and that serious morale problems persist among working controllers."[1] This was precisely the view expressed in the 1970 Corson Report, the Report by the National Transportation Safety Board, and subsequently the General Accounting Office/Flight Safety Foundation studies.

Four years after the strike, in an effort to determine what conditions existed in the system after the strike, the U.S. General Accounting Office conducted a study in 1985 to assess how controllers, supervisors, and managers viewed the system. The GAO utilized the Flight Safety Foundation (FSF), an international, independent membership organization dedicated solely to the improvement of flight safety, to evaluate the study and its results. The 1985 study found a variety of conditions in the air traffic control system that had not been addressed and that remained serious safety and efficiency problems. Most disturbing was the wide difference between controllers and their immediate supervisors and the organization's managers concerning an assessment of the conditions in the system and the morale of the flight controllers. For the most part, controllers believed they controlled too many airplanes, did not receive adequate breaks from controlling activities, worked with less-than-optimal hardware and software, were not provided adequate training, and so forth. A preponderance of controllers rated morale in the organization as low. Supervisors, in general, agreed with these observations. Managers, on the other hand, indicated that all was well and that morale was high.

The GAO study observed that the 1985 study "showed essentially that FAA had not met its target number of FPL [full performance level] controllers at many major facilities and air traffic growth had caused controller work load to reach a point where controllers were stretched too thin. Despite FAA assurances to the contrary, controllers and their supervisors expressed serious concerns about their ability to maintain the proper margin of safety."[2]

During the 1985 study, the GAO asked the FSF to compare the condition of the system in 1985 with what existed prior to the strike in 1981. The FSF "concluded that conditions within the controller work force had changed since its 1981 evaluation and that although the 1985 system was not unsafe, it did not provide the same level of safety as before the FAA controllers' 1981 strike."[3]

During the 1981–1985 period, the volume of air traffic had increased from 66.7 million flight operations in 1981 to 71.4 million flight operations in 1985. However, the number of FPL controllers was 13,205 in 1981 as compared to 8,315 in 1985–4,890 fewer FPL controllers four years after the strike.

The FAA had expanded the number of "developmental controllers" from 3,039 in 1981 to 4,217 in 1985 and had instituted a category of support personnel called air traffic assistants (ATAs). However, owing to complaints about the inadequacy of training for the "developmentals" and the fact that the ATAs preformed primarily clerical support functions, there can be little wonder that many of the problems identified by the controllers went unmet.

In 1989, the GAO conducted a second follow-up study of conditions in the nation's air traffic control system. Again, the GAO utilized the services of the FSF to provide guidance and objective perspective on the study results. The GAO summarized the persistent and consistent divergence between controllers and supervisors and the agency's managers that Secretary Lewis said he was going to fix. Specifically, the report showed: (1) "Managers agreed that there was a shortage of controllers. However, they did not believe controllers handle too much traffic or work too long without a break."[4] (2) "A majority of controllers believed the quality of several essential areas of training for developmentals is inadequate. Facility managers do not agree."[5] (3) "Over 40 percent of controllers—the largest response group—viewed their own morale as low. Most managers did not perceive controllers' morale to be low."[6] (4) "Despite FAA assurances to the contrary, controllers and their supervisors expressed serious concerns about their ability to maintain the proper margin of safety."[7]

Several specific problems identified by the controllers included: (1) "[A] majority of controllers (59 percent) said they were typically required to work too long without a break during peak periods. FAA's work period guideline states that controllers normally receive a break after 2 hours continuously at one air traffic control position. On the basis of responses, 32 percent of controllers typically exceeded FAA's 2-hour limit and 87 percent had exceeded the limit at least once in the previous month."[8] (2) "Forty-three percent of controllers said their own morale was low while 29 percent said their morale was high. Thirty-six percent of their first-line supervisors said their own morale was low and 38 percent said their morale was high. Managers, however, viewed controller/supervisor morale as high. The Flight Safety Foundation viewed this disparity of controller/supervisor and management views as a serious problem."[9] (3) "Most controllers and supervisors rated the overall safety of the air traffic control system as 'adequate,' 'good,' or 'excellent'; however, some controllers (16 percent) and supervisors (8 percent) rated the system as 'poor' or 'very poor.'"[10]

In contrast to these feelings about the system, "[f]acility managers do not believe that controllers are overworked. Few managers (5 percent) said controllers handle too much traffic, few managers (7 percent) said FPLs work too long without a break, and most managers (70 percent) said the amount of facility overtime was appropriate."[11]

Reading the remainder of the GAO report, one feels as though he or she is reading a document that was prepared two decades earlier. After almost ten years of turmoil, the expenditure of billions of public dollars, the destruction of homes, families, and careers, and the ever-present rhetoric that conditions will change, the following statements confirm that little real improvement has occurred. The GAO report observed: "Controllers expressed their concerns about various working conditions, including too few controllers, too much work, overtime, inadequate quality of developmental training, and low morale. Additionally, they viewed airlines and pilots as contributing to controller difficulty and, from an air traffic system perspective, rated factors that make it difficult to keep the air traffic system safe."[12]

Once again, the gap between the operational professionals who wrestle with the volume of traffic, inadequacies in the hardware, insensitive management practices, long hours, ad infinitum, and the feelings by senior management is striking and disturbing. One can only wonder how a system such as this one, in which most of the supervisors and some of the managers rose out of the ranks of controllers, which is relatively small and intimate, can perpetuate such a divergence of opinion. What is clear is that the system was not fixed as Secretary Lewis promised and one could argue that it was in some sense worse.

Thus, eight years after the controllers' strike, the GAO and FSF found that conditions within the system had not improved substantially and that safety conditions remained at about the same level as during the 1985 study. There had been an increase in FPLs to 9,858 in 1988 as compared to 13,205 in 1981, while the volume of flight operations had risen to 80.4 million in 1988 from 66.7 million in 1981. There were still considerable complaints about the hardware and software supporting the system; overtime requirements and inadequate breaks from controlling activity; the volume of traffic controllers handled, particularly in larger control areas; inadequate training; and so forth.

The FSF reviewed the 1989 GAO study and compared the results to the two earlier time periods. While there had been modest improvement in several categories and modest deterioration in several others, the FSF concluded that while the system was not unsafe, due to the problems remaining in the system, it did not provide the margin of safety that is needed for ongoing long-term system safety. The FSF found similar divergence between controllers/supervisors and managers as were found in the earlier studies. Most significant were the differences relating to employee morale. Nearly half—43 percent—of the surveyed controllers characterized controller morale as low. However, FAA managers characterized controller morale as high. "The Flight Safety Foundation viewed this disparity of controller/supervisor and management views as a serious problem."[13]

Controllers and supervisors attributed some of the problems in the air traffic control system to airline practices and the use of the system by general aviation pilots. The utilization of major "hubs" for more efficient airline operation led to congestion around major airports. In addition, the practice of airlines scheduling airplanes to arrive or depart at the same time provided increased strains on the system. The primary complaint about general aviation traffic was the inability of pilots to communicate well and follow controller instructions.

There were several areas of agreement between controllers and managers. Managers agreed that FPL controller staffing was too low and that airline scheduling and utilization practices adversely affected the system. However, managers did not feel that controllers were overworked; that they controlled too much traffic; that they worked too long without a break; or that the amount of overtime was excessive. Managers generally felt that training was adequate. In the 1989 study, no manager rated the safety of the overall air traffic control system as less than adequate.

Nevertheless, the review of the 1989 study by the FSF led to several disturbing conclusions. The response patterns in the 1985 and 1989 studies were similar. The FSF concluded, "Although some shifting of emphasis and areas of concern occurred, the air traffic control system appeared to have changed little, and the 1989 responses offered no basis for altering its 1985 assessment of the system's safety. While the system is not unsafe . . . the margin of safety remains essentially unchanged from 1985 and is less than desirable."[14]

In spite of these findings, the FAA continued to assert that the air traffic control system was working well and that there were no serious safety concerns. The FAA attempted to streamline and improve its recruitment and hiring programs to improve the quality of new controllers. In addition, the agency initiated a "pay demonstration project" in June 1989 to provide supplemental pay—

up to 20 percent bonus pay—to staff performing safety-related functions in "hard-to-staff" locations. These initiatives may have had some impact on the system, but the primary problems controllers contended were contributing to adverse working conditions and low morale remained intact.

In the aftermath of the August 3 strike, the public showed overwhelming support for the president's actions. After all, the administration's public relations machinery had effectively muted the ineffective attempts by the PATCO to make the PATCO rationale for the strike. However, the euphoria of the public did not last long. As the real conditions in the air traffic control system became more known, public criticism began to grow about the manner in which the Department of Transportation and the Federal Aviation Administration handled their personnel relations. The first response by administration officials was that there was no substance to allegations of insensitive and possibly belligerent personnel policies and procedures. However, as prior studies, most commissioned by the FAA, and several independent studies repeatedly demonstrated, there were serious problems in how FAA managers related to and responded to employee concerns and problems.

Obviously, Secretary Lewis has not been responsible for the entire period since the strike, and therefore it may not be reasonable to place the entire burden on him for the lack of progress. That is true. However, what is also true is that the secretary was on the scene during the period before the strike and therefore had intimate knowledge about conditions, practices, and policies; and he was directly responsible for several years of operation after the strike. In light of every report or study that showed clearly that the system was out of balance, the secretary apparently did little to bring it back into balance. If he did take decisive actions, those actions were either ineffective or ignored. The secretary must be held accountable for that process.

THE NATIONAL ASSOCIATION OF AIR TRAFFIC CONTROLLERS

While this study is not designed to bring the story of the air traffic controllers up to the present, it is instructive to note that the current status of the system—fifteen years after the strike—remains at less than an optimal level. The new air controllers' union, the National Air Traffic Controllers Association, points to continued problems in basic management practices, the automation process, long hours, understaffing, and many of the same problems that contributed to the 1981 strike. It isn't clear what should be made of current conditions, but it is not unreasonable to suggest that many of the statements made about how the FAA and DOT were going to respond to controller interests and concerns have simply not been carried out. Who is responsible for the state of the air traffic control system cannot be precisely determined. Each FAA administrator and each secretary of transportation can say that he or she inherited a difficult set of problems and tried to do his or her best within resource constraints. It is difficult to argue with these ideas, but they don't address the basic problems.

One thing is certain: Most of the problems in the air traffic control system are not money problems. To hide behind the shield of budgetary constraints is disingenuous at best. While certainly there are budgetary issues concerning automation and staffing, the issues related to managerial style and the apparent inability of FAA management to develop labor-management relations processes that avoid or minimize conflict can be addressed outside the budgetary processes. In fact, from the material contained in this study, it is clear that even if the FAA were to implement the most sophisticated computer system that current technology permits, there would be lingering and important problems in the labor-management sphere. The NATCA may have developed a more amicable working relationship with the FAA—and that deserves praise. What is clear, however, is that many of the problems that existed before still exist today. Therefore, one must wonder whether the more cordial relationship is what is needed to bring balance into the system. The NATCA has been the exclusive bargaining agent for the air traffic controllers for about nine years. Have the labor-management relationships in the air traffic control system improved in those nine years to warrant praise of these relationships? It is difficult to tell. One still hears of long hours, compulsory overtime, working beyond the hours standards set by the FAA, inadequate computer systems, and a host of related problems, all reminiscent of the early 1980s.

The NATCA, in its own Internet home page, raises questions about system safety and the status of labor-management relations in the FAA environment. The NATCA concludes that the air traffic system is basically safe but that the lack of resources, inadequate computer hardware, and other limitations make the system vulnerable. These kinds of ideas come fifteen years after a disastrous strike that was purportedly motivated by many of those same concerns.

Is the FAA automation program feasible? Is there any hope that the system, as currently envisioned, will achieve its goals in a reasonable time frame? These questions are complex, but the evidence available is not encouraging. As recently as the middle of 1994, writers for the *Washington Post* observed that "despite huge expenditures and a major improvement program dating from 1981, some of those computers [in air traffic control facilities] run in part on technologically extinct vacuum tubes that until recently could be acquired only from factories in Poland and Czechoslovakia. Others come from China."[15] Further, "At sprawling Los Angeles International Airport, the radars that monitor planes on the ground on often fog-enshrouded runways depend on tubes made only in a British factory. The FAA has no way to test them other than by plugging them in."[16]

Some may snicker at the thought of vacuum tube hardware in a system as complex and important as the U.S. air traffic control system. How a system like this could find itself in such a position is a classic case of bureaucratic mismanagement and the inability of federal contractors to deliver their products and services at contract prices. In purely money terms, when the FAA proposed its Advanced Automation System (AAS) in 1981, its estimated cost was $2 billion. Seven years later, after spending about $700 million on "research and development," a contract was let to IBM for about $4.3 billion. By September 1994, the estimated cost was $4.7 billion. By year's end, the estimate was $5.9 billion. In March 1995, the estimate was about $7 billion for a system that was less sophisticated than the one envisioned more than a decade earlier.

Thus, the FAA developed a "plan" for air traffic control automation that was nearly three and a half times as expensive as the original plan. Importantly, the FAA seems no closer today to bringing the system on-line in an enhanced computer environment than it was fifteen years ago. In fairness to the FAA, one must say that the task at hand is Herculean, at best. The air traffic control system handles considerable volumes of traffic with a much reduced personnel level than what existed before the strike.

In late 1994, FAA administrator David R. Hinson suspended work on the massive AAS program. Subsequent to the suspension, several reviews indicated that the prospects of success were small. The administrator canceled the AAS program, and the NATCA supported his decision. However, the union expressed concern that the administrator reported that the system was 99.4 percent reliable. The union believes that statements such as these tend to distort many of the real problems still existing in the air traffic control system. Consequently, the union argued for increasing funding for the system, hiring 1,500 to 2,000 new controllers, implementing a program to attract seasoned controllers to the busiest facilities, and reforming the procurement program to ensure the newest technology is adopted into the system while it is still new technology.

After the FAA pulled the plug on the AAS program, work started on an even more expansive system. Labeled "free flight," the new technology will permit airplanes to chart their own courses, will rely on expanded use of collision-avoidance technology, and will utilize satellite communications systems. In the FAA's words, the free flight system will remove the air traffic control system from a "centralized command-and-control" system to a "distributed system that allows pilots, whenever practical, to choose their own route and file a flight plan that follows the most efficient and economical route."[17] While these conceptual systems hold great promise for aviation in the twenty-first century, they are far from perfected, and implementation is decades in the future. In the meantime, controllers continue to work long hours in systems they feel are unreliable.

PRIVATIZING THE AIR TRAFFIC CONTROL FUNCTION

Undoubtedly due in part to simple frustration with the complexity of the system and partly to the policy, generally, of privatizing governmental functions, the FAA has proposed letting the air traffic control function slide into the hands of private entrepreneurs. There is considerable support for and opposition to the idea. Opponents argue that "bottom line" pressures will compel cutting corners and shortchanging the flying public in relation to air safety. Proponents argue that the only way to insulate the FAA from political pressures is to privatize it. Several influential congressional leaders such as James Oberstar are unconvinced that privatization is needed. Proponents argue that only privatization has a chance to rescue the struggling system.

The Clinton administration has expressed some interest in reviewing the privatizing of some parts of the FAA while letting other parts function as a governmental organization. Specifically, in 1994, the administration was considering a "split" function that would "send the air traffic control functions to a government-owned corporation, something like the Tennessee Valley Authority."[18] The primary individuals who would go into the new corporation would be the air traffic controllers, the computer specialists who maintain the system, the mechanics, the electricians, and other specialists directly involved in the day-to-day operation of the air traffic control system. Those not going into the new corporation would be current FAA employees who are responsible for regulating aviation safety, for establishing training requirements for pilots and flight attendants, and for airport security programs. The administration rejected a proposal to bring the entire FAA into the new government-owned corporation or the complete privatization of the FAA in the form of a private sector corporation.

Other organizations such as the Aircraft Owners and Pilots Association (AOPA) are skeptical of the privatization proposals. The AOPA believes that the character of air traffic control is so critical to the nation's welfare that it should not be privatized. Rather, AOPA supports maintaining the system as a governmental function with broad and informed oversight. The National Business Aircraft Association (NBAA) has adopted a position similar to AOPA's.

The unions, and particularly NATCA, generally oppose privatization. There is a certain irony in this position in that one of the purported goals of the PATCO was the privatization of the FAA so that it, the PATCO, could negotiate with the new organization as a "private sector organization." In discussions with controllers in NATCA, government officials found that many controllers were concerned about job security, pensions, and other types of issues that would be part of a privatization process. The administration was ineffective in addressing the specific changes in working conditions and employee security programs that would emerge in the new corporation.

SUMMARY

Why has the FAA had such a difficult time developing an air traffic control system that is responsive to the needs of the U.S. aviation industry? There are many possible answers. Several will be outlined here, but readers will have to form their own judgments.

The cynic may argue that the budgetary process over-powers the safety process. Specifically, the types of automated systems needed to support a nation-wide, high technology, high reliability system are staggering. System concepts alluding to system development in the single digit billions seems to escalate to double-digit billions. Even with resource estimates in the multiple billions of dollars, the contractors and FAA administrators seem unable to initiate a work-able development strategy. Thus, budgetary considerations are vitally impor-tant and there is no question that they have played an important role in prevent-ing a viable system from emerging.

A second possible answer may be the FAA's history of not only initiating and implementing a workable, state-of-the-art system, but rather embarking on a system of staggering complexity. It seems that soon after the hoopla for the newest "mega-system" settles down, it becomes obvious that the FAA cannot make it work. After hundreds of millions of R and D in conjunction with proto-type systems, the infamous "plug is pulled" and the FAA is left empty handed. Almost immediately, of course, the FAA initiates its next development program. One must wonder how many times the FAA will embark on a new venture without demonstrating its ability to carry out a development program? Critics watch this process of proposing bigger and more complex technological sys-tems, seemingly without any compunction about their ability to complete them. The FAA responds that they cannot simply sit back and let the system totally collapse. This is true. However, it may be prudent to not always shoot for the stars. Wouldn't it make sense to structure a less grandiose system, implement it within budget, and make it operational? Until this happens, the FAA will re-main open to understandable, severe criticism.

A third possibility may be related to the tenure of the top FAA administra-tors. There have been 13 Administrators of the FAA and its predecessor, the Federal Aviation Agency since November 1958. These individuals and their terms of office follow:

Elwood R. Quesada	11/01/58 – 01/20/61	27 Months
Najeeb E. Halaby	03/03/61 – 07/01/65	51 Months
William F. McKee	07/01/65 – 07/31/68	37 Months
John H. Shaffer	03/24/69 – 03/14/73	48 Months
Alexander Butterfield	03/14/73 – 03/31/75	24 Months
John L. McLucas	10/24/75 – 04/01/77	16 Months
Langhorne M. Bond	05/04/77 – 01/20/81	43 Months
J. Lynn Helms	04/22/81 – 01/31/84	34 Months
Donald D. Engen	04/10/84 – 07/02/87	33 Months
T. Allan McArtor	07/22/87 – 02/17/89	19 Months
James B. Busey IV	06/30/89 – 12/04/91	30 Months
Thomas C. Richards	06/27/92 – 01/20/93	7 Months
David Hinson	08/10/93 – 11/09/96	39 Months
Jane F. Garvey	08/04/97 – Present	

During these thirty-nine years, the Administrator with the longest tenure in

Office was Najeeb E. Halaby, the second administrator, who remained in office for four years and three months. John Shaffer, the fourth administrator, spent four years in office. Three other administrators served between three and four years. All others spent less than three years in office. The average tenure for the thirteen administrators was two years and seven months.

The nation's air traffic control system is a complex, constantly in motion, stressful environment. It has been compared to playing chess, fighting bulls, or juggling. In the final analysis, it is probably some combination of all of these activities. The FAA has attempted to identify short-term and long-term strategies to alleviate some of the stress that controllers experience. The FAA's efforts have, for the most part, been ineffective. Billions of dollars have been spent studying the system and crafting intervention strategies. The most recent element in that process is "free flight." While the intent of free flight is to enhance operational efficiency and, inferentially, safety, it is interesting that the concept of safety does not take center stage in the development strategy. In fact, in the FAA's documents available on the Internet, the concept of more efficient airline operation seems to be the focus of the free flight program.

The nation's air traffic control system is a complex, constantly in motion, stressful environment. It has been compared to playing chess, fighting bulls, or juggling. In the final analysis, it is probably some combination of all of these activities. The FAA has attempted to identify short-term and long-term strategies to alleviate some of the stress that controllers experience. The FAA's efforts have, for the most part, been ineffective. Billions of dollars have been spent studying the system and crafting intervention strategies. The most recent element in that process is "free flight." While the intent of free flight is to enhance operational efficiency and, inferentially, safety, it is interesting that the concept of safety does not take center stage in the development strategy. In fact, in the FAA's documents available on the Internet, the concept of more efficient airline operation seems to be the focus of the free flight program.

The FAA will say that safety always has been and always will be its primary focus. Maybe letting pilots select their own routes to enhance efficiency will simultaneously lead to greater safety. Maybe letting pilots utilize satellite technology and enhanced communications procedures to produce greater efficiency will simultaneously increase safety. There are many possibilities. However, it is important to note that while not mutually exclusive, efficiency and safety are often antithetical. Every pilot wants to fly the most direct route, at the optimum altitude, with the most advantageous tailwind component. This routing will be the most efficient, but one must question whether or not it will also be the safest.

NOTES

1. "Air Controller Problems Resurfacing," *Washington Post*, March 18, 1982, p. A7a.

2. U.S. General Accounting Office, *Aviation Safety: Serious Problems Continue to Trouble the Air Traffic Control Work Force*, GAO/RCED-89-112 (Washington, D.C.: GPO, April 1989), pp. 2–3.

3. Ibid., p. 3.

4. Ibid., p. 2.

5. Ibid.

6. Ibid.

7. Ibid., p. 3.

8. Ibid., p. 4.

9. Ibid., p. 5.

10. Ibid.

11. Ibid., p. 6.

12. Ibid.

13. Ibid., p. 5.

14. Ibid., pp. 7–8.

15. Richard M. Weintraub and John Burgess, "U.S. Seeks Shift in Air Traffic Control," *Washington Post*, May 2, 1994, p. A1.

16. Ibid.

17. Federal Aviation Administration, "What Is Free Flight?" Internet: http://asd.orlab.faa.gov/files/ff_ov.htm#what, March 3, 1997.

18. Weintraub and Burgess, "U.S. Seeks Shift in Air Traffic Control," p. A3.

Chapter 10

Summary, Lessons, and Conclusions

Who was responsible for the PATCO debacle? The answer to this question is not simple. Those who believe that every strike is caused by unions will undoubtedly argue that the PATCO was responsible for its actions—it rolled the dice and lost. Others will argue that while the PATCO initiated the strike on August 3, 1981, there were mitigating circumstances that cannot be overlooked. These individuals will argue that in a free society persons cannot be compelled to provide their labor services against their free will. Furthermore, if conditions are sufficiently unacceptable, proponents would argue that employees who must withhold their labor services should not lose their jobs.

These types of arguments will continue as long as there are two sides to the labor-management process. What might be useful is to summarize this event in American labor history by examining the conclusion of the event and the lessons we have learned.

August 3, 1981, is a pivotal day in federal sector labor-management relations. There had been concerted actions by federal employees before and certainly there had been hundreds of strikes by state and local employees both before and after August 3, 1981. Many of the strikes involved functions that affected the health and safety of American citizens. Virtually all affected the "general welfare." Firefighters, police, teachers, sanitation workers, postal workers, and many others have "withheld their labor services." Each of these actions invariably led to protestations about the necessity, efficacy, or legality of public sector work stoppages. In virtually every instance, some method was found to resolve the problem, not necessarily to everyone's satisfaction but to permit the functioning of the struck institution to resume.

What makes August 3, 1981, unique in public sector labor-management relations is that it is the first time that the Federal government destroyed a federal union. *Destroyed* may sound like too harsh a term, but the sum and substance of the federal government's actions was the decertification of the PATCO as the exclusive bargaining agent for the nation's air traffic controllers and the destruction of the union. Without exclusive bargaining rights, a union cannot survive in contemporary society. Other unions immediately exert their bargaining rights for these workers, and in that process, the decertified union is nonfunctional, that is, destroyed.

For federal unions, the breaking of the PATCO was a sobering event. Union leaders believed that if the government succeeded in breaking the PATCO, it would only be a matter of time before other federal unions would be the target of similar actions. The unions representing the nearly 1 million postal workers—the National Association of Letter Carriers and the United Postal Workers Union—have had a less-than-cordial relationship with the U.S. Postal Service. While the U.S. Postal Service is a quasi-public corporation and therefore operates by somewhat different rules—as does the Tennessee Valley Authority, Bonneville Power Authority, among others—the postal unions were justifiably reticent about their relationship. At the very least, breaking the PATCO served to diminish the aggressiveness of the postal unions in the negotiation process. The U.S. Postal Service consummated a new agreement with its employees shortly after the PATCO was destroyed.

In spite of the fear that federal unions felt about the PATCO situation, it was apparent that they were reluctant to get too close to the PATCO. There was some fear that being closely aligned with the PATCO would make them the next target for reprisal; many union members believed that the PATCO was being greedy about its salary demands; the AFL–CIO took a more or less hands-off attitude toward the strike; and the administration had the support of a majority of Americans for its actions.

Nevertheless, federal unions did not want the PATCO to fail because of the potential "next step." Therefore, they cautiously provided support at various levels that was as much symbolic as real. The American Federation of Government Employees, the National Treasury Employees Union, the National Federation of Federal Employees, and the two major postal unions provided some financial support but, more important public relations support, legal assistance, legislative lobbying support, and other forms of in-kind assistance such as babysitting for PATCO strikers walking the picket lines, actually walking the picket lines for PATCO members, and so forth. The financial support provided assistance to strikers' families to pay mortgages, buy food, and help with other critical expenses.

The PATCO strike was disastrous for the organization's members, but in terms of safety in the national air traffic control system, there was little perceived impact. PATCO officials and members argued that safety was compromised, as did controllers in Canada, but the evidence supporting their arguments was not compelling. There were some data indicating that near misses increased, but whether or not the strike affected how these events were reported is not known. Pilots and controllers may simply have been more inclined to report near misses during the strike than they were in more settled times. However, one must be careful to note that the ongoing problems with outdated hardware, long work schedules, and all the other issues related to safety remained unchanged.

How could the strike have happened? Who miscalculated the fortitude of the president? Why didn't other unions support the strike? Was the president looking for an event to make his point? Was the PATCO leadership out of touch with its membership? Did the overwhelming vote of rejection of the government's offer represent arrogance, lack of information, or misinformation? These and other questions about what many believe was one of the most damaging strikes to the credibility of American labor unions was the focus of this book. The questions are not easy to answer, but hindsight in the sweep of history provides one with insights into leadership in the union and in the country, the conditions of organized labor as major players in the U.S. economy, and the role of public opinion in these types of cataclysmic events.

A case can be made that no organization other than the federal government could have consummated the firing of over 11,000 employees and survived the public pressures to resolve the issues. What organization in the public or private sectors could withstand the removal of fully two thirds of its employees and still remain operational? Incredibly, while there were reduced volumes of air traffic, some—particularly pilots—argued that the system worked better after the strike than before the strike. What made it doubly intriguing was the fact that the strike occurred in an industry that is intensely concerned about safety and that has highly skilled employees who seemed irreplaceable. These employees worked long hours under stressful conditions. How could reducing the number of controllers by fully two-thirds improve system operation? The administration was lucky in many ways in addition to not having other unions and public opinion to contend with. A single major airplane crash would probably have turned the public against the administration and could have reversed the fortunes of the PATCO. However, there were no serious accidents that could be attributed to the strike, traffic was reduced in volume but flowed well, and replacement FAA employees were able to gear up quickly for their new assignments.

What could possibly have happened to precipitate a strike by federal employees that ended in their wholesale dismissal? Were errors made in the overall strike strategy? Was the strike destined to fail before it began because of a new administration's need to "stake out its turf?" Did events during the strike coalesce into a situation from which neither side could move? Were their "missed opportunities" by leaders on one or both sides to resolve the problem?

In the aftermath of an emotional, traumatic confrontation that ultimately cost over 11,000 professional air traffic controllers their jobs, resulted in a less safe—but, other than the PATCO, few argued unsafe—air traffic control system, and set the stage for federal labor-management relations for over a decade, it is little wonder that there is no consensus about what caused the problem. Many, both inside and outside the labor movement, blamed Robert Poli for taking on the entire federal government early in a new administration. Poli's critics blamed him for lack of foresight, inflexibility, ego fulfillment, and poor judgment. They blamed him for not consulting with other parts of organized labor before setting and carrying out a nationwide strike. They blamed him for not taking the necessary steps to educate the public about the *real* controller issues, that is, stress, antiquated equipment, and poor management, among others. There is evidence to support all or most of these arguments. However, they do not constitute the whole story.

Robert Poli was new to the presidency of the PATCO, but he had served as PATCO vice president for six or seven years prior to becoming president. He had worked as a controller and understood the issues and environment. He knew that the controllers sat at a critically important spot in the U.S. aviation industry. He was certain that if most or all of the controllers struck, the system of air traffic control would grind to a halt. He believed that the new president would not want to risk major disruption of this critical industry when he was trying to get the economy moving again. Poli believed that the new president would not want to risk a major air disaster early in his presidency and therefore would find some way to accommodate the union's demands. He also knew that few government employees had ever been permanently discharged for exercising the strike option. Poli knew that newly elected President Reagan had praised Lech Walesa and Solidarity for striking against the belligerent regime in Poland. All of these factors suggested that Poli's decision to take the controllers out was a prudent tactic in the overall bargaining strategy.

But there is still more. Robert Poli met with candidate Reagan in Florida to discuss the needs of air traffic controllers, and from that meeting, the PATCO decided to endorse Ronald Reagan for president. This decision was counter to the AFL–CIO's posture on the campaign, and as a consequence, Poli lost favor with Lane Kirkland and most National Union presidents. While the precise content of the Poli-Reagan discussion is not known, it must have been sufficiently substantive and supportive of the union's goals to have produced an endorsement. Correspondence between Poli and candidate Reagan provided unambiguous support by the soon-to-be president for PATCO goals. It is not unreasonable to assume that Robert Poli believed he had the ear and understanding of the soon-to-be-elected candidate. It is not unreasonable to assume that Poli believed that because of his new-found relationship that when push came to shove, the president would side with the controllers.

While Poli was central to the decision to strike and the entire poststrike process, might there not be other factors of importance in assessing the final outcome? Consider the reaction of the Air Line Pilots Association to the strike. As picket lines went up across the country, ALPA pilots ignored them. ALPA members even complemented the effectiveness and professionalism of the remaining controllers as they—the pilots—utilized the system. If a single event could have turned the tide toward the PATCO, it would have been the honoring of the PATCO picket lines by ALPA pilots. While the government could and did replace large portions of the 11,500 striking air traffic controllers, they could not have replaced the 40,000 ALPA pilots, all of whom were employed by private sector airlines and not the federal government. Since ALPA pilots decided to cross the picket lines and continue flying, the PATCO strike was seriously weakened.

Is it reasonable to assume that Poli expected the ALPA pilots to honor the PATCO picket lines? There had been a subtle, long-term feud between airline pilots and air traffic controllers. The pilots frequently argued that the air traffic controllers had too much control over flights and that the pilot's rights and professionalism were infringed upon. Air traffic controllers have long countered that their role is indispensable, equally or more stressful, and much lower paid. One of the persistent demands of controllers over the years has been to raise their salaries to those of airline pilots. One does not hear much about the issue today because the salary structure of pilots may not be as far out of line as the PATCO suggested in earlier years. In comparative terms, PATCO leaders and members were clearly thinking about the $100,000-plus pilot flying a heavy jet and *not* the $35,000 pilot flying a regional commuter piston or turboprop airplane.

Knowing these types of historical sticking points, it probably should have occurred to Poli that the ALPA would not honor the PATCO picket lines. However, the event that made ALPA support impossible was the manner in which Poli had achieved the presidency of the PATCO and how he failed to "mend the fences" in the labor movement. John J. O'Donnell, ALPA president, made clear by his actions that he disliked Poli and had no intention of supporting Poli's actions. This one aspect of the overall strategy, even if recognized by Poli, would probably not have been sufficient to prevent the strike. Even if Poli had believed that ALPA would not support the strike, he believed strongly that it wouldn't really make any difference. It wasn't until after the strike started and its success became doubtful that the full effect of ALPA's actions became apparent. What is most clear is that Poli did not adequately stroke not only ALPA but other unions that he would ultimately come to rely upon. By the time he realized he really needed the rest of organized labor, it was too late.

THE STRUCTURE OF PATCO AND THE PROBABILITY OF SUCCESS

A union must weigh the probabilities that a particular concerted action will meet its objectives. There are no guarantees in this process, but in general, it is believed that certain characteristics of an organization or its market provide strong indicators of success or failure. If one were to examine the size, function, and operational characteristics of the PATCO during its fourteen-year history objectively, there would be little doubt that it would rank near the top of a list of organizations that, most would argue, could be successful in concerted actions such as strikes, slowdowns, and picketing. The organization had relatively few members—about 15,000; members were highly skilled and highly paid; they occupied a critical position in an important national industry; they were employed in the public sector; they seemed to have the ear and sentiment of the Congress; and so forth. In the context of collective bargaining, these and other characteristics suggested that the PATCO possessed considerable bargaining strength.

While there were elements suggesting considerable strength, one characteristic that suggested an area of weakness was the management style in the FAA. *Rigid, insensitive, directive, militaristic,* and other similar terms were used to describe the FAA's approach to employee relations and the collective bargaining process. Possibly, the presence of the union pushed the FAA into this management style, but more likely, it was the character of the organization and the types of people attracted to the organization that produced this system. In any case, from the early days of unionism in the FAA, there were clashes between the employees' representatives and the FAA management. There seemed to be continual confusion about what each side wanted in the bargaining process. The FAA virtually always said publicly that the *only* thing that the PATCO wanted was more money. This was an effective ploy because out of the other side of the FAA's mouth came the idea that controllers were among the highest paid civil servants. If this was the only thing that controllers wanted, the cards were stacked against them. The FAA continued to surface information that suggested that working conditions—overtime, length of periods between breaks, the workweek, and so forth—were well within what a "reasonable" person would accept.

The PATCO, on the other hand, did ask for more money. There is no question that money was an important demand, but it clearly was not the only demand and arguably not even one of the most important demands. It is likely that if the FAA had given the PATCO members all or most of the money they were asking for, the success of this action would have been short-lived. Additional money would have placated controllers for awhile, but with the other documented problems—stress, insensitive managers, antiquated equipment—remaining unresolved, one can be certain that future problems would have occurred. It is likely that FAA and DOT managers also realized that simply complying with the money demands would not "fix" the system. They, too, read the studies and heard the testimony about the outdated equipment, hours, and other problems that were part of the system.

Rather than money being the primary issue, Poli argued, "Our main goal is to assure people who enter the controller profession that they have a reasonable chance of completing their chosen careers without being cut off in the prime of life and discarded into the medical retirement statistics. That is why we have also been focusing on hours of work and retirement. I think that is both reasonable and responsible."[1] Lane Kirkland referred to information indicating that the psychological and medical aspects of the air controller profession resulted in early burnout. He noted specifically that "PATCO members claim that few of their number last long enough on the job, 25 years, to collect full retirement benefits. They point to FAA statistics, obtained by the union through the Freedom of Information Act, showing that between 1976 and 1979 about 89 percent of U.S. controllers who retired did so for medical reasons before they were eligible for full retirement benefits."[2] No profession finds upward of 90 percent of its members leaving the profession early for medical reasons. There can be little doubt that controllers were justifiably concerned about this problem.

THE LESSONS

Whatever the characteristics of the PATCO, a primary lesson of the PATCO debacle is that unions must be very careful in the assessment of strategic strength. Even when all the elements of a successful stoppage are apparent, resolve, power, and luck by the opposition can lead to defeat for the union. This is doubly important if a union does not have strong ties to the rest of organized labor and does not have effective public relations programs.

As the PATCO sized up its relative strength in the aviation industry, in addition to the institutional characteristics identified earlier, there were a number of additional indicators that suggested that its power was substantial. From the very first action by the PATCO in 1968, it realized that its actions would have a significant impact on the industry and economy. As noted in the 1970 Corson Report, the PATCO slowdown in the summer of 1968, orchestrated under the rubric of a program called "Operation Air Safety," precipitated an immediate crisis in the aviation industry. The PATCO instructed air traffic controllers to comply strictly with the letter of all FAA regulations governing the control and separation of aircraft.[3] From this and several other events in the next several years, PATCO came to see that its concerted actions imparted considerable power to the union. It could, it thought with impunity, engage in actions that would put pressure on the FAA and the industry to meet the union's demands.

A second lesson that may be separate but related is the care and feeding of the organization's potential or actual allies. Poli and the PATCO were misguided in their treatment of ALPA and, for that matter, the leadership of the AFL–CIO. Poli seemed to believe that other unions would rush to PATCO's defense simply because they were labor unions. Clearly, the outcome of the strike action could have been very different if the ALPA had honored the PATCO picket lines and refused to fly. Similarly, more focused and aggressive support by the machinists—those who maintain and repair the airplanes—and the flight attendants would have put extraordinary pressure on the aviation system. These unions did provide some support, but in isolation, it was not enough. Even the support from controllers in other countries was weak and ill-focused. The International Federation of Air Traffic Controllers Associations tiptoed around the periphery of the process and provided no meaningful support. Foreign governments were able to quickly push their domestic controllers back to the radar scopes and away from supporting the PATCO.

In the context of interunion support, it is important to recognize that labor unions are political organizations headed by individuals with considerable egos. These egos must be stroked carefully. Poli's rise to the leadership of the PATCO created distaste in the mouths of many union leaders throughout the labor movement and particularly, as noted earlier, John O'Donnell, the president of ALPA. Poli was essentially an unknown person in the American labor hierarchy because of the roles he played. On the other hand, John Leyden, his predecessor, was a longtime, respected union leader who had worked hard to build bridges between the PATCO and other unions. After his abrupt rise to leadership, Poli did little to convince these leaders that he was sensitive to their concerns and that his leadership would help PATCO and the labor movement overall become stronger. In fact, he seemed to go out of his way either to ignore other union leaders or to show them that he could take PATCO anywhere that he wished without their assistance or support. It is significant that in the first several days of the strike Poli and Lane Kirkland did not meet or talk about the situation. One would have thought that a national union leader would be in close and constant contact with the leadership of the AFL–CIO. In hindsight, this tactical blunder weakened the PATCO's position when the strike most needed support. It is impossible to conclude that the strike would have been successful with the support of other unions, but certainly the crossing of picket lines by ALPA pilots and the refutation of Poli concerning air safety by O'Donnell and other ALPA representatives served to weaken Poli's position in the early days and weeks of the strike when public opinion was most sensitive.

Lesson three relates to unions and the external political system. Did the administration and specifically President Reagan want to break the union? The answer to this question may never be known, but there are a number of signals that help us understand how the president came to take an intransigent position. At the outset, it is fair to postulate that the president did not set out to destroy the PATCO as a union. After all, the PATCO was one of a few labor organizations that openly supported Ronald Reagan for president. There was no reason for the president to take on and destroy an organization that could be useful in the future.

In addition, there is evidence that the president understood and supported the need for improving conditions in the air traffic control system. Whether the president would have ultimately helped the controllers achieve their many goals is also unknown, but there is little doubt that the PATCO had the ear and general sympathy of the new president—before the strike.

On the other side of the ledger, the leadership in the Department of Transportation and the FAA was less sympathetic to the union. The style of leadership and the long history of acrimonious relationships between the FAA and its controller unions were legend in the labor movement. Therefore, the new president had a group of senior managers and administration officials who were less sympathetic to, and one might argue antagonistic toward, the PATCO and the goals it sought.

As a consequence, it probably took little persuasion by the president's advisers to convince the president that the aggressiveness of the PATCO and the perceived greediness of the organization spelled problems with several of the other goals the president had established. Most important was the president's drive to bring the federal budget under control through reduced spending and taxes. While the PATCO proposals were inconsequential in the overall budgeting process, it would have been difficult for the president to permit the PATCO to succeed in its quest for large salary increases while the President was holding the line in other spending categories.

If the president sought to break the PATCO, this decision undoubtedly came *after* the strike was under way. Once the PATCO had initiated the strike, a number of fortuitous relationships unfolded. First, there was no question that the PATCO was violating a federal law, and therefore, the president could take the high road of upholding the laws of the land regardless of who violated them. Second, since few unions supported the president, this was a vehicle for possibly repaying the labor movement for nonsupport. Third, it was early in the administration, and the president, always a signal sender, determined that a strong position with the PATCO would dampen the enthusiasm other unions might have to expand their agendas.

Robert Poli missed or misinterpreted the importance of the political process in federal labor-management relations. He misjudged the president's commitment and resolve; he misjudged the influence DOT and FAA officials would have on the president; and he misjudged the ability of the government to isolate and mischaracterize the PATCO's issues.

There is also another dimension of the political processes that swirled around the PATCO strike. Poli made it known that he and the president had a "meeting of the minds" about the PATCO and its issues. This came to light in the congressional hearings, which to a large extent backfired on Poli. Once it became known that Poli and Reagan had worked out an "understanding" or what some would call a "deal," the president had no choice other than to play hardball. If the president had given into the PATCO demands, he would have been strongly criticized for giving into the union. The president simply could not accommodate a prounion label.

A fourth aspect of this fluid situation may have involved the type of advice the president was receiving from his advisers. They were taking patently inflexible public positions on every aspect of the strike, and the president, too, took early positions that would have been impossible to back away from in a settlement process. As a consequence, the position of the president hardened very early and very quickly. The new president was not one to "eat crow," and his early pronouncements on the strike would have required that to happen. Advisers with more experience in negotiating and in the collective bargaining process might have advised the president to be more tactful in his public announcements by leaving a little "wiggle room" for a future settlement process.

Admittedly, since there were no aviation disasters that could be tied to the absence of qualified controllers and since the president ultimately won the battle and the war, one might argue that the advice the president received was right on target. Whether that assessment is true or not, the point here is that the president did not relish the notion of breaking the PATCO, and only after the strike was in motion did his resolve to destroy the union come to the fore. Once this position arose, the president did little to assist in the settlement of the dispute. In fact, he and Secretary Lewis both said publicly that they had no interest in talking with Poli or any other PATCO officials as long as the PATCO was on strike.

In addition to all this, the president and the administration took extraordinary risks by breaking the PATCO. The administration knew that a single major aviation accident could turn the tide of public opinion away from the administration. The system was set up for just such a calamity, too, but it never happened.

In the sweep of history and with hindsight as a guide, an important question is whether President Reagan was prudent and correct in his destruction of the PATCO. Those who supported the president will resoundingly answer yes. Those who did not support the president's actions will just as resoundingly answer no. The historical fact is that the union was destroyed, and that fact cannot be changed. Did PATCO commit a capital crime that warranted its destruction? In the jargon of jurisprudence, did the punishment fit the crime?

What specifically was the crime? This question seems easy to answer, but in fact it is difficult to be precise about the answer. There is no question that the PATCO violated a federal law. A reasonable question might be, So what? Organizations and individuals frequently violate federal law in ways that are more egregious and damaging to the American system than PATCO's strike. There was actually little more than inconvenience of the public in the aftermath of the strike. Should this have been the rationale for breaking the union? As Aboud and Aboud argued earlier, strikes may produce public inconvenience and disruption. However, freedom is not a costless process. A society that cherishes freedom must be prepared to tolerate some disruption and inconvenience as the quest for universal freedom unfolds.[4] Since little more than inconvenience occurred (disruption was minimal), did it make sense to carry the process to conclusion?

Arguing on the other side, it's important to note that this was not the first concerted action by the PATCO. The organization had engaged in other actions earlier that resulted in both inconvenience and disruption. For example, the discharge of sixty-seven controllers for participation in the sick-out in 1970 was a clear signal that the PATCO was prepared to exercise its muscle. Under civil service appeals, twenty-seven of the controllers were reinstated, and Secretary of Transportation John A. Volpe ordered the rehiring of the remaining ones in February 1972.[5]

The four years between 1972 and 1976 were ones of relative peace between the PATCO and the FAA. What is perhaps most important, however, is that the problems that had precipitated the earlier job actions did not go away. Controllers remained concerned about safety in the system; about long workweeks; about compulsory overtime; about management's apparent disinterest in the controllers' ideas; and about their inability to communicate these concerns effectively. John Leyden, a skilled leader and peacemaker, could not change many of the fundamental problems in the system that continued to fester. He bought time and kept the lid on controller frustrations, but it was only a matter of time before new problems would arise, and arise they did.

While there were a series of threatened and actual slowdowns and stoppages throughout the 1970s, the final disruption by the PATCO prior to the 1981 strike occurred at Chicago's O'Hare Airport. The FAA refused a PATCO demand for an annual tax-free bonus of $7,500. The reason for the bonus demand was to compensate controllers for stress on the job at O'Hare. After the FAA rejected their demand, PATCO members initiated a slowdown that caused delays in air traffic and cost the air carriers over a million dollars in wasted fuel.[6] This series of concerted actions gave credence to the idea that the PATCO knew exactly what it was doing and that if the 1981 strike had been averted or stopped by either side, there would be further actions in the future. Was this realization enough to warrant the union's destruction? Maybe.

On the PATCO's side, there is considerable evidence that the FAA and the Department of Transportation were less than forthright and honest bargainers. Some may argue that management was tough and shrewd in its bargaining strategy, but there is considerable evidence that the FAA went out of its way to frustrate the PATCO and other federal unions in both bargaining and nonbargaining activities. It's easy to be tough and shrewd when one has virtually unlimited resources including access to the media, legal support, public opinion, and financial resources. As reported in *U.S. News and World Report*, controllers became a fanatical group after years of acrimonious relations with the Federal Aviation Administration.[7] Robert Poli, testifying before the House of Representatives, was pointedly critical of the FAA's linkage between labor-management issues and deficiencies in the air traffic control system. He argued that the PATCO had been the target of scurrilous attacks that had questioned not only the integrity of the PATCO as an organization but more important, the air traffic controllers as a profession.[8]

He suggested that the FAA repeatedly tried to "trivialize" safety problems in the system by publicly confusing the importance of these issues with the internal labor-management problems in the relationship. Poli argued that the FAA's cavalier attitude insulted the air traffic controllers' professional integrity and the flying public. He asserted that these facts led to an opposite and disturbing conclusion about the FAA. He suggested that the FAA used labor-management relations as a vehicle to deflect attention away from the deficiencies in the air traffic control system.[9] This was Poli's view, of course, and the FAA vehemently disagreed with this assessment.

There was little doubt in 1981—and there is little doubt today—that there were documented problems within the air traffic control system that contributed to serious safety problems. Frequent power outages due to antiquated hardware, long work hours, management attitudes and capabilities, lack of training, and numerous other problems provided avenues for potentially disastrous conditions. In support of this idea, Poli pointed to the frequent failures of computers supporting air traffic control. In one year, 1979, FAA computers failed 6,651 times. In spite of this astronomical failure rate, the FAA claimed that that PATCO's concern with this issue was a ploy for fueling labor disputes.[10] For a system that must provide reliability approaching 100 percent, hardware failures of this magnitude should have sounded the alarm for somebody inside the FAA and in the Congress.

CONCLUSION

The Professional Air Traffic Controllers Organization and the Federal Aviation Administration provided a classic example of labor-management relations at its worst. They provided numerous examples of precisely what not to do. They provided numerous examples of power bargaining that spun out of control. There can be no question that the PATCO was legally wrong in its strike action. There was without question reasonable support for extracting a pound of flesh for the PATCO's actions. The real question, of course, was where that pound of flesh came from and whether it was appropriate to destroy the organization in the extraction process. The president won both the battle and the war in the early weeks of the strike. After that was demonstrated to the satisfaction of everybody, would it not have made more sense for the nation, the individual controllers, and the aviation industry to find a method for resolving the impasse? After international support for the strike evaporated and the decertification proceedings were clearly on track, it would have been prudent for the president to find ways to bring the controllers back to their jobs. However, he failed to take that step. As a consequence, the system has lurched from one untenable situation to another for the better part of fifteen years. There may be some small improvements in the operational systems, and there are more improvements promised in the future. The costs to the nation and the industry to rebuild the air traffic control system have been significant. Nobody has attempted a complete compilation of the costs, both short term and long term, of the PATCO strike, but one can be sure they are in the double-digit billions of dollars.

In the final analysis, the costs to the nation and the industry may not be the most important issue. What may be the most important issue is that relating to the effects of the strike on labor-management relations and the character and role of unions in the American economy. The percentage of unionized American workers is quickly approaching the single-digit level. The power of unions in the American economy is also approaching a post–World War II low.

There seems to be no end in sight. All of the causes of these declines have not been carefully studied, but one must argue that the attitudes related to the

PATCO debacle and twelve years of sustained antiunion bias in the White House have taken their toll. However, it is much too early to begin constructing the final resting place for American unionism. American workers today, in 1998, are experiencing relatively good times. Real wages are increasing slowly as the rate of inflation has slipped to less than 3 percent per year. The nation is in the mature stage of the longest sustained growth period in the last forty years. Consumer optimism and confidence are relatively high and stable.

However, there are also ominous clouds on the horizon. Corporate downsizing, outsourcing production to foreign vendors, increased competition from foreign producers, and other types of changes are under way. American workers are resilient and resourceful. In good times, they don't think much about joining unions. However, if some of the processes noted earlier continue to threaten jobs and provide pressure on labor standards, the interest in a common voice provided by unions could quickly reemerge.

There will be PATCO scars on the American union movement for many decades to come. However, these scars are relatively healed, and the trauma that caused the scars is fading from the psyche of most Americans. In some ways this is good because the nation and its unions must put the past to rest and move forward. It is not good in the sense that we forget those things that are unpleasant and thus fail to learn from those experiences. This book's purpose is to bring some semblance of perspective to a difficult time in American labor history. It was an important time for many reasons. The PATCO debacle sits at the very beginning of the Reagan Revolution and, many would argue, set the tone for the Reagan administration's relationship with all American workers. The manner in which the president handled the strike told Americans a lot about the man. Much of what they saw, they liked—focus, toughness, a sense of right. However, there were some things they didn't like—rigidity, lack of compassion, an unforgiving nature.

We cannot go back in time and would not choose to go back even if we could. The air traffic controllers who lost their jobs have restructured their lives, and many undoubtedly have gone on to bigger and better things. Many were not as fortunate. The PATCO strike and its aftermath are worthy of more attention than they have been provided. After all, over 11,000 of our countrymen and women were swept up by a process and event that changed their lives. Even though most Americans were not affected substantially by that event, it's important to understand as fully as possible what happened and why it happened. The author hopes this book has taken a small step in that direction.

NOTES

1. Robert Poli, "Letters to the Editor: The Air Traffic Controllers Reply," *Washington Post*, August 7, 1981, p. A7.

2. "Kirkland Blasts Attempt to Bust Air Controllers," *AFL–CIO News*, Vol. 26, No.

33, August 15, 1981, p. 12.

3. Senate, Committee on Post Office and Civil Service, *Air Traffic Controllers*, 91st Cong., 2d sess., Report to Accompany S. 3959, Report No. 91-1012 (Washington, D.C.: GPO, July 9, 1970), p. 25.

4. Antone Aboud and Grace Sterrett Aboud, *The Right to Strike in Public Employ-ment*, Key Issues Series—No. 15 (Ithaca, NY: New York State School of Industrial and Labor Relations, Cornell University, 1974), p. 9.

5. Gregory L. Karam, "The Legal Consequences of a Deliberate Air Traffic Control-lers Slowdown," *Northern Kentucky Law Review*, Vol. 8, No. 1, January 1981, p. 170.

6. Ibid., p. 171.

7. "Challenge to the Government," *U.S. News and World Report*, August 17, 1981, p. 18.

8. House of Representatives, Committee on Post Office and Civil Service, Subcom-mittee on Investigations, *Air Traffic Control*, 96th Cong., 2d sess. (Washington, D.C.; GPO, September 30, 1980), p. 16.

9. Ibid.

10. Ibid.

Epilogue

After the principal parts of this book were complete, an interesting study entitled *Flying Blind, Flying Safe* [1] was published. Excerpts from the book were published recently in *Time* magazine. The comments that follow relate primarily to the material in the *Time* magazine article. Written by former DOT inspector general Mary Schiavo, the book describes the problems the FAA has had over the last couple of decades with maintaining safety in the aviation industry. It is a powerfully important book, written by a knowledgeable professional. One cannot read what Schiavo has written without being deeply angered, frustrated, and fearful of conditions in the American aviation industry. Schiavo examines a number of systems and conditions in the American aviation industry that jeopardize safety. Not only is the air traffic control system utilizing old, antiquated hardware, but as Schiavo reports, the FAA has not effectively policed the aviation industry and its suppliers. She documented massive use of "bogus" parts in airplanes of all types, lapses in airport security, and other safety problems that appear pervasive in the aviation sector. The Federal Aviation Administration is, of course, the federal agency responsible for setting standards and policing the industry to ensure those standards are met.

No one can read Schiavo's analysis of conditions in the aviation sector and feel good about American aviation safety. The patterns of evidence are too pervasive and too sustained to be simply quirks in the system. She alleges cover-ups, deception, false public statements, attempts to quiet those who are critical of the FAA's processes, ad infinitum. It is a chilling commentary on a department, agency, and industry that should be the pride of every American. It alleges that dollars come before safety, that senior managers and political officials are puppets of the aviation industry, and that the agency changes direction in response to the loss of life rather than anticipate and correct problems. Ms. Schiavo indicates that the FAA has been labeled the "Tombstone Agency" because it apparently lacks the ability to regulate the aviation industry effectively and simply counts the tombstones to see how well it is doing.

While her work focuses primarily on the inspection and maintenance of aircraft, it also provides some insights into the air traffic control system. Describing the initiatives the FAA has taken since the 1981 PATCO strike, Schiavo is critical of the agency and the substantive Congressional Oversight Committee. Writing in *Time*, she faulted Congressman James Oberstar and his House Aviation Subcommittee for failing to "hold the agency's feet to the fire" in the development of a modern ATC system.[2] In addition, she was sharply critical of the massive waste of money and time by the FAA in its attempt to construct "cutting-edge, glittering new systems—the newest generation of whiz-bang electronics, avionics, software and hardware, many of them custom-designed to keep up to date with the needs and desires of American aviation."[3] As she noted, and as noted in this book, after more than a decade of research and development and the expenditure of over a billion dollars, no functional system emerged. In fact, the proposed system was an "utter failure," and administrator Hinton canceled the entire development process in 1994 to begin the development of the "free flight" system.

There are plenty of reasons to be pessimistic about the FAA's new air traffic control initiatives. The agency's track record raises serious concerns about its ability to initiate, develop, and maintain complex, state-of-the-art electronic and computer systems. Even when technology is known, tried, and tested, the agency seems to find it difficult to establish and maintain an implementation schedule. Schiavo points to the delays in the installation of Doppler radar systems to provide pilots and controllers with information about airport wind-shear conditions. Doppler radar technology is well tested and used extensively in meteorology and weather reporting programs. Even small television and radio stations use the technology to enhance their weather reporting capabilities. However, according to Schiavo, the FAA seems unable to establish a responsive process for the installation and use of this technology in major airports across the nation.[4]

One must wonder how long the existing ATC hardware and software can be used before there is a catastrophic failure. Maybe there are sufficient redundancies in the system to permit backup systems and backup of backup systems to keep the ATC system operating indefinitely. There was a recent event at Washington's National Airport in which, during the morning rush hour, the primary communications electronics and the backup system for the communications electronics failed. The backup system for the backup system kicked in, and the airport was able to maintain communications with aircraft on a reduced volume basis. It is unclear what would have happened if the second backup system had failed. Events such as these are troubling and the prospects for cataclysmic failures send chills up the spines of those who think about these things. Maybe the FAA has become so accustomed to responding to system failures that a whole new operating scheme has evolved, namely, crisis management on an ongoing basis. One would hope this is not the case, but the track record of the agency in recent decades suggests this process as a real possibility.

The unions and the air carriers have been crying "wolf" for over two decades. The thrust of their concerns has been the imminent collapse of the air traffic control system. The unions argue that the only glue holding the system together is the air traffic controller. There is a strong case for that position. After all, the hardware and software side of the system has not responded to the state-of-the-art technology available in the United States today. No one can explain or justify vacuum tube technology in any system, let alone one as complex and critical as the air traffic control system.

There are those, of course, who argue that the cries of "wolf" are alarmist and largely miss the mark. After all, air transportation remains the safest mode of transportation on an accident or death per mile basis. This observation is, of course, true. However, since the FAA has not provided the needed hardware in the system to effectively bring the system into line with expanding air traffic, the aspect of the system that must be keeping it functional and safe is the air traffic controller. This is not to say that it is only the air traffic controller who makes the system safe. There are many participants in the safety equation, that is, pilots, aircraft manufacturers, mechanics, flight attendants, and many others who contribute to the nation's safety record.

Some believe that the role of the air traffic controller will diminish over the next several decades. In fact, the free flight concept has precisely that outcome. What is likely to happen, however, is that the role of the air traffic controller will not diminish: rather, it will change. If free flight becomes operational, controllers may relinquish some direct control over aircraft during the routine, enroute segments of their flights but become more involved in the beginning and end points of each flight. As airspace becomes more congested, the role of the controller is likely to expand rather than contract. If free flight cannot or does not work, the precise role of air traffic controllers becomes increasingly unclear. One thing seems certain: Air traffic controllers will remain the "glue" holding the system together, far into the future. There are many possibilities and opportunities for enhancing the role of the air traffic controller in the safe and efficient operation of the aviation industry. That was, after all, the reason for initiating the air traffic control system in the first place.

NOTES

1. Mary Fackler Schiavo with Sabra Chartrand, *Flying Blind, Flying Safe* (New York: Avon Books, April 1997).

2. "Flying into Trouble," *Time*, Vol. 149, No. 13, March 31, 1997, p. 60.

3. Ibid.

4. Ibid.

Selected Bibliography

Aboud, Antone, and Grace Sterrett Aboud. *The Right to Strike in Public Employment.* Key Issues Series—No. 15. Ithaca: New York State School of Industrial and Labor Relations, Cornell University, 1974.

"Air Controllers' Strike." *Facts on File*, Vol. 41, No. 2136, October 23, 1981.

"Air Strike Starts to Wear Down All Sides." *U.S. News and World Report*, August 31, 1981.

Anderson, W. E. "Medical Observations of Flight Service Specialists." In Hearings before the Subcommittee on Post Office and Civil Service, House of Representatives. *Air Traffic Control.* Washington, D.C.: GPO, September 30, 1980.

Bowers, David B. "What Would Make 11,500 People Quit Their Jobs?" *Organizational Dynamics*, Winter 1983.

"Challenge to the Government." *U.S. News and World Report*, August 17, 1981.

Chiles, James R. "Preparing for Takeoff as Air Traffic Controllers." *Smithsonian*, Vol. 20, No. 10, January 1990.

Federal Supplement. Vol. 313, F. Supp. 181. St. Paul, Minn: West Publishing Co., 1970.

"Flying into Trouble." *Time*, Vol. 149, No. 13, March 31, 1997.

General Accounting Office, *Controller Staffing and Training at Four FAA Air Traffic Control Facilities*, CED 81-127 (Washington, D.C.: GOP, July 9, 1981).

Hanslowe, Kurt L., and John L. Acierno. "The Law and Theory of Strikes by Government Employees." *Cornell Law Review*, Vol. 67, No. 6, August 1982.

"House Approves Plan to Rehire Former Air-Traffic Controllers." *Congressional Quarterly*, April 2, 1988.

"How Air Travel Stands One Year after Strike." *U.S. News and World Report*, August 3, 1982.

Hurd, Richard W., and Jill K. Kriesky. "Communications: The Rise and Demise of PATCO Reconstructed." *Industrial and Labor Relations Review*, Vol. 40, No. 1, October 1986.

Karam, Gregory L. "The Legal Consequences of a Deliberate Air Traffic Controllers Slowdown." *Northern Kentucky Law Review*, Vol. 8, No. 1, January 1981.

"Kirkland Blasts Attempt to Bust Air Controllers." *AFL–CIO News*, Vol. 26, No. 33, August 15, 1981.

Nordlund, Willis J. *A History of the Federal Employees Compensation Program.* Washington, D.C.: GPO, August 1992.

Northrup, Herbert K. "Reply." *Industrial and Labor Relations Review,* Vol. 40, No. 1, October 1986.

Northrup, Herbert K. "The Rise and Demise of PATCO." *Industrial and Labor Relations Review,* Vol. 37, No. 2, January 1984.

"Should the U.S. Grant Amnesty to Air Controllers?" *U.S. News and World Report,* August 24, 1981.

U.S. General Accounting Office. *Aviation Safety: Serious Problems Continue to Trouble the Air Traffic Control Work Force.* GAO/RCED-89-112. Washington, D.C.: GPO, April 1989.

U.S. General Accounting Office. *Controller Staffing and Training at Four FAA Air Traffic Control Facilities.* CED-81-127. Washington, D.C.: GPO, July 9, 1981.

U.S. General Accounting Office. *FAA's Definition of Its Controller Work Force Should Be Revised.* Report to the Chairman, House Subcommittee on Investigations and Oversight, Committee on Public Works and Transportation. GAO/RECD 88 14. Washington, D.C.: GPO, October 1987.

U.S. House of Representatives. Committee on Government Operations. Subcommittee on Government Activities. *Problems Confronting the Federal Aviation Administration in the Development of an Air Traffic Control System for the 1970s.* 91st Cong., 2d sess. Report No. 91-1306, Union Calendar No. 623. Washington, D.C.: GPO, July 16, 1970.

U.S. House of Representatives. Committee on Post Office and Civil Service. Subcommittee on Investigations. *Air Traffic Control.* 96th Cong., 2d sess. Washington, D.C.: GPO, September 30, 1980.

U.S. House of Representatives. Committee on Post Office and Civil Service. Subcommittee on Investigations. *Federal Labor-Management Relations and Impasses Procedures.* 97th Cong., 2d sess. Serial No. 97-50. Washington, D.C.: GPO, February 24, April 29, May 4, July 22, 1982.

U.S. House of Representatives. Committee on Post Office and Civil Service. Subcommittee on Investigations. *Working Conditions and Staffing Needs in Air Traffic Control System.* 100th Cong., 1st sess. Serial No. 100-26. Washington, D.C.: GPO, July 29–30, 1987.

U.S. House of Representatives. Committee on Public Works and Transportation. Subcommittee on Investigations and Oversight. *Examining Circumstances Surrounding the 1981 Firings of Air Traffic Controllers at the Chicago Air Route Traffic Control Center.* No. 100-35. 100th Cong., 1st sess. Washington, D.C.: GPO, March 10, 11, September 14, 1987.

U.S. Senate. Committee on Post Office and Civil Service. *Air Traffic Controllers.* 91st Cong., 2d sess. Calendar No. 1016, Report No. 91-1012. Washington, D.C.: GPO, July 9, 1970.

U.S. Senate. Committee on Post Office and Civil Service. *Air Traffic Controllers.* 91st Cong., 2d sess. Report to Accompany S. 3959, Report No. 91-012. Washington, D.C.: GPO, July 9, 1970.

Weintraub, Richard M., and John Burgess. "U.S. Seeks Shift in Air Traffic Control." *Washington Post,* May 2, 1994, p. A1.

Index

About the Author

WILLIS J. NORDLUND is Dean of the School of Business at the College of West Virginia. He is former Regional Director of the Office of Workers' Compensation Programs, U.S. Department of Labor, and served as Special Assistant and Executive Assistant to the Under Secretary of Labor between 1977 and 1980. He is the author of *The Quest for a Living Wage* (Greenwood, 1997) as well as numerous professional articles. He is also a multi-engine, instrument-rated pilot.

ISBN 0-275-96188-5